LETHAL WARRIORS

WHEN THE NEW BAND OF BROTHERS CAME HOME

DAVID PHILIPPS

First published in hardcover in 2010 by PALGRAVE MACMILLAN® in the US—a division of St. Martin's Press LLC, 175 Fifth Avenue, New York, NY 10010.

Where this book is distributed in the UK, Europe and the rest of the world, this is by Palgrave Macmillan, a division of Macmillan Publishers Limited, registered in England, company number 785998, of Houndmills, Basingstoke, Hampshire RG21 6XS.

Palgrave Macmillan is the global academic imprint of the above companies and has companies and representatives throughout the world.

Palgrave® and Macmillan® are registered trademarks in the United States, the United Kingdom, Europe and other countries.

ISBN: 978-0-230-12069-3

The Library of Congress has catalogued the hardcover edition as follows:

Philipps, David.
    Lethal warriors : when the new band of brothers came home / David Philipps.
        p. cm.
    ISBN 978-0-230-10440-2 (hardback)
    1. Post-traumatic stress disorder. 2. Iraq War, 2003—Veterans—Mental health. 3. United States. Army. Parachute Infantry Regiment, 506th. I. Title.
RC552.P67P545   2010
616.85'212—dc22

2010028192

A catalogue record of the book is available from the British Library.

Design by Letra Libre

First PALGRAVE MACMILLAN paperback edition: April 2012

10 9 8 7 6 5 4 3 2 1

Printed in the United States of America.

CONTENTS

ACKNOWLEDGMENTS

This book would not have happened without the gracious help of many people. Thank you, first and foremost, to the soldiers of the Lethal Warriors/Band of Brothers, both named and unnamed, who helped explain what happened even if they would have rather it be forgotten.

At the *Colorado Springs Gazette,* thanks to Joanna Bean, a good friend and a great editor, and Tom Roeder and Dennis Huspeni, whose reporting laid the foundation for mine. And thanks to editor Jeff Thomas and publisher Steve Pope for having the guts to publish the articles that later grew into this book.

Thanks to my agent, Will Lippincott and my editor, Alessandra Bastagli, who both saw the growing importance of this issue and championed the book. And thanks to all the people at Palgrave Macmillan who helped make it a reality.

Thanks to Mark and Carol Graham for all you have done.

Thanks to the Colorado Springs Police Department, especially Derek Graham, Joe Matiatos, and Brad Pratt. Nice work fellas.

Thanks to the Colorado Public Defenders, especially Sheilagh McAteer.

Thank you mom, for always being willing to read copy.

Thank you Whitman for reminding me that the world is wonderful, and most of all, thank you Amanda, the earth under my feet and the stars over my head. I love you.

"This book is to be neither an accusation nor a confession. It will try simply to tell of a generation of men who, even though they may have escaped its shells, were destroyed by the war."

—Erich Maria Remarque,
All Quiet on the Western Front,
1929

JANUARY 2012

In December 2011, the final American combat convoy rolled out of Iraq, nine years after the start of a war that was supposed to last six months. Nearly 4,500 U.S. troops died in the war. Another 32,000 were wounded. At least 104,000 Iraqi civilians were killed. And, with the exception of removing Saddam Hussein, almost nothing was accomplished. When the last truck rumbled over the line into Kuwait and the border crossing gate closed behind it, one soldier turned to a newsman next to him and said, "That's it, the war is over," as if just getting out of Iraq was victory enough.

The same week, I got an email from a retired cop in North Carolina. "My son, my hero, was the all-American young man," he wrote. "Captain of his football team, winner of the home run derby, captain of his high school wrestling team. He joined the Marine Corps in 2003 as a junior in high school and did two tours in Iraq. He is now a disabled vet (PTSD, back, knee injuries, etc.). After coming home he became a firefighter. He now sits in prison for the kidnapping and rape of two prostitutes. When my son was arrested, he looked at me and said, 'Dad, don't get me out.' I never understood the severity of his PTSD, what it could do to someone."

———

It was one of several emails readers have sent since *Lethal Warriors* first came out in 2010, all suggesting the same thing: The war is not over. Not even close.

Just a few weeks earlier, I got an email from an Iraq vet wondering what he could do to help his best friend, a young Special Forces veteran of Iraq and Afghanistan, who blacked out while drinking at a hotel and came to in a police car, arrested for stabbing someone. He had no idea what had happened. I asked if other guys in the unit were having similar struggles. The vet who emailed said they all were in one way or another, adding, "Anyone who tells you that life has been coming up roses since they went to war is lying like a banker in front of a congressional subcommittee."

A few weeks before that, I ran into a soldier from the Lethal Warriors at a bar in Texas. He had two bronze stars and had turned down two purple hearts. After being honorably discharged in 2008, he went to college on the G.I. Bill. He was in his last year of a sociology degree. He had done OK as a civilian. "I'm not saying I can sleep all that well," he said with a sideways glance, "But I never went psycho." Still, he said, civilian life did not seem to have much purpose, and he was getting ready to drop out of school to go back to Iraq as a highly paid security contractor. "I don't know why the hell I want to go back there," he said. "But I do."

The war is not over, even if we wish it was.

This summer I was invited to read at a four-day meeting of Veterans for Peace. As its name suggests, it is a group of thousands of combat veterans whose collective experience has taught them that wars, while easy to start, are hard to stop, and often hurt civilians most. Because of this, they actively promote nonviolence. Most of the members are Vietnam vets, which means they are almost all grandfathers now. They come together to read poetry, plan protests and, like all old vets, tell war stories. During the days I spent with them, I saw many men stop midsentence to silently weep into their gray beards. forty years later, the memories were still as sharp and painful as the day they were made.

The war is not over. It won't be for a long, long time.

Just days after the final pullout from Iraq in 2011, journalist Tom Ricks pondered what would be a fitting memorial to the Iraq war on National Public Radio. "The Vietnam Memorial is a gash in the ground, like a grave," he said. Since Iraq accomplished almost nothing, he said, "I think the Iraq War memorial probably would ideally be a dead end." A dead end might even be too optimistic. After all, for thousands of troops and the people who care about them, the end has yet to come. More fitting might be a memorial whose borders imperceptibly leach into the surrounding cityscape, suggesting the Iraq War will be present long after it has lapsed from national attention. And it might make sense to intertwine it with a memorial for the War in Afghanistan—since the same men and women fought both wars, against insurgents who learned from each other's viciousness—and link it by a murky, slippery path to the 9/11 memorial.

If problems persist in returning troops, it is not entirely the fault of the military. The United States military has shoveled resources at Post-Traumatic Stress Disorder, Traumatic Brain Injuries, and other problems in volumes that only it could. In 2010 alone, the Department of Defense spent over $800 million on PTSD research. Scores of projects are searching for better ways to detect and treat these injuries. But the old complications still exist. There is a stubborn stigma against troops getting help. The inability to tell which troops are faking and which troops truly need treatment continues to vex the leadership. And perhaps because of this confusion, the leadership at Fort Carson and other military bases still finds backdoor ways to kick out struggling soldiers, rather than give them the help and benefits they deserve. Where will all these men end up?

Will the influx of cash and PTSD research change the game? Will it make warfare somehow less costly and more humane? Will anyone learn from the story of the Lethal Warriors? These questions are still unanswered.

But it seems likely that as long as the United States fights wars like the one in Iraq, we will keep seeing stories like the one in this book. The latest to hit the headlines is the saga of the Fifth Stryker Brigade in Afghanistan. Like the Lethal Warriors, they were foot soldiers deployed to a deadly province. Like the Lethal Warriors, they suffered almost daily attacks by hidden bombs but rarely fought an armed enemy face to face. And like the Lethal Warriors, they started killing civilians and planting weapons on them to fake an attack. In 2011, twelve soldiers were court-martialed for those murders and other crimes. Others have committed suicide or been arrested for other crimes. One deserted the unit and showed up on a crowded street in downtown Salt Lake City in full infantry gear, toting an assault rifle like the one he carried in Afghanistan. He was killed in a shootout with police.

Perhaps the most important lesson the story of the Lethal Warriors can offer is that anyone who experiences the horror of war can be poisoned by it. Those affected by it should know they are not alone. Their struggles do not indicate a defect of character, but rather a natural reaction to an unnatural situation. And they are not alone. Not by a long shot.

INTRODUCTION

A man delivering newspapers found Kevin Shields's body.

It was 5:00 A.M. Saturday, December 1, 2007—four years, seven months, and eleven days after the start of the Iraq War. The deliveryman was rolling in his Ford pickup through a century-old neighborhood packed with crooked bungalows on the west side of Colorado Springs. The block was dark. The sky was clear. Bare branches hung over the predawn street like a black net swimming with stars. The thermometer stood at 14 degrees and the still air had painted frost on the rows of parked cars. Most of the sprawling city of 600,000 on the high, dry prairie at the foot of the Rockies was still asleep. The jagged silhouette of the mountains on the western edge of town stood cloaked in darkness except for a single light shining from the very summit of 14,000-foot Pikes Peak. The quiet yards reeled past the pickup's open window, one after another, and the soft thud of copies of the *Colorado Springs Gazette* falling on the sidewalks and porches sounded the peaceful cadence of the start of another day.

Then there was the body.

The deliveryman pressed on the brakes, a newspaper still in his hand, shoved the shifter into park, and craned out the window for a closer look.

Kevin Shields was sprawled faceup across the sidewalk, his head near the gutter, just inches from the pickup's front tire. He looked young, maybe twenty years old, was clean shaven with smooth boyish cheeks, had a military buzz cut, and was wearing no hat or gloves despite the cold. His half-open eyes stared blankly at the net of stars. His feet almost touched a white picket fence hung with red ribbon for Christmas. His head was tilted slightly downhill and blood spilling from his nose and mouth had trickled back and pooled around his eyes, drying in the perfect shape of a mask. A barely smoked Camel lay on his chest where it had landed after falling from his lips.

"Hey, buddy! You OK?"[1] the deliveryman shouted.

Kevin Shields did not answer.

A bullet had punched a small hole through his right cheek, right where a beauty mark might be. It had splintered the thin shell of his skull and torn apart his temporal lobe—the part of the brain that attaches meaning to complex, nuanced images like black branches lacing the night sky or red bows on a white picket fence. A second bullet had pierced his neck, jabbing up through his skull and destroying the part of his cerebellum that acts as the internal metronome bringing balance, time, and space together. A third shot through his tongue and throat before clipping his spinal cord. A fourth tore through the blood-rich muscles of his left thigh.

Kevin Shields was dead.

The deliveryman dropped the rolled-up copy of that day's *Gazette,* fumbled for his cell, and dialed 911.

The paper that hit the pavement not far from Shields's body that morning held a grab bag of news typical of any city of 600,000: TEACHER CUTS HAIR FOR CHARITY, BUDGET CUTS WORRY EMERGENCY OFFICIALS, MOUNTAINS MAY GET FOUR FEET OF SNOW. But tucked away on page three was news unique to Colorado Springs: BRIGADE LIKELY WILL BE HOME BY CHRISTMAS.

Colorado Springs is perhaps the most military city in America. Take away the backdrop of the Rocky Mountains and in many ways Colorado Springs appears to be any modern western American city, punctuated by inoffensive earth-toned suburban sprawl. The town regularly racks up "best city" awards from glossy magazines. Most residents are transplants attracted by good jobs, low crime, clean air, and sunshine. Roots are shallow. History is short. There is no regional accent, cuisine, or industry. The biggest nongovernmental employer is Wal-Mart. Neighborhoods are often distinguishable only by the neon clusters of chain stores and restaurants. It could be Mesa, Arizona, or Santa Ana, California, or Salt Lake City, Utah. In many ways, the defining culture is a lack of a defining culture.

At the same time, Colorado Springs is far from typical because it is surrounded by military bases. To the north is the U.S. Air Force Academy, where elite cadets train to be pilots and officers. To the east is Schriever Air Force Base, where pilots who wear jumpsuits but almost never leave the ground control a shadowy armada of military satellites and drones. To the west, burrowed more than a thousand feet into the solid granite of Cheyenne Mountain, is NORAD, where Cold War–era computers scan every inch of earth's orbit for incoming nuclear missiles. And to the south sits Fort Carson, the third-largest army base in the country. Around the cluster of military installations swirl an orbit of defense contractors. The annual local economic impact of the military is estimated to be about $4 billion. One out of every three dollars spent in Colorado Springs flows through the U.S. Department of Defense.[2]

The morning Kevin Shields was shot, many of the more than twenty thousand troops at Fort Carson were in their second, third, or fourth deployments in the wars sparked in the wake of the terrorist attacks of September 11, 2001. The Iraq War—a conflict that military commanders initially said would last six months, tops—was grinding through its fifth and bloodiest year.[3] And the war in Afghanistan, which was predicted to be just as quick and easy, was in its seventh.[4] The troops were increasingly weary and worn out, and so was the country's appetite for war. By late 2007, much of America's initial flag-waving fervor for the wars had either drifted to other distractions or dug in to predictable positions of partisan rhetoric and email forwarding.

But in Colorado Springs, the war was not an abstract policy question or another partisan fulcrum. It was day-to-day life. War was seen not so much as a question of right or wrong but as a professional duty. No matter what the troops thought of George W. Bush or the Taliban or Saddam Hussein, or the whole multibillion-dollar adventure, if they were summoned, they went and did their job. The families left behind usually focused not on the big-picture headlines coming out of Washington or on the squabbling of commentators on cable, but on the daily bulletins of small victories and defeats—good news and bad news—that could change their lives forever.

The top story in the *Colorado Springs Gazette* lying near Shields's body that day was a rare scrap of good news in a year that had been mostly bad. It announced that the 3,900 soldiers of the 2nd Brigade Combat Team, 2nd Infantry Division would be home for Christmas. The brigade had left home to spend twelve months in Baghdad in October 2006 at the height of vicious sectarian clashes between Muslim factions in the city. Then the surge to retake the city came and the unit's tour was extended for three months. In that fifteen-month tour, 64 men in the 3,700-soldier brigade were killed in combat. Another 240 were seriously wounded. The brigade, which made up only a fifth of Fort Carson's population, claimed more than half of its casualties. The unit's corner of Baghdad was so infested with roadside bombs, sniper fire, and revenge killings between warring factions that when the brigade commander, Colonel Jeff Bannister, spoke on the phone to the *Colorado Springs Gazette* for the story about their homecoming, he proudly said things were clearly getting better: there hadn't been a single attack for 24 hours. "That's huge," he told the reporter.[5]

In fact, there *had* been an attack on the brigade that day. And another death.

Kevin Shields had served as a machine gunner in the 2nd Brigade for two tours. After growing up in a small town in Illinois, he joined the active-duty army in 2003 at age twenty. Since then, like everyone in his unit, he had spent more time deployed than he had at home. He had seen the worst of Iraq and come back a broken man—suicidal and addled by brain injuries. He had spent so much time away from his wife and three-year-old son that he sometimes felt he barely knew them.[6]

He had gone out alone the night before his murder to celebrate his birthday. Now he was dead. The reasons for his murder had almost nothing to do with what he did or said that night, or the aging neighborhood of bungalows where his body was found. They had much more to do with things that happened months and years before and thousands of miles away in Iraq—things that people who had never deployed to Iraq, even people in a military town like Colorado Springs, could not understand.

Days later, after some good detective work and a lucky break, police caught the killers and were surprised to discover Shields had been shot by his fellow soldiers. The cops arrested two veteran machine gunners, Louis Bressler and Kenneth Eastridge, and a twenty-one-year-old medic, Bruce Bastien. Eventually all were sent to prison. But police would soon learn that Shields was not the first to be killed by soldiers from the brigade, or the last.

Shields's five-hundred-soldier battalion within the brigade had started the war as the 506th Infantry Regiment, a unit famously known since World War II as the "Band of Brothers."[7] It was a hallowed fighting team with a long reputation for heroics in the face of impossible odds. But through several changes in command over two combat tours, the army renamed the battalion the "Lethal Warriors." The rolled-up *Colorado Springs Gazette* not far from Shields's body reported that the Lethal Warriors would be home from the war in just a few weeks. What it did not mention was that, true to the name, the unit would bring the war home with them.

A few days later, the bold black headline reporting the arrest of Kevin Shields's killers revealed new, more disturbing crimes: CARSON GI: CIVILIANS SHOT AT, MAN FACING MURDER CHARGE TALKS OF VIOLENCE IN IRAQ.[8] Under the headline, the arrested men stared from mug shots with hooded eyes and cold, expressionless mouths hanging from pallid faces. They looked like the undead.

Major General Mark Graham scanned the newspaper story and the faces of the young soldiers and felt a sad remorse. The fifty-three-year-old officer had a thick thatch of silver hair, large, coffee-colored eyes, a strong jaw, and a hard-set love for the army. He had taken full command of Fort Carson in September 2007, just two months before Shields was killed. At the post, the general commanded 21,000 troops and civilians—more employees than anyone in Colorado except the governor. He also oversaw every National Guard and Reserve soldier west of the Mississippi, all 190,000 of them. With the war in high gear, Fort Carson was in the midst of deploying combat brigades at such a frenetic pace that there was barely enough time to train, resupply, and fill vacancies in the force before shipping out again.

In spite of the commotion and the size of Graham's assignment, which often meant his workdays started before 7:00 A.M. and pushed late into the night, it was the small, sometimes overlooked aspects of the job that interested him most. For Graham, the greatest part of the army was the individual soldiers. The general made it a point to visit wounded troops at the post's hospital every chance he could and sat quietly in the front row of every memorial service for those killed in Iraq and Afghanistan. Busy as he was with the big picture, he never seemed too preoccupied to see each individual portrait.

Graham had grown up in a small town in Illinois. His father had died of a heart attack when Graham was eleven years old. His mother worked on a washing-machine assembly line and later as a bookkeeper to provide them a simple living. Graham joined the Reserve Officers Training Corps (ROTC) at eighteen as a way to pay his way through Murray State University in Kentucky. He was reluctant to join the military because he did not want to cut his long hair, but he knew his mother couldn't afford to send him to school. He was commissioned a second lieutenant of field artillery in 1977. In the post-Vietnam era, when military service wasn't exactly cool, and with no history of military service in his family, Graham had every intention of leaving the army as soon as he fulfilled his service obligation. It never happened. The strong friendships he formed in the army always kept him from leaving. "He never had much family. He never had any brothers," his wife, Carol, later said. "So the army became his brotherhood. It became his family."

But the road had been hard on the general in the last few years. Hard in ways he would have thought unimaginable before the Iraq War. He had taken command of Fort Carson at its most out-of-control point in decades. Multiple deployments were straining soldiers and their families to the breaking point, leaving a trail of divorce, arrests, and suicide. But it went far deeper than that.

Graham was now a two-star general. The names of his grown sons, Jeffrey and Kevin, were engraved on the underside of the silver stars he wore on his shoulder straps. Both had admired their father as much as he had admired them. Both had joined the ROTC in college, just like him. Both now were dead.

That morning, looking at the pallid mug shots in the newspaper, Graham felt, in a way, as he felt when he looked at every soldier since his sons died, whether it was a soldier standing rigid as a commander pinned a bronze star on his chest or an image of a soldier who had gone AWOL and slit his wrists in a motel room. He looked at them as if he were looking at his own sons—as if his own family members were standing accused of murder. He felt the contradictory stabs of emotion that often follow a family tragedy: disbelief, shame, a fleeting urge to disown or blame, anger, a search for excuses, an upwelling of grief, then the solemn emptiness of acceptance that can only be filled with questions: "How did this happen? What did we miss? What could I have done better?"

It was a question he was doomed to ask over and over. In the twelve months after Kevin Shields was shot, soldiers from the returning brigade killed five more people. Others were shot or stabbed, intentionally run down by cars, beaten, or raped. The arrest rate for troops in the city tripled, compared to peacetime levels. The crimes were only the tip of a pyramid of destruction that included everything from manslaughter and drunk-driving fatalities to assault, domestic violence, drug abuse, and divorce. In the four battalions that made up the brigade, the carnage was especially high among one: the Lethal Warriors. One soldier started gunning down random pedestrians on the street near his apartment with an AK–47. Another beat his ex-girlfriend so savagely that homicide detectives searched his house for a weapon, incredulous that he could do such damage with his bare hands. In the year after the battalion returned from Iraq, the per-capita murder rate for this small group of soldiers was a hundred times greater than the national average.[9]

Alone, each of the murders might not have meant much beyond the communities they savaged or the families they destroyed. The country had already seen several such killings without raising much alarm. In towns large and small, headlines told similar stories of men back from Iraq: IRAQ WAR VET CHARGED IN SHOOTING DEATH OF FELLOW SOLDIER[10] in Kansas; ARMED IRAQ VETERAN CHARGED IN APARTMENT SHOOTING[11] in Idaho; WAR STRESS BLAMED IN IRAQ VET SHOOTINGS[12] in Las Vegas; VET ACCUSED OF KILLING WIFE WEEPS AS PROSECUTORS OUTLINE CASE[13] in Chicago. But these uncharacteristic bursts of violence were isolated. They offered anyone trying to decide what role the wars played in the crimes only a confusing blend of suspicion and skepticism: suspicion that combat had something to do with the crimes, and skepticism that such a notion offered too generous an excuse. Few people pondered the news, and often when someone suggested that combat was to blame, military officials were quick to note that all troops are screened for mental health problems and offered every possible resource.[14]

Kevin Shields could have been one more forgotten name on the roster, another headline read in the morning and tossed away by afternoon. But as more soldiers from his unit were arrested for murder, the question of what lay behind all the killings became harder to ignore. Eventually the national media, Congress, and even the army took notice. This one senseless death was the start of a wave of crime that eventually changed how the government thinks about the connection between war and violence. After long denying it, today the army acknowledges that combat can contribute to crime. It is developing programs that aim to inoculate soldiers against the toxic stress of war and treat them when they return. The moment Kevin Shields's body hit the ground can be seen as the beginning of a turning point in how the military thinks about the lingering psychological wounds of war, often called post-traumatic stress disorder (PTSD). In large part, the Lethal Warriors and the havoc they wreaked on Colorado Springs forced the army to begin to address these hard issues.

———

Colorado Springs is an average city with an average amount of crime. It regularly ranks right in the middle for major American cities. Double the city's murder rate and you would have New York City's. Quadruple it and you would have Los Angeles's. Increase it ten times and you would have Detroit's. But increase it one hundred times? That starts to look less like a city and more like a war zone. It starts to look like Iraq.

I grew up in Colorado Springs, so close to Fort Carson that I could hear the booming of artillery at night. Growing up, I counted an ever-changing cadre of army brats as my friends. That was during the Cold War, when deployment often meant nothing more than a few years in West Germany or Korea. Times have changed.

Just a few weeks after the war in Iraq started in 2003, I went to work as a reporter at the *Colorado Springs Gazette*. From the newsroom, I started to see a different side of the army than the one I knew growing up. It was not the Cold War anymore. Soldiers were returning from long, grueling, and deadly combat tours only to be told to get ready to go back again. At home, civilian life chugged on as if Iraq did not exist. As the war ground through two, three, and four years, more and more soldiers were getting in trouble with police. I watched friends stationed at Fort Carson go from eager and idealistic to worn down and disillusioned. The arrest rate of military personnel in town doubled and then tripled. Assaults in the city set records. At the newspaper, we reported on huge brawls that grew to several hundred people outside bars popular with GIs. The police had to form special task forces to try to control the crowds. At the same time that this fiercely Republican city was brandishing SUPPORT THE TROOPS bumper stickers, you could see the malaise seeping into all walks of life.

Then the murders started.

When it was one soldier, then another, arrested for killing, it made you shake your head and wonder if the cause was Iraq or something inside the man that made him pull the trigger. But when three, then six, then eight, then ten soldiers were arrested for murder or attempted murder, and all of them came from one particularly hard-hit brigade, their shared experiences in war started to become a more likely culprit. The killings raised several questions: Why this one unit out of hundreds? What had happened to these Lethal Warriors, as the soldiers in this unit called themselves? How much was due to who they were before they joined the infantry? How much was due to the untold things they saw and did in Iraq? How much was due to their treatment when they came home?

People are naturally reluctant to believe that war could turn someone into a killer. We think of ourselves as fixed, concrete personalities. Experiences may leave a noticeable patina on our character, but we like to believe they can't fundamentally change who we are—certainly not enough to make a good person bad, or turn a calm man into a killer. To admit that such a thing is possible is to admit that none of us really know ourselves—that we are at the mercy of experience. But that is what has happened time and time again to soldiers returning from war. Murder is an extreme example, but the stark changes combat can forge are so common that the refrain of friends and family describing a young veteran's return has become cliché: he came home different.

Looking at the mug shots in the newspaper of the men who murdered Kevin Shields, I was struck by how young they were. Most had joined the army out of high school and were of college age by the time they were arrested. Instead of spending those formative years at a university, they had spent them at war. Looking at the photographs, I thought of these young men and all the life-building events guys their age usually experience—the challenges, mistakes, triumphs, and relationships that are the raw materials of maturity. These guys had few of the normal experiences. Instead, they had Iraq and more Iraq.

If I had watched my best friend die at that age, had seen people killed pointlessly in a crossfire, had shot Iraqis only to realize that killing was not like not anything shown in the movies. If I had been almost killed by a roadside bomb one morning and then ordered to go out the next day and the next and the next on the same road—if I had been an infantryman in the Lethal Warriors—who would I be when I graduated from that experience? Would I be another mug shot in the paper? I honestly was not sure.

After the murder of Kevin Shields, and the murders that followed, Fort Carson was at first quick to dismiss any suggestion that the experience of war led soldiers to commit crime. The army repeatedly pointed out that it had screening processes to look for things such as depression and post-traumatic stress disorder, and a whole floor at Fort Carson's hospital was dedicated to soldiers' mental health. Many in the army suggested that the cause of the crimes was not war or poor mental healthcare but the men themselves. "Anybody that does crimes of that nature, it goes deeper and farther back than anything in the U.S. Army," Lieutenant Colonel Brian Pearl, the 2–12's commanding officer, told the *Los Angeles Times* after the murders. "Nothing here has trained them to do what they are charged with."[15]

Many officials dismissed the significance of the killings by pointing out that the vast majority of the soldiers in the unit had not committed any crimes, but that in every bunch there would be a few bad apples. They pointed out that the soldier demographic of men eighteen to twenty-four naturally included the section of the population with the highest violent crime rate. But that alone could not explain the jump in violence. The Lethal Warriors had a murder rate twenty times greater than young men as a whole.

To me, it seemed unwise to judge where these soldiers had ended up without a thorough inquiry into where they had been. The only way to really know what happened to the Lethal Warriors was to talk to the men themselves. In researching this book, I spent months interviewing soldiers, sergeants, officers, mothers and fathers, brothers, lawyers, and police. I listened to the stories of men in prisons, trailer parks, parents' basements, and wherever they had washed up after combat.

Lethal Warriors is their story.

———

It is true, as the authorities have said, that most of the soldiers who come back from Iraq never end up in jail. Many veterans whom I have met in the course of my research are kind, law-abiding, and selfless beyond belief. But it is important to tell the story of this critical few in order to offer what the army would call an "after-action review"—an inspection of what happened, why it happened, and what can be done to keep it from happening again.

So what did happen to the Lethal Warriors? In short, hundreds of teenagers volunteered for the most dangerous job in the army. They were conditioned through months of specialized drills to be disciplined, tough, brave, and utterly lethal. Then they were sent to the deadliest places in Iraq. They came home to a hero's welcome but were given little in terms of actual support for the invisible psychological wounds of war. Many were paranoid and quick to anger. Many felt unsafe and alienated back in the United States. Reintegration into civilian life was brief, and, by many soldiers' estimations, a joke. The army spent months and sometimes years teaching them to be warriors, then Iraq taught its own harsh lessons, but on return, these young soldiers, many just barely adults, were expected to figure things out on their own.

Many people I've spoken to don't believe that the wars in Iraq and Afghanistan pack enough intensity to inflict much psychological damage on soldiers. After all, the conflicts have generated little of the all-out combat associated with World War II, and only 5,631 U.S. troops were killed in the conflicts by the summer of 2010—a fraction of the 58,000 killed in Vietnam in about the same number of years. But the lack of massive offensives and the smaller number of deaths conceal the true toll.

Iraq and Afghanistan are new kinds of wars with new kinds of casualties. Though the wars have produced relatively few American dead, that is, to a large extent, because of new advances in body armor, armored vehicles, and sophisticated lifesaving techniques. In the Civil War and World War II, one in three soldiers wounded in combat died from his injuries. In Vietnam it was one in four. In Iraq and Afghanistan it is somewhere around one in fifteen.[16] This stunning advancement does not even count the thousands who, because of better armor, were never seriously wounded in the first place. A massive explosion that could have evaporated an infantry company in the Civil War might cause little more than a concussion to troops in an armored Humvee in Baghdad. Many of the soldiers later arrested for murder had been blown up half a dozen times and received barely a scratch. But that does not mean modern combat does not inflict wounds. These modern conflicts have produced tens of thousands of walking wounded hidden in the force. Nothing illustrates the new dynamic better than this: by 2009, while the United States was engaged in two separate wars, more soldiers died from suicide, drugs, and alcohol than died by the hand of the enemy.[17]

Many aspects of war have not changed for centuries. What General William Tecumseh Sherman said in 1879 is just as true of Iraq as it was of the Civil War: "War is hell." Fear, blood, courage, grief, rage, violence, hope, and hate have not changed much since Sherman's day or since the earliest kickings of civilization. The smell of death and the sense of loss are the same. The shame and confusion are the same. The human psyche, which must process all these emotions, has not changed much in forty thousand years. Warfare has evolved, but the human brain's ability to cope with it is still stuck in the Stone Age.

The character of combat operations in Iraq and Afghanistan also may create a unique kind of casualty. The conflicts occur mostly in occupied cities and along highways. And the foe is disguised in the civilian population. Real enemies on this unconventional battlefield are hard to identify, and every target appears in a cloud of doubt. Enemy or innocent? Every combat action potentially carries an extra-heavy burden of ambiguity and regret. Mistake the foe for a friend, and perhaps die; mistake a friend for the foe, and die inwardly. Many soldiers understandably begin to mistrust and hate the people they are charged with protecting, extending their fears to the entire population. The same toxic situation produced an estimated 50,000 cases of PTSD in Vietnam that still haunt us forty years later.

At the height of the Iraq War, over 60 percent of American deaths were from improvised explosive devices (IEDs).[18] Troops had few effective means of detecting or defeating these concealed weapons and no clear enemy to counterattack, leaving them only a tense, helpless fear they experienced day in and day out. Hopelessness, helplessness, and uncertainty are some of the most toxic emotions that lead to damaging doses of combat stress, which means the modern type of warfare may not be as loud or bloody as the invasions of D-day or the Tet offensive in Vietnam, but it is no less vicious, and because there are no battle lines in Iraq or Afghanistan, troops almost never get a break. Troops like to say it is 360/365—all around, every day.

One of the truly new aspects of these conflicts is how the military is encouraging soldiers to cope. In past conflicts, soldiers showing signs of combat stress were given what the army called "three hots and a cot"——rest away from the fighting and a few good meals to allow their mind to naturally heal. In the course of my research, I interviewed a sergeant named John Lally who served with the 506th in Vietnam and I asked if his unit had a combat stress doctor that troops could visit. He laughed and said, "The only combat stress doctor we had was Jack Daniels." Now the military is using prescription drugs to tame combat stress for the first time.

Things have changed. Psychiatrists in the field in Iraq and Afghanistan have dispensed untold hundreds of thousands of antidepressants, antianxiety pills, and sleep aids such as Ambien. The army's own data suggest that in 2007 about 22,000 soldiers in Iraq and Afghanistan were taking prescription antidepressants or sleeping pills.[19] These drugs may be given with the best intentions and may be providing needed help, but in the case of the Lethal Warriors, the drugs also allowed the military to keep rundown troops in combat, which just caused the psychosocial effects to pile up until they came home.

———

The unique mix of lifesaving technologies, mood-stabilizing drugs, and vicious Vietnam-style fighting in the current wars has minted a new generation of veterans who return home in one piece even though, inside, they may be in pieces. The effects are evident across the force. In 2009, the army was giving 225,000 soldiers some form of behavioral health care. Almost half of them were on mood-stabilizing prescription drugs. Ten percent of the entire force had a prescription for narcotic painkillers—overwhelmingly OxyContin. Even the army admitted there was likely widespread abuse. Most returning veterans are amazingly strong and resilient. With the help and support of families and communities, they can heal. But a few of the hardest hit by the war need special attention. In the case of the Lethal Warriors, many never got it. So the war spilled out into the suburbs of America, and a number of innocent people died.

It is critical that the lessons the Lethal Warriors have to teach not be ignored, because the ongoing wars in Afghanistan and Iraq have the potential to create new soldiers just like them every day, and future wars will pose the same challenges. By ignoring the needs of these soldiers and others like them, the nation does a great disservice to its war fighters and to itself—one whose consequences became evident in the streets of Colorado Springs. If there is a lesson in the senseless bloodletting of the Lethal Warriors, it is that the nation needs to press for the safety, well-being, and healing of combat veterans, even after the bullets have stopped flying. Doing this for the sake of the soldiers themselves would be enough to justify the cost and effort, but as the story of the Lethal Warriors shows, it is not just the soldiers who pay the ultimate price for the neglect. We all do. It is critical that we deal openly, honestly, and intelligently with the true costs of war, and weigh them before we decide to wage it, or we will suffer the consequences.

CHAPTER 1

"Y'ALL CAN FORGET GOING TO IRAQ"

It was raining in Kyonggi-Do, South Korea. But it almost always rained in Kyonggi-Do, at least during the summer. The province, which lies at the western end of the border with North Korea, sees around fifty inches of rain during the summer monsoons. Water dribbled off every leaf in the thick deciduous forests, saturating the soil and feeding trickles and rills that tumbled down the mountainsides. The rough, low hills looked like a foggy corner of the Appalachians. If not for the orderly quilt of flooded rice paddies spread across the valley floors, the scene could easily be mistaken for West Virginia or eastern Kentucky.

That is what Kenny Eastridge thought when he first saw the Korean landscape. He had grown up in Kentucky, and when he arrived in Kyonggi-Do as a lanky, awkward army private in the winter of 2004 he was surprised at how much this distant corner of Asia looked like the hills back home. Now, on this hot summer night, the rain dripped off the rim of his helmet, soaked into his fatigues, and gleamed on a big machine gun he had slung over his shoulder. Eastridge was a pale scarecrow of a soldier—five feet ten, 140 pounds, with short brown hair, wire-frame granny glasses, and an adam's apple that stuck out like a knot on a tree. He looked like an extra in a war movie—not the strong-jawed hero or the mean sergeant but the young, sensitive small-town kid, the skinny one with the accent and just enough charisma and heart to doom him at the climax of the picture.

Somewhere nearby in the dark he could hear the diesel growl of tank. Around him, other soggy soldiers tramped through the ceaseless rain on a training mission. After nine weeks of basic training and a few weeks of specialized infantry training stateside, the nineteen-year-old private had been sent with a handful of new recruits to the 1st Battalion, 506th Infantry Regiment, stationed on the North Korean border. Its mission was to guard against a massive Communist attack. The troops trained relentlessly to be ready at a moment's notice. They lugged their heavy guns up mountain ridges. They stayed out for days at a time on foot. And that night, they marched through the rain, sinking deeper and deeper into the Kyonggi-Do mud.

Somewhere in the dark morass of tanks and men marched Kevin Shields and Louis Bressler, two other new recruits barely out of high school. None of them really knew the others, and none had ever expected to find themselves in rural South Korea, but that spot, more than any, marked the starting point of a journey that literally circled the globe, through four years and two combat tours, only to eventually crash in Colorado Springs.

The battalion's five hundred soldiers were stationed in a remote cluster of low, Cold War–era cinder-block barracks called Camp Greaves. The camp, which had been the battalion's home since 1987, sat about two miles from the Demilitarized Zone and was the American outpost closest to North Korea. The barracks stood tucked among the green hills and flooded rice paddies on the north bank of the wide, slow Imjin River. Two bridges spanning the Imjin sat within shouting distance of the camp. The first was a rickety, narrow steel trestle called the Freedom Bridge, because thousands of prisoners of war had walked south across the bridge to freedom in 1953 when the Korean War wound down. The second, a few hundred meters upriver, was the Unity Bridge, a four-lane modern span built as a gesture toward reunification of the North and the South. Both bridges were strung with razor wire and packed with explosives.

In the event of an all-out attack from the north, the battalion was supposed to blow both bridges, scramble into Black Hawk helicopters, and retreat across the river to defensive positions to brace themselves against the onslaught of North Korea's estimated one million troops. Casualties in the battalion were expected to be upward of 90 percent. The role of Eastridge and the others was only to slow the advance. In short, commanders told the unit—joking in a way that let everyone know they were dead serious—"We are the speed bump."[1]

When they arrived, the new grunts were taught that because they were assigned to the 506th Infantry Regiment, they were now part of one of the most hallowed, heroic, and respected units in the entire U.S. Army. They called themselves the Band of Brothers. Few of the fresh privates knew much at all about the history of the Band of Brothers when they arrived in Korea, but they all had it practically memorized by the time they left.

———

The Band of Brothers was formed at the start of World War II as a new kind of fighting force. It was an experimental paratrooper unit manned entirely by volunteers—no draftees—and trained in a way the army hoped would render it especially lethal in combat. During World War II, soldiers often went through basic training together but then were sent off to different units. The Band of Brothers was different. They all lived and trained together for months, then shipped off to Europe together as a unit. The idea was that soldiers who trained together knew how to work together better. They knew each other's strengths and weaknesses. They would trust each other in combat. Combined, these factors would make them a better fighting team.

Almost every day and on many nights, the infantry recruits of the original Band of Brothers had to run two miles from their training camp in Toccoa, Georgia, to the top of an 800-foot mountain called Currahee—a Cherokee word meaning "Stands alone." The mountain became a symbol both of their individual strength and their shared struggle. Over half a century later, and half a world away, soldiers in the Band of Brothers stationed in a rainy corner of Korea still saluted their officers by shouting, "Stands alone!"

The experimental unit proved its worth again and again fighting the Nazis. The Band of Brothers plunged into the flak-filled night over Nazi-occupied France on the eve of the D-day invasion in June 1944. They were told they would be in the fight for three days. Instead, they fought every day for a month; a quarter of the unit was injured and another fifth was killed while taking a number of key enemy positions. In December, the Band of Brothers helped stop a German offensive at the Battle of the Bulge. The outgunned infantry unit—with little food, water, or ammunition and no winter clothing to guard against subzero temperatures—dug in and held off a much larger German force. One-third of the soldiers were killed, but they never abandoned their posts. The unit became famous for bravery and loyalty.

The nickname "Band of Brothers" was adopted from a few lines in the St. Crispin's Day speech in Shakespeare's *Henry V*, in which the king remembers how his sick and drastically outnumbered army triumphed over the French years before:

From this day to the end of the world,
But we in it shall be remembered—

We few, we happy few, we band of brothers;
For he to-day that sheds his blood with me
Shall be my brother; be he ne'er so vile

Adopting "Band of Brothers" as a moniker was the soldiers' way of saying the bonds of friendship in battle would always unite them, no matter what happened down the road. The nickname originally only referred to the men of the battalion's Company E, but over time the whole battalion adopted it.

In Vietnam, the battalion was reactivated and traded parachutes for helicopters. Once again, the soldiers found themselves in the worst of the worst, fighting back the repeated assaults of the Tet offensive and throwing platoon after platoon against the bloody, entrenched Vietcong bunkers on a promontory soldiers called Hamburger Hill.

The status of the regiment got a sudden boost when its heroics were turned into a bestselling book by historian Stephen Ambrose in 1992,[2] then spun into a ten-part miniseries on HBO in 2001. New soldiers like Shields and Eastridge watched the series over and over in the barracks. If they got bored with it, they could play a video game on PlayStation based on the bloody jungle warfare the Band of Brothers encountered in Vietnam. Everywhere they went, they had to salute superiors by saying "Stands alone!" Even the trays in the chow hall bore the Band of Brothers logo.

Soldiers hoping to be sergeants had to memorize the history of the unit—every parachute jump in Europe and every assault in Asia. When young officers joined the battalion, they went through a decades-old ceremony in which they had to drink from a special grail. The other brothers mixed a brew of tomato juice, symbolic of the blood spilled by past brothers, whiskey for the soldiers who are "strong, smooth and full of fight,"[3] and a pinch of dirt from Currahee Mountain (or, if no dirt was available, coffee grounds) to give them strength to "stand alone." The grail holding the mix had handles fashioned from the metal pull tabs of the Airborne's reserve parachutes. The cup was forged from melted-down silverware the Brothers pilfered from Hitler's vacation home. For the humble grunts of 2004, the lore boosted morale by linking their often humdrum existence to the heroes they saw on TV.

"We thought it was awesome," Jose Barco, a private in the unit who became one of Eastridge's best friends, said years later. "Wearing that 506th patch on your shoulder was one of the coolest things in the world."

In World War II, the Band of Brothers had been a blend of young men of almost every background—country and city, privileged and poor, Jewish and Catholic, virtuous and verging on criminal. Their only common bond was a willingness to volunteer for a job in the army that seemed almost recklessly dangerous. The Brothers marching through the mud of Korea sixty years later were not so different. Every shade and accent was represented—guys from the city and guys from the middle of nowhere, guys with college degrees and guys who never graduated from high school, guys from good homes and guys from the slums, homeschooled Christians and godless delinquents. The one thing they all had in common was that they had voluntarily joined the army—and not just the army, the infantry.

———

Kenny Eastridge had joined at age nineteen in 2003 to save himself from a life that never had much chance of being anything but a disaster. He had grown up in a poor part of Louisville, Kentucky, with his mother. His father worked across town as a mechanic, but Kenny rarely saw him. One day, when Eastridge was about nine, his mom took him to Toys "R" Us, bought him a video game, then dropped him off at his dad's house, saying she needed to run some errands. She didn't come back for three years. He later was told she had become a crack addict. His father took him in, but was not around much. He would pick up fast food for dinner, bring it home, and then go out again. Kenny was left to entertain himself.

One afternoon on May 7, 1996, when he was twelve years old, he invited one of his best friends, Billy Bowman, and two other boys over to play video games. They were messing around, doing what kids do when parents are not home, when Eastridge pulled out one of his father's antique shotguns to show off. He carefully broke open the breech and removed the shells, since he knew his dad always kept his guns loaded. Then he handed it over to his friends, the skinny arms of each boy straining under the cold, heavy metal. They passed it around with nervous smiles. They weren't supposed to play with guns, but that was part of what made it cool. They pointed the gun at each other, pretending they were the Terminator or Rambo or any of a number of other characters from the movies they loved.

"All right, we better put it back up," Kenny said after a while. He broke open the shotgun and slid the shells back into the chambers. Then he tried to slam the breech shut with one flick of his wrist, John Wayne style. The long steel barrel swung up and clicked closed, but he couldn't hold the weight with one hand. He fumbled for the stock with his free hand and caught the trigger. The gun went off. Billy Bowman was watching from a few feet away. The blast hit him square in the chest.

When the cops came, Kenny was crying. He had just killed his best friend. He was arrested and eventually pled guilty to reckless homicide. He did no jail time, but was ordered to have counseling as part of his probation. The court also required him to live in a house with no firearms, but his father refused to give up his guns, so Kenny went to live with his grandmother for a while in rural Shepherdsville, Kentucky. When his mom heard about the killing, she immediately checked herself into rehab. When she sobered up, she remarried his dad and they put together a steady life and got permission for Kenny to move back in with them.

After Billy died, the smell of gunfire, or any burnt-metal smell, always made Eastridge shaky and nauseous. He did not want to think about what had happened. He wasn't a bully or some kind of black-trench-coat sociopath; he was a clever and affable slacker who liked to read, watch movies with friends, smoke pot, play video games, and tell funny stories. On his MySpace page he listed his major as "marijuana."

By the time Eastridge was seventeen and his other friends were graduating from high school, he was so far behind from the murder charges, the counseling, the moving, and general slacking off that he was still only in ninth grade. School felt increasingly awkward. He had no prospects for college. He had no job skills or good chances for meaningful employment. The days of good blue-collar manufacturing jobs in the United States were quickly drawing to a close. The future was a thicket of dead-end jobs. But Eastridge was smart. He knew if he just found the right way to prove himself, he could do something with his life.

The army commercials on TV seemed to offer a chance. Kenny had always been fascinated by the war stories of his grandfather, who was an infantry soldier in World War II, and loved playing shooter video games and watching war movies. The terrorist attacks of September 11, 2001, and the buildup to the Iraq War seemed like a sign to him that his generation was being called to serve. He decided to drop out of school, get his GED, and join the army. He would not only be serving his country, he would be building a career. His mother heartily supported his decision to join. She said it would be good for him.

Eastridge started calling recruiters as soon as he turned eighteen. On his first call in 2003, he learned that the army would not take him. Anyone with a collection of minor criminal convictions or one big one—like the killing of Billy Bowman—needs a waiver from the army to enlist. Recruiters have to interview the soldier to see if they are deserving. The bigger the crime, the higher up the chain of command the waiver has to go. They are not rare, and have become more common as the wars have stretched on. From 2004 to 2009, the army issued 80,403 waivers, with more than half going to recruits with drug and alcohol abuse, misdemeanors, or felonies.[4] When Eastridge mentioned on the phone that he had a felony conviction, the recruiters would say something like "We may be able to work around that." When he said it was a homicide, some would pause, dumbfounded. Some would laugh. "You mean you killed somebody?" one said. "I don't think so." Eastridge kept calling dozens of recruiters across three states, trying to find one who needed to meet a quota. When he grew too embarrassed to call, his mother would. Finally, after six months, a major in Nashville told him, "Son, it sounds like you just need someone to give you a chance. I want to be that guy."

After boot camp at Fort Benning, Georgia, Eastridge landed in South Korea, where on that rainy night he was trudging through the mud, a nineteen-year-old private carrying a twenty-two-pound machine gun slung over his shoulder. The gun's official name was the M–249 squad automatic weapon, but soldiers called it the SAW, partly because of its ability to cut down the enemy. It was the biggest gun that Eastridge's light infantry unit carried. Grunts used it to lay down a suppressive fire in quick burps of sixteen bullets per second. Being a SAW gunner was considered an honor. The job was given to the best, most dependable private in every infantry team. With the machine gun, body armor, extra ammo, water, and required supplies, Eastridge carried almost a hundred pounds. And he loved it. He had finally found something he was good at.

———

Louis Bressler, who would become one of Eastridge's closest friends, marched behind him. There was nothing immediately distinctive about Louie. He was five feet eleven with a solid build, mousy brown hair, a wide, round head, pale blue eyes, and a slightly crooked smile. Other soldiers did not think of him as especially loud or quiet, bright or slow. He was just another guy, cool and fun to be around, but not someone who stuck out from the crowd.

Bressler, too, had joined the army to try to make something of himself. He had grown up across a handful of southern states where his father, Big Lou, sold cars. Out of Louie's three brothers and four sisters, his mother, Theresa Bressler, always described him has as a "new soul"—a child for whom every detail of life was fresh and mysterious. "Some kids might know not to touch a hot stove," she said. "With him, he had to try everything and see."[5]

Big Lou had been a marine in Vietnam. He never said much about the fighting he had seen, but he always talked to the boys about the Marine Corps like it was the greatest thing in the world. He told them stories about survival training. He taught them how to make fires in the woods and live on bugs and berries. He wanted them to be tough and self-reliant like their old man. He let

Louie and his little brother, Drew, settle their differences with their fists. Louie idolized his father. He wanted to be just like him.

Louie always liked being outdoors. He loved playing football. When he was nine years old, Big Lou bought the kids motorcycles, and dirt bike racing became his passion. But school was a struggle. Neither Louie nor Drew could sit still in class. His mother tried Ritalin, and Louie settled down, but she felt uneasy about drugging her kids and tossed the prescription. By the time Louie was eighteen, he had dropped out of high school. He had two kids by a girl he met in school. They lived with his parents but showed little interest in their prospects for the future. Louie drifted through a few low-end jobs at places like Arby's and KFC, occasionally helping Big Lou sell cars.

One day Big Lou, tired of seeing his son sitting around the house playing video games, said it was time for him to be a man. Take responsibility for your life and your family, he said.[6] Get out of the house. You are grown up now. Act like it. They got into a fight. Louie told his father to leave him alone, but he knew Big Lou was right.

After the 9/11 attacks, Louie decided to join the marines to make his old man proud. But because 9/11 had stirred the hearts of so many young men, the marines were flush with new recruits. Louie didn't score high enough in aptitude tests to make the cut. He was so heartbroken he started to cry. His mother took him aside and said, "You can still do it. Go for the army instead. My father did, and he was in all his life. It will be good for you."

Marching through the mud in the dark and the rain, Bressler felt like he was finally making Big Lou proud. He made a point of knowing the regulations and making sure his gear was in perfect shape. He liked the all-night maneuvers, the survival tactics, and the shooting. He liked that he had been chosen to carry a heavy, powerful SAW. He wielded it with pride and took interest in learning all the details of soldiering. The army was cool, and he was good at it.

"Bressler was a stud," his lieutenant, Erwin Godoy, said, recalling his soldier years later. He copped an attitude sometimes, like all new soldiers, the officer said, but he also showed a zeal for the work. "We would run every day with vests, rifles, the full battle rattle. He was always up there with me in the fast group. He wanted to be a soldier. He just needed some guidance."

Also marching in the mud was Kevin Shields, whose background was a near carbon copy of the others'. He was raised in a small town in Illinois by his grandparents after his mom, Deborah Pearson, who was in and out of jail, lost her custody. He never met his father. Shields had three younger siblings—all partially raised in foster homes. By the time he joined the army, he had not seen any of them in years.

Kevin's grandparents had an even-keeled Midwestern kindness and provided a stable, loving home. His grandfather, Ivan Shields, who was a retired stamp-mill foreman, became his closest friend. He never let Kevin shoot so much as a BB gun. Instead he steered him into sports, where he thrived. "He was a smart kid. Everything I showed him, I only had to show him once," his grandfather said.[7] Both shared a love of bowling. Kevin's lifetime average was 200. His grandparents watched him pick up almost every sport in high school: baseball, basketball, golf, and wrestling. He didn't want to go out for football, his grandfather said, because "he did not like hitting." But he loved to snowboard on family trips to Wisconsin. Anything that included being outside with his friends was his kind of thing. Maybe that is why in 2000, when Kevin was seventeen and army recruiters came to his high school, he decided to join the National Guard. A few months after September 11, he told his grandfather he was going to join the infantry full-time.

"Are you sure? You know it might not be like you think it will be," his grandfather said. He had been around long enough to know that war and an eighteen-year-old's idea of war are two different things. He wanted Kevin to really think it through. But Kevin was adamant. He had left high school as a junior and gotten a GED diploma. Since then, like Bressler, he had worked a handful of dead-end jobs at chain restaurants.

"I just feel like it is something I have to do," Kevin said to his grandfather. And that was that.

———

In many ways, the three soldiers' life stories were common in the battalion. A frequent refrain of new recruits usually included some version of "If I hadn't joined the army I'd probably be dead or in jail." Everyone had volunteered for a reason. Usually because their life back home was nothing worth sticking around for.

"Almost all of these soldiers were troubled kids," Lieutenant Godoy said. "We got kids with rough backgrounds, and you took care of them, taught them teamwork, taught them respect. A lot of times it was the first real discipline they ever had. I was mom, dad, boss, judge, and jury."

Every Brother had problems in his past. Eastridge's roommate, Marcus Mifflin, was homeless before he joined. Eastridge's best friend, David Nash, said he had been in a shootout back home in New Orleans. Their medic, Ryan

Krebbs, had dropped out of college, then had been kicked out of his father's house because he was just sitting around smoking pot. The guy across the hall, eighteen-year-old Jose Barco, had never really been outside the Cuban barrios of Miami. He claimed he had been shot multiple times while in high school.

"Doing what?" Eastridge asked.

"Doing something I shouldn't have been doing," Barco said.

He told Eastridge the bullets were still embedded in his side.

At first, Eastridge didn't believe Barco. The baby-faced soldier looked like he was about fifteen years old. He had a lady-killer smile and a drive to please his commanders. He was so sheltered that he had never seen a can of chewing tobacco before he joined the army. But you could never tell. No one believed Eastridge when he said he had accidentally blown away his best friend with a shotgun. With his granny glasses and his skinny neck holding up a big helmet, he looked more like a bobblehead figure than a convicted killer. It just showed that you could not judge a soldier by looking at him. Months later, Barco went to the aid station complaining of twin lumps under his skin. The medic removed two bullets.[8] He kept them for years on his mantel.

That was the thing about this new Band of Brothers. Every soldier had his issues. If he didn't, he probably wouldn't be in the infantry. One in ten needed a waiver for past criminal activity to get into the army. But everyone had also consciously chosen to leave the past behind and seek a better life by joining the military. Later, after the murders started, some blamed the killers' civilian backgrounds for their crimes, but, at least in some ways, soldiers like Bressler, Eastridge, and Barco were not exceptions in the battalion, they were typical.

Their commanders were not overly concerned with whether a soldier was an Eagle Scout or a dropout before joining the Band of Brothers. What mattered was the soldier. He either followed orders or he didn't. He was able to hit the target or he was not. He complained about having to carry the SAW or he sucked it up and marched on. In soldier speak, he was either "squared away," or he was a "shit bag."

If a soldier was squared away, he could work his way up, slowly earning the respect of his sergeants, his fellow grunts, and himself. If he was a shit bag, he could expect punishment from the sergeants. They called it "getting smoked."[9] Usually getting smoked meant push-ups, endless jumping jacks, or less-than-choice duty: scouring garbage cans, scrubbing toilets, or watching the phone all weekend while the others were on a pass. Eastridge, Bressler, and Shields all got smoked now and again when they first arrived for mouthing off to superiors.

"They thought they were tough guys," Godoy said. "But they soon realized everyone there is a tough guy and got humbled a bit. But they were motivated. They performed well."

The training the soldiers received, encouraging them to suck it up and push their problems aside, would come back to haunt them years later, as it led them to ignore the warning signs of PTSD. Acknowledging problems meant a soldier was not able to handle himself. Not being able to handle yourself meant you were a shit bag. Being a shit bag meant you had no place in the Band of Brothers. And many of them loved the Band of Brothers above all else.

Dr. William Nash, a navy psychiatrist at the National Center for Post-Traumatic Stress Disorder who is a leader in the study of the psychiatric toll of war, notes in his book *Combat Stress Injury Theory, Research, and Management* that infantry soldiers' "profession requires them to remain calm, focused and in control regardless of adversity. Psychiatric labels imply, for them, not only weakness but a failure in their core to live up to the warrior ideal. Like weapons found on close inspection to have defective components, psychiatrically labeled war fighters can lose the trust of their superiors and peers, and their own trust in themselves. Many modern warriors would rather be diagnosed with cancer than with depression, anxiety or—worst of all—post-traumatic stress disorder."[10]

The training the Brothers received in Korea did not include tactics for overcoming this natural stigma toward mental health care. They were mired in a Cold War standoff with a Cold War mindset, perpetual readiness but no combat. Over the decades, the army had learned a lot about instilling discipline but very little about treating combat stress. Few of the battalion's commanders had any experience with real combat or any training in how to handle PTSD. When the war came, many soldiers ignored their symptoms and insisted they were still squared away, even as they were slowly losing their minds.

In draft-driven wars like the war in Vietnam, the infantry was the place a grunt generally ended up if he did not have the smarts or the connections for a safer assignment. By 2004 that was no longer true. In the all-volunteer army, thousands of young men signed up to be foot soldiers by choice. The infantry was not the dregs or a dumping ground. Compared to the army as a whole, infantrymen had average intelligence test scores and an average number of criminal waivers. If anything, the infantry considered itself the elite core of the force—the real army. They were willing and able to do things that would send more upstanding, well-adjusted human beings crying to their mommies. Not everyone could be infantry. But the idea of fighting on foot with nothing more than a rifle, a few grenades, and a handful of other fearless thrill-seekers drew a certain type of man like a flame draws moths.

"They tend to be a little crazy," Jeffery Althouse, a platoon sergeant in the Lethal Warriors, said years later. "But a lot of times that is the mentality you are looking for. Those loose cannons sometimes are the guys who are going to be good in a fight."

Kenny Eastridge, with his hard-luck past, was one of the craziest guys. He drank heavily when not training. His uniform was not always up to neatness standards. He seemed to excel at demanding training exercises but to founder when given any free time. Some sergeants warned other incoming soldiers: "If you want to do well in the army, stay away from that guy."[11]

Eastridge wanted nothing more than to become an infantryman. He wanted to hump through the mud with a big SAW over his shoulder. He loved going to the range. He qualified as an expert in every weapon. After basic training, he could have signed up for almost any other job—fixing trucks, firing artillery, filing papers—but, he said, "I wanted to do all the crazy war stuff only the infantry gets to do." Most of the others felt the same way. They wanted to stay out in the field for days on end, lugging rucksacks up mountains, sleeping in the mud and the rain, then getting drunk when they came back and hopefully getting laid. More than anything, though, they wanted to go to war. That was their job. They saw it as their ultimate test.

"I wanted to kill bad guys," Jose Barco said later. "I didn't join the army to end up behind no desk."

Eastridge felt the same way, or thought he did. But most people, when it really comes down to it, don't actually want to kill other people. Humans are social animals, and the natural aversion to taking another person's life is so strong that, some studies suggest, left to their own instincts soldiers often will not fire their weapons, even in the heat of battle. This phenomenon was first described during World War II by a brigadier general named S. L. A. Marshall, who surveyed thousands of soldiers in the Pacific shortly after battles to see how many had fired their weapons. He found only about 20 percent ever had. The rest simply held their guns, unable or unwilling to fire.

Through his research, Marshall surmised that the main reason for the astonishing lack of firing was that soldiers simply did not want to kill. When the time came and they had another person in their sights, their humanity overcame their training and they could not pull the trigger. The "problem," argued Marshall, who was an official military historian focused on creating more effective and deadly army units, stemmed from the fact that the army was training soldiers to fire at targets and not at people. He proposed the military "apply the proper correctives."[12]

In the intervening decades, historians have challenged Marshall's data, and some now dismiss them. Others defend them. But the army wholeheartedly embraced his findings and began training soldiers with a new program to overcome the natural aversion to killing. It is called "reflexive fire" and is still used to this day. Soldiers start by learning to aim and operate their weapons shooting at classic bull's-eyes. Then they move on to paper outlines shaped like people. Eventually they graduate to lifelike battle simulation ranges of rolling hills and trees where human-shaped targets pop up for a few seconds. The soldier must immediately aim and shoot. In close-quarters handgun training, soldiers' silhouettes pop suddenly from behind corners and barriers and soldiers have to shoot twice into the center of mass. They are rewarded for hitting targets and reprimanded for missing. Through repetition, conscious thought is minimized, and as the name of the technique suggests, firing becomes a reflex.

Reflexive fire is classic psychological conditioning—the same process Ivan Pavlov used to get a dog to salivate at the sound of a bell in the often-used psychology textbook example. And it is extremely effective. Army studies show that by the Vietnam War the rate of fire had jumped from 20 percent to 90 percent.[13]

"They drill it into you over and over," Eastridge said, looking back at his training. "Until it is all muscle memory."

The jump in firing is a victory for fighting forces, but can have dangerous side effects for the individuals who do the fighting. Soldiers overcome thousands of years of social evolution with a few months of conditioning. And being able to pull the trigger though muscle memory is not the same as being able to reconcile with the act afterward. "The ability to increase this firing rate comes at a hidden cost," Lieutenant Colonel Dave Grossman writes in his authoritative guide to killing in combat, *On Killing*. "Severe psychological trauma becomes a distinct possibility when psychological safeguards of such magnitude are overridden."[14]

This is not to say that reflexive fire training removes all conscious decision making. Just as a big league slugger who practices swinging at thousands of pitches until he can hit a ball without thinking will not suddenly and impulsively start swinging while walking down the street, a soldier will not lose control of his ability to decide when to shoot and not shoot after months of reflexive fire training. But in the right situation, just like the batter, he will be able to shoot without conscious thought. And one of the ageless safeguards against violence is switched off.

In 2004, most of the new privates in the Band of Brothers did not give much thought to the psychological impacts of the training they received. They had joined the army to kill bad guys, and they were getting to fire cool guns like the SAW. Besides, most of them had inadvertently put themselves through years of desensitization before joining the army by playing hours and hours of lifelike first-person-shooter video games.

Not only that, they were itching to fight. Eastridge, Bressler, and Barco were so eager to go into battle that they were initially disappointed when they found out that after basic training they were going to South Korea instead of Iraq. South Korea counted as a deployment. It was a hardship tour for which the soldiers got an extra $150 pay every month—a little thanks from Uncle Sam for living far from home in a dangerous area. No army unit had ever been sent from one hardship deployment to another. "So ya'll can forget going to Iraq," Eastridge's sergeant said when he first arrived.

Maybe, once the Band of Brothers redeployed back to the United States in another year, then stayed in the States at least a year, there would be a chance of going to Iraq, the sergeant said. But with the top brass of the military predicting in 2003 that the Iraq War would last at most six months, there would not be much action left. The show would be over.

Instead, the battalion's assignment was to spend a year as the speed bump standing defensively against the Democratic People's Republic of Korea. The Band of Brothers was part of a larger, 3,900-soldier unit called the 2nd Brigade Combat Team of the 2nd Infantry Division. A brigade combat team is a bit like a string quartet—one group made of four distinct units, each having a different expertise that allows it to do the job. The brigade had a heavy artillery battalion (the big, long-distance guns), a mechanized infantry battalion with light, tank-like personnel carriers called Bradley Fighting Vehicles (medium guns), and two air-assault infantry battalions trained to rapidly deploy foot soldiers from helicopters (small guns). The idea was that a single brigade combat team would include every resource needed to fight a small war.

Eastridge, Bressler, Shields, Barco, and the others eventually realized that sitting in South Korea, missing out on Iraq, was not so bad. An attack by the Communists was not very likely. Though the Korean War was still technically being waged (both sides declared a truce in 1953 but never made peace), neither side had fired a shot in years. The demilitarized zone, 2.5 miles wide, 155 miles long, and fenced and guarded by both sides, had unintentionally grown into a leafy, peaceful nature preserve. When Eastridge arrived late in 2003, the only barrages being lobbed across the border were rhetorical. From his barracks he could hear the massive loudspeakers on the Communist side of the DMZ blaring old Marxist marches and praises to the Dear Leader and his utopian egalitarian state all night. The South countered by blasting western-style pop and cheery discourses on democracy. They went back and forth, on and on, as they had for years and years.[15]

One part of life in Korea that Eastridge learned to love was Sergeant Sean Huey, his squad leader. The twenty-eight-year-old from Pennsylvania had a strong sergeant's jaw without a sergeant's snarl. He was stern but fair. He demanded a lot, but it only served to make the squad better. And when things were bad, he always had a joke. Eastridge had never grown up with much discipline, and at first he chafed under the tight control of the army. But eventually he started to realize that Sergeant Huey's demands were making him a stronger, better person. He marched the men up and down through the mountains of Kyonggi-Do for days at a time. They slept out in the frigid mud and practiced with their weapons until they were all dead shots. He wanted them to know they could be more than they were. They could do anything if they worked hard. "He was a total badass and a great guy," Eastridge said later. "Everybody loved him."

The Band of Brothers' remote camp was populated entirely by men. Families were required to stay stateside. American women were nowhere to be seen. The isolated infantry camp had a bowling alley, a movie theater, and, to make the Americans feel at home, a Burger King. Most American soldiers were not allowed to drive in Korea. There was a nightly curfew to keep soldiers from causing trouble in the local villages. Without much to do, the men trained for an eventual attack over and over: sound the alarm, grab your gear, heft your SAW, fall back to the Black Hawks.

When soldiers got a break, they usually took a bus to the nearby military town of Sonjuri, where a seedy red-light district had grown full and robust in the fifty years of American patronage. Soldiers referred to it and a dozen districts like it in different towns near bases across South Korea as "the Ville." Dark, sleazy clubs called drinky-girl bars, aimed at young GIs, crowded the narrow street. Tangles of wires strung above the dirty pavement fed power to neon signs hanging over the sidewalks: BMW CLUB, JOHNNY BAR, CLUB LIBERTY, and CLUB USA. The drinky girls, scantily clad young women who were employed by the bars, smiled and waved outside the clubs to lure soldiers in with "Buy me a drinky?"

The setup inside the bars was always the same. Soldiers could buy the girl a sweet, nonalcoholic cocktail for about twenty dollars. The cocktail would entitle the Joe to a little conversation. With the right girl, a few cocktails might get him a peek under her shirt or a quick rub under the table. Many of the girls were prostitutes, and most could at least introduce a soldier to a prostitute.

Most of the girls were from Russia or the Philippines. Shadowy traffickers imported them on "entertainment visas," claiming they planned to employ them as singers. The traffickers then rented them out to bar owners. The girls worked in modern indentured servitude. The bar gave them room and board. The girls had to sell between two hundred and four hundred drinks a month to pay their rent. A girl who didn't sell enough drinks to pay her rent went into debt with the bar. The easiest way to get out of debt was through prostitution. A girl charged about $150 to take a soldier upstairs. She was allowed to keep about $40. The rest went to the bar owner.[16]

Some guys cruised the Ville more than others. Soldiers in the unit estimate about half did not go at all. Shields bought drinks regularly for a Russian girl named Svetlana and they ended up getting married. After patronizing the Ville for a few months, Eastridge married a Korean drinky girl. Eastridge's close friend, David Nash, was known to come off weeklong training missions in the mountains and go straight to the whorehouses without even taking a shower. The platoon's medic tried to make an example of him by publicly announcing to the barracks he was treating Nash for venereal disease yet again, but it did little good. That, along with a general lack of hygiene and a dirty sense of humor, earned the private the name Nasty Nash, or simply Nasty.[17]

The infantry battalion took great pride in instilling soldiers with some of the noblest human traits: bravery, honor, fidelity, and unity. But many grunts took just as much pride in wallowing in some of humanity's most debasing vices: getting stumbling drunk and getting in fights with soldiers from other units, then blowing their pay at a whorehouse. Such behavior was not something to be ashamed of in the unit. If anything, it was fodder for a good story during the next march in the mountains. Soldiers said many superiors tacitly condoned it.

Officially, soldiers were not supposed to patronize the drinky bars, but punishment for patronizing prostitutes and brawling in the Ville was often mild compared to what it would be in the United States. What would have been a felony assault stateside was often just dealt with via sergeants at the platoon level. Sometimes they would assign no punishment at all. Sometimes they would even encourage soldiers. Later, many soldiers said they thought the lax party atmosphere of South Korea was in part to blame for their wild behavior when they returned to the United States. Other units saw heavy combat, but the soldiers of the 506th saw heavy combat after being immersed in a world where things like prostitution and brawling in the streets had few consequences. "Stuff you wouldn't get in trouble for over there became a big deal," Jose Barco said, remembering his return to the States. "That was a big shock."

————

After being assured there was no way the Band of Brothers was ever going to Iraq, suddenly, in April 2004, there were rumors. A specialist from Texas got a call from his mom, who had a brother in army intelligence. He heard they were all going to Iraq. Then another soldier heard it, too. Then CNN reported it.

"We're not going to Iraq," soldiers remember hearing Charlie Company's commander, Captain William Jones, saying. "We're right in the middle of Expert Infantryman Badge training."[18]

The battalion had been practicing for weeks to take the test for the prestigious badge. To qualify, soldiers had to pass thirty-three skill tests, including setting booby trap; throwing hand grenades with deadly accuracy; and learning to assemble, load, and fire the ten different guns used by the infantry well enough to do it with their eyes closed. It was a ticket to going to Ranger School and becoming a truly elite warrior, which is all that most of them dreamed of doing. The test was just days away.

Eastridge and Bressler had been practicing over and over, and were confident they would make it. Both thought the whisperings about Iraq really were just rumors. After all, the Band of Brothers was already deployed in a hostile area. Some guys in the unit had not seen their families in the United States for over a year. No unit in recent history had ever been sent straight from one warzone to another. There was no way the army would send them to Iraq.

Their hunch probably would have been correct if the Iraq War had gone according to plan. The invasion strategy had called for a quick, deadly wave of 130,000 troops that would ebb to about 30,000 troops by the end of 2003.[19] But things had not gone according to plan. After the March 2003 invasion, looting and disorder crippled many of the cities. The American decision to disband the Iraqi army that spring created hundreds of thousands of armed, trained, and now unemployed enemies. A fresh wave of attacks rippled through the country. In August 2003, a truck bomb destroyed the United Nations offices in Baghdad. Another series of shrewdly placed truck bombs threatened to turn Kurdish factions in the north against one another. In December, Saddam Hussein was captured, which American commanders thought would quell the unrest, but the violence only seemed to spread. Suicide bombers targeted Iraqi police stations and army recruiting sites. The number of roadside bombs aimed at American troops grew daily. In February 2004, insurgents rained grenades and gunfire on a convoy carrying the U.S. senior commander in Iraq, General John Abizaid. In April 2004, 129 troops died in combat—making it the deadliest month since the war began. Intelligence officials had not found any weapons of mass destruction, but they had unearthed a seventeen-page Al Qaeda document detailing a plan to spark a civil war and "prolong the duration of the fight between the infidels and us."[20]

By the spring of 2004, troops that deployed during the invasion were worn out. Reinforcements were needed. In May 2004, the Band of Brothers commander canceled training for the Expert Infantryman Badge. That night, around midnight, Eastridge, Shields, Bressler, and Barco were hanging out in the barracks when their sergeants told them to get up to the command post and stand in formation. They hurried up a set of stairs to a hill near the top of Camp Greaves. In the dark they filed into their platoons. Shields in first platoon. Bressler in second. Eastridge and Barco in third. They stood in silence as the captain of Charlie Company walked to the front. "The rumors are true," he said. "We're going."[21]

Eastridge scanned the neat ranks of Charlie Company for reactions and saw one face after another silently glancing around, just like him, looking for a reaction. No one said anything. No one knew how to act. Eastridge felt the competing twinges of excitement and fear. He wanted to serve his country. He wanted to kill terrorists. At the same time, he didn't want to leave Korea and his new wife, and though he would never have admitted it at the time, he was a little scared.

Barco was pumped. His older brother, already in Iraq, kept telling him badass stories. He was ready to get some of his own. Bressler called his father, Big Lou, to tell him the good news. He was excited and proud. He could not wait. Shields was hesitant. He had just found out that his wife, Svetlana, was pregnant. He knew he would miss the birth of his son and was afraid he might not live to see him. He threatened to desert the army, but his lieutenant got wind of it and told him if he ran, his new wife would probably never get a visa to the United States.

"I think he questioned whether he could kill anyone," his grandfather said. "On the whole, he was not very happy about going."

The Band of Brothers spent a frantic two months during the summer monsoons preparing for their mission in Iraq. They traded their Black Hawk helicopters for Humvees. They built a mock Iraqi village among the lush Korean hills and trained for urban combat. Over and over in the rain, they practiced things commanders thought they would need in the desert, like what to do if a mass of crazed jihadis rushed their outpost. They practiced guarding convoys by keeping the muzzles of their rifles "porcupined out" of the open windows of their Humvees. They met up with armored battalions from their brigade in a massive training exercise where they marched next to tanks in the rain and the mud. "It was stuff we never ended up doing in Iraq—stuff that would get you killed over there," Eastridge said, recalling the drills. But at the time, no one knew. Almost none of them, even the men in charge, had ever been to Iraq.

As the Band of Brothers prepared for their tour, the situation in Iraq grew more dire. The country's Shiite Muslims—an oppressed majority that, White House officials predicted before the invasion, would welcome the occupying troops "as liberators"[22]—began forming armed militias and violently took three cities from coalition forces. While the Band of Brothers marched in the drizzle, terrorists began kidnapping foreign civilians and beheading them on Internet videos. As the soldiers loaded into planes and ships, the Iraqi army, which by 2004 was supposed to take the reins from the Americans, was in such complete disarray that not even one battalion was capable of establishing order.[23]

The Band of Brothers left Korea on August 4, 2004. In the last rainy days before the flight, the mood among the troops grew more tense and festive and wild; the whole battalion was so juiced up on excitement and fear that all hell broke lose. They watched endless war movies. They fast-forwarded to the best battle scenes of the Band of Brothers series, then watched them again and again. They got roaring drunk. They did not know where they were going. They did not know if they would ever come back. Many stayed out after curfew in the drinky-girl bars. Bressler and another soldier got so drunk that they shared a prostitute. After downing uncounted bottles of beer and whiskey, the grunts started to wreck their barracks, ripping doors off hinges and smashing windows. A couple of soldiers wedged themselves up into the crawl space under the roof and came crashing down through the ceiling. Eastridge ran up and down the hallways spraying beer on everybody, then stumbled with a crew of drunken soldiers across the drizzly grounds and broke into the camp's bowling alley. There they started smashing everything with bowling pins and left the place a ruin.

To say that this behavior sullied the glorious reputation of the World War II unit would be inaccurate. Some soldiers in the unit had always been outrageous to the brink of criminality. William "Wild Bill" Guarnere, a legendary sergeant in the original Band of Brothers, had grown up fighting and stealing on the rough streets of South Philadelphia. In his book, *Brothers in Battle, Best of Friends,* he told a story about trashing the barracks in France in 1944: "Me and a couple other sergeants went out and robbed about twenty cases of champagne. We threw a party in our barracks, got drunk as skunks, and trashed the joint. We ripped the bunks out of the floor, threw them out the windows, broke everything we could get our hands on, lit things on fire, just destroyed the place. . . . I was a wild man. I was like Jekyll and Hyde, a troublemaker outside of combat, but in combat I was focused." [24]

The soldiers in the modern Band of Brothers climbed into planes bound for Iraq and watched through the windows as the green mountains of Korea disappeared. In the months to come, they realized what was true for Wild Bill's generation was true for theirs: some of the worst soldiers at home were some of the best when the bullets started flying. "We were a bunch of dropouts and criminals, but that is what the infantry needed," Ryan Krebbs said years later. "War is a dirty, nasty thing, and you need dirty nasty people to do it."

CHAPTER 2

A WALT DISNEY FAMILY

In the predawn quiet, Mark Graham got out of bed and fumbled toward the shower. It was 5:30 A.M., February 19, 2004. Graham, who was an army colonel, had recently moved to Fort Sill, Oklahoma, with his wife, Carol, after three years stationed in South Korea. Moving to a new post every few years might have taught other families to pack light, but the Grahams were attached to their mementos. The house was full of photos and reminders of their grown children: Jeffrey, Kevin, and Melanie.

Carol got up with her husband. When he went to the bathroom, she sat down at her computer. In the glow of the computer screen, Carol scanned her in-box for a note from Jeffrey, as she had every day in the three months since her oldest son left for Iraq. He usually only had time to send one every couple of weeks, and they tended to be upbeat but brief. Still, she liked to hear that he was all right.

The twenty-four-year-old was a second lieutenant leading a platoon in the 1st Battalion, 34th Armor Regiment, of the 1st Infantry Division, better known, because of the division's distinctive red and white shoulder patch, as "The Big Red One." The unit was based at Fort Riley, Kansas, not far from his parents, but deployed in the fall of 2003 to a dangerous swath of Iraq called the Sunni Triangle—so called because the patchwork of towns and farmland populated primarily by Sunni Muslims formed a triangle between the Tigris and Euphrates Rivers in the center of country. The cities of Ramadi, Baghdad, and Tikrit stood at the corners. Before the war, when the region popped up in discussions in America at all, it was usually because it was known as the Fertile Crescent, or the Cradle of Civilization in ancient Mesopotamia, where farming, writing, herding, and even the wheel got their first, shaky start. But by late 2003 the region increasingly captured America's attention because it had emerged as a stronghold for Sunni Muslims loyal to Saddam Hussein and the birthplace of an unexpectedly fierce resistance to the United States forces.

The Big Red One left for the Triangle with only four weeks notice, and expected at first to do some light peacekeeping. The shock and awe of the initial invasion of Iraq had met little organized resistance. In May 2003, President George W. Bush landed on the deck of the aircraft carrier USS *Abraham Lincoln* in the Pacific in front of a now infamous MISSION ACCOMPLISHED banner and announced "major combat operations in Iraq have ended."[1] Like the Band of Brothers, many in Jeffrey's tank battalion were frustrated that they appeared to have missed the excitement. They expected to spend their deployment rebuilding schools and training a new Iraqi army. The Sunnis in the Triangle had other plans.

The Iraqi army that had melted away in the first shock waves of the war had stashed uncounted tons of machine guns, grenade launchers, ammunition, and artillery shells in fields and houses all over the Triangle. When the Big Red One arrived in September 2003, insurgents were just starting to unearth the weapons caches.

Six months after the invasion, Jeffrey's battalion had a simple mission: highway patrol. A four-lane highway stretched through the Triangle from Ramadi to Baghdad. During the invasion, the United States military had given every major highway in Iraq code names—most drawn from American college and professional sports teams. The highway through the triangle was called Route Michigan, after the University of Michigan Wolverines. For this mission, the tank crews were given Humvees and rifles instead of heavy armor. They were supposed to keep the Michigan safe and open, and keep order in the few small towns along the way. It turned out to be a nasty task. The farm fields and reed-choked marshes between the highway and the Euphrates River became fertile ground for insurgent ambushes. Suicide bombers along the highway splintered Iraqi police stations using cars packed with explosives and strafed Iraqi army checkpoints with machine-gun attacks from fast-moving pickups. It was a message to the rest of the population: work with the Americans and you will die.

The insurgents also went after the Americans. They set traps for the division's soldiers all over the Triangle using IEDs. Locals crafted these weapons out of everything from fertilizer to propane tanks, but the ambush weapon of choice seemed to be the 155 millimeter artillery round. The hundred-pound shells looked like a bullet the size of a harbor seal. They were designed to be lobbed several miles by howitzers and explode in a burst of hot, jagged metal, creating a fifty-meter "kill zone." All of the Iraqi army howitzers capable of firing such a round had been destroyed or confiscated during the invasion, but the resistance had managed to make off with uncounted thousands of shells. Insurgents soon discovered these big shells were gruesomely effective when buried in the roadside and detonated on passing Humvees. On average, an IED hit Jeffrey's brigade every day for twelve months. It was a relatively new tactic, one the U.S. military was so unprepared for that most of its Humvees lacked any armor. The soldiers in them had almost no defense against the hidden shells. Sixty-two Big Red One soldiers were killed in the yearlong tour. Another 530 were seriously wounded.[2] For all of their struggle, Jeffrey's brigade made little progress. The Triangle was no safer when they left than when they arrived, and the brigade that replaced them suffered an almost identical number of casualties.

A little town called Khalidiya quickly established itself as one of the battalion's flash points. In Arabic, Khalidiya means "immortal place" or "eternal place"—a fitting name since tribes of one kind or another had claimed this ground since the dawn of civilization. The town's one main road was surrounded by a sun-bleached maze of ramshackle houses. It wasn't even big enough to show up on most maps. But in the first four months of the tour, four soldiers from the brigade were killed there in separate bomb blasts.

Jeffrey arrived in Iraq in November 2003 to replace a lieutenant who had had his lungs ripped out of his chest by an IED near Khalidiya. Showing up with red cheeks and a big grin, Jeffrey looked like he was about fifteen years old. The platoon called him "Smiley" behind his back, one soldier said, but he quickly won their trust. He seemed eager to learn from them and was reluctant to put his foot down prematurely, just to pull rank. "He never lost his cool," said his medic, Anuar Valdez. "He seemed to care as much about the men as about the mission, so he quickly earned our respect." Jeffrey, like his father, always seemed to make time to check that the lowest ranks of soldiers were doing all right. He would even make coffee at 2:00 A.M., while some other officers were asleep, and visit the lonely, unheated radio room to tell funny stories to help the grunts on night duty pass the time.

In the first half of the tour, the battalion raided the Triangle relentlessly, searching for bomb-making supplies and detaining hundreds of men of fighting age in an attempt to restore order, but their tactics only seemed to throw fuel on the fire. The Pentagon blamed the growing unrest on a few Al Qaeda–trained terrorists sneaking in from Syria.[3] But the American military's habit of searching houses in the middle of the night, shutting down the main road for hours at a time, and destroying shops and houses during firefights seemed to make enemies as quickly as Al Qaeda found followers. In early February 2004, seven hundred Iraqis protested outside Jeffrey's base, demanding that the army stop raiding their houses and taking their sons.

Jeffrey never mentioned any of this in his emails to his mom. He would only say that he was lucky enough to be in charge of a great platoon, and that they were making slow but steady progress. He would assure her he was doing well, always ending his emails by saying "Pray for my platoon."

When Carol did not see a new email from her son that February morning in Oklahoma, she clicked back to her home page. An article from the BBC at the top of the page's newsfeed caught her eye: IRAQ ROADSIDE BOMB KILLS THREE.[4] She clicked the link and read. "Two U.S. soldiers and an Iraqi interpreter have been killed by a roadside bomb near the city of Khalidiya, U.S. officials say. A similar attack on an American convoy in Baquba, northeast of Baghdad, reportedly wounded an Iraqi policeman earlier in the day. Both cities are regarded as centers of resistance to the coalition forces. American troops detained . . ." She stopped reading.

"Mark?" she said, walking into the bathroom, where Graham was shaving.

"The news says two soldiers were killed in Khalidiya today. Would anyone know yet if it's Jeffrey or not?" she asked.

Graham paused with the razor still resting against his neck.

"No . . . Probably not yet," he said. He would ask at work.

She ducked out of the bathroom without saying more. Later that morning she walked down to the Fort Sill chapel to pray.

When she left the bathroom, Mark stared unblinking into the mirror. The Grahams' other son, Kevin, had died eight months before. Mark still did not like to talk about it. But at that moment he thought about it.

"It just could not be true," he thought as he stared into the mirror. "Not again."[5]

———

Mark and Carol Graham used to joke that they had a Walt Disney family, so wholesome it was straight out of a fairy tale.

Carol is thin and pretty with delicate, almost elfin features, long, light brown hair, and a personality much bigger than her five-foot-four frame. She is infectiously friendly and takes the southern hospitality of her native Kentucky so seriously that she can talk for hours to a perfect stranger. If she meets people more than once, chances are the petite woman will greet them with what one friend called "a big ol' neck hug."

Mark is a model of Midwestern reserve and self-discipline—calm, humble, and hardworking with an aw-shucks kind of modesty. People almost immediately describe him as smart and genuinely kind. As an officer, he isn't afraid to take control of a situation, and his leadership skills pushed him to the top of the ranks, but he prefers listening to giving orders. He is an old-fashioned gentleman, always holding the door for his wife and referring to her as "my bride." His only vices are a steady supply of Dots candy in his desk drawer and an appreciation for a good cigar on a summer afternoon in the backyard.

Since they married at the end of college in 1977, Mark and Carol had built a deep level of companionship. Carol was the officer's most valued counselor. As someone outside the strict chain of command of the army, she was free to respond with bare-knuckle honesty and a vital infusion of humor. Their sons Jeffrey and Kevin were best friends growing up. The oldest, Jeffrey, and Kevin, two years younger, were so close they developed their own language, mostly used to swindle their parents at cards. They called it Grahamanese. "They were two parts of a whole. They really were," Carol said looking back on their childhoods.

Jeff was the outgoing son—instantly charismatic, bold and a natural leader, the one who literally dated the prom queen. Kevin was taller but quieter—more pensive. His mother described Kevin as "more academic" and Jeffrey as "more athletic," though it was a tricky dichotomy since both boys earned top grades, and both excelled at sports. Jeffrey graduated from college with honors in civil engineering. Kevin completed the army's demanding airborne jump school.

As boys, the two were close enough in age to share friends but never competed for them. Whenever Jeffrey was a captain picking teams for a neighborhood pickup team of baseball or football, he would always choose his brother first. Jeffrey kidded his younger brother that whenever they made a new friend the person initially liked Jeffrey better but in the long run ended up liking Kevin more. During the Persian Gulf War in 1990, their father deployed to Saudi Arabia. At the time, Bette Midler's song, "Wind Beneath My Wings" played constantly on the radio or as a sound track to montages of soldiers in the desert. The boys, who missed their father, naturally made it their favorite song. One night, when Carol was tucking the boys into bed, she remembers Kevin, who was seven years old, saying, "Jeff, you always pick me first for teams when you don't have to. You are the wind beneath my wings."

Jeffrey said, "No, Kevin, you are always telling me how smart I am when you are the smart one. You are the wind beneath my wings."

It was one of those family moments that later sounds almost too corny to believe, Carol said, but as a parent, in that moment, it made her practically burst with pride and love.

Jeffrey, Kevin, and their younger sister Melanie all went to the University of Kentucky, starting in 1998, where they got an apartment together. At the time, their parents were stationed in South Korea. In college, Jeffrey and Kevin both joined the ROTC, as their father had. Jeffrey wanted to lead soldiers in combat, then become a civil engineer. Kevin wanted to be an army doctor. Both were fierce fans of Kentucky's basketball team, like their mother. During March Madness one year they painted the tournament brackets on a wall in their living room, then built stadium seating out of tables and desks so that as many as sixty of their friends could watch the games with them. Their dad thought the parties were ridiculous. Their mom thought they were kind of cool.

———

In his junior year, Kevin started to change. He stopped caring as much about things like golf and basketball that he used to love. His record of straight A's started to slip until he was failing organic chemistry. He knew it would jeopardize his plan to become a doctor. He could not concentrate at all. He spent more and more time alone. One day in 2002, walking into the library, he noticed a booth offering screening for depression. He went down the list of questions and checked yes to almost all of them. The school referred him to counseling. That night, in one of his nearly daily phone calls to his mom in Korea, he said, "Mom, did you know that depression is an illness and not just a feeling?"

Carol was caught off guard. She had been a high school guidance counselor and was used to helping young adults talk through their problems. But her sons had never had any problems. "You're a Graham kid," she thought to herself. "What have you got to be depressed about?" To her son, she was more sympathetic. She understood everyone got the blues sometimes and asked him to tell her more about why he was feeling the way he did. But she was not too concerned. She thought it was just something he would work through.

Kevin went to counseling at the university and was prescribed Prozac. Carol called regularly from South Korea to make sure he was exercising, eating right, and at least occasionally going to church. Little things like that always made her feel better, and she thought they would give Kevin a boost, too. But he continued to struggle. His father noticed that Kevin would seize on small, negative details of his life and brood over them.

"Look, if the pressure is getting to you, you can take some time off and come home," his father said one day on the phone. "You can get out of ROTC. We'll repay the scholarship."

"But Dad," Kevin said, "you remember the soldier's creed."[6]

The creed is a motto every soldier repeats over and over during basic training until it is seared into memory, "I am an American Soldier . . . I will put mission first. I will never accept defeat. I will never quit."[7] Like the Lethal Warriors, the young ROTC soldier wanted to press on at all costs rather than be diagnosed with depression.

On May 9, 2003, Kevin's older brother Jeffrey was commissioned a second lieutenant. That same semester, Kevin was picked as the top ROTC cadet in his class and chosen to go to an elite cadet leadership training school that summer. But going to the school meant divulging on an army form that he was taking an antidepressant.

This presented a problem in the military, since mental illness tends to be viewed with distrust. The soldier's creed includes a line that says, "I am disciplined, physically and mentally tough." It equates being mentally squared away with being a good soldier, and suggests behavioral health problems are a fundamental failure. For generations, stretching back at least a hundred years, army psychiatrists and commanders often eyed mental illness suspiciously as a form of malingering, an excuse for soldiers trying to fake their way out of duty. At best it was a weakness. At worst it was deceitful cowardice. Even if commanders believed depression and PTSD were real, they tended to look at a mental condition on a medical form as a red flag. After all, promoting a young officer is not so different from picking a guy for a pickup baseball game. Did other soldiers want the one who was depressed on their team? Would they be able to count on him? Was he squared away? Depression and other mental health issues were seen as career killers.

The army culture developed a kind of psychiatric "Don't Ask, Don't Tell" policy. Most troops silently assumed that a diagnosis of depression, PTSD, or any other mental issue would lead to a denial of security clearances or bar them from promotions or special assignments. So if they had those problems, they did not list them. If they needed help, they got it secretly through civilian doctors.

When twenty-one-year-old Kevin finished the school year and prepared to go to ROTC camp, he decided to suck it up and soldier on. Like the creed said, he was mentally tough. He quietly stopped taking his Prozac. A year later, in 2004, the U.S. Department of Agriculture started requiring makers of Prozac and other similar antidepressants to put a bold "black box" warning label on the drugs, saying they increased the chances of suicides in children. In 2007, it expanded the warning to young adults like Kevin.[8] At the same time, the USDA warned against suddenly stopping the use of antidepressants like Prozac, because withdrawal can cause side effects including paranoia, panic attacks, aggression, and deeper depression. The Grahams did not understand the risks Kevin was taking. Neither did he.

In her regular calls to Kevin from South Korea, Carol tried to stay upbeat, thinking that her cheeriness would rub off on him. And he seemed excited to go to ROTC leadership school that summer. He carried his depression quietly. His brother and sister both thought he was fine. But sometimes his dark thoughts would sneak out.

On June 20, 2003, Carol called her son. He said he had just spent three days in his living room playing a video game that simulated modern American life. "I did everything the world says is success. I went to the right schools, married the right girl, got my kids in the best East Coast boarding schools, worked my way up the corporate ladder. At my retirement, even the president came." He paused, then said, "I hate the way the world measures us."

"Hon, you need to get some sleep. Stop playing that stupid video game," Carol said. She was unsure what else to tell him.

"Do you know what Henry David Thoreau said?" Kevin said. "He said, 'The mass of men lead lives of quiet desperation.'"[9]

The next morning, June 21, 2003, Kevin was supposed to meet his older brother for a game of golf. When Kevin did not show up, Jeffrey called the apartment and told Melanie to roust him out of bed. With the phone still cradled at her cheek Melanie, who was two years younger than Kevin, opened his bedroom door and found him hanging by his neck from the ceiling fan.

"Come on, Kevin, stop messing around," Jeffrey heard her say through the phone. Then she started screaming.[10]

Kevin was buried on a hillside in Frankfort, Kentucky, not far from Daniel Boone's grave. The family said little about the death to anyone but their closest friends. Others who found out seemed reluctant to talk about it, as if they were ashamed. In a way, the Grahams were ashamed, too. Mark Graham rarely spoke of the suicide, and certainly not in public. He kept asking himself what he had done wrong. Both he and his wife felt like they had failed Kevin. They tortured themselves by replaying all the things they could have said or done differently. Mark had tried to educate his children about the dangers of alcohol and drugs and sex, but his own ignorance of mental illness left him unable to recognize and respond to depression. He had thought it was something Kevin could just work through. Years later, Mark said, "I will blame myself for the rest of my life for not doing more to help my son."[11]

The day Kevin died, Jeffrey put his golf clubs away and said he would never play again. He slipped his brother's driver's license into his pocket and carried it everywhere. It was in his pocket in the summer of 2003 when the army offered him a noncombat assignment because of Kevin's death; he turned it down. It was in his pocket that fall when he explained to his fiancée his decision to go to Iraq, saying, "The only thing worse than war is a soldier not at war."[12] It was in his pocket in November 2003 when he deployed to the Sunni Triangle. And it was in his pocket on February 19, 2004, when his platoon set out on foot patrol one morning in Khalidiya.

———

The foot patrol was a new attempt by the battalion's command to try to defuse the growing Sunni Triangle insurgency with kindness. Fighting the insurgency with conventional force only seemed to make it grow stronger, so the battalion's operations officer had devised a strategy of moving soldiers off the big base and into the neighborhoods, getting them out of their tanks and Humvees and onto the sidewalk, and forcing them to get to know the locals.[13] The idea was that every family recruited through friendship and basic services like water and trash pickup was a family that wouldn't join the terrorists. The intention was to show that soldiers and locals could work together. So that February morning, the mission was simply to go out on a meet-and-greet. Jeffrey's platoon stuffed their pockets with candy and small toys to hand out to the kids of Khalidiya and filed off, a group of soldiers walking on each side of Route Michigan.

By noon they had walked for hours and passed out almost all of their candy. Everyone was tired, and they were just blocks away from their outpost. They passed by a bridge over the Euphrates that had been the site of several large IED blasts. Anuar Valdez, the platoon medic, walked directly across the four lanes from Jeffrey. He watched the lieutenant walking at the front of the line of soldiers with his radioman and an Iraqi police officer and an interpreter. Valdez bent down to give a lollipop to a little girl and watched as she smiled and shied away. Then *boom!* The deafening, unmistakable blast of a 155 mm shell turned the still air into a hot fist that knocked the medic and everyone else to the ground. The blast had come from the other side of the road. Valdez tried to shake the ringing out of his ears and scan the scene. Dust choked the area, and clutches of civilians clambered to their feet and scattered. A few bursts of gunfire from the platoon cut the air. Jeffrey and the others had disappeared in the smoke and fire and dust on the other side of the road. Valdez sprinted across the four lanes of Michigan to search for wounded. The damage was so severe that at first the medic could not tell who was who. The policeman had no head. Both of the interpreter's arms and one of his legs were torn off. The radioman had disappeared entirely. The platoon found his body later, half a football field away, caught in the branches of a tree. Jeffrey was recognizable only by the name stitched on his body armor.

Just before the blast, according to the army, Jeffrey had halted the line after spotting what appeared to be a bomb. As he was turning to warn the others, someone detonated it remotely with a cell phone. He died almost exactly eight months after his younger brother.

———

"We all took it real hard. We were never the same. I still think about it every day," Anuar Valdez said one night, six years later. "Jeffrey Graham had every quality you could hope for in a leader. You know, like his dad. He had the potential to be great."

The day Jeffrey was killed, Carol Graham came home from praying at the post chapel to find her husband in the living room with the commanding general of Fort Sill, David Valcourt. He had personally given the news to Mark and they had both returned to the house to wait for Carol. When she saw the general, she knew it could only mean one thing. She collapsed in her husband's arms and cried. It was a surreal and perplexing moment. The Grahams loved two things: the army and their family. Now one had taken the other. It was hard to know how to go on.

The community's response to news of Jeffrey's death was markedly different from Kevin's. Flowers came from all over the world, sent by members of the Graham's army family. Locals in his town made his fiancée a quilt. The newspaper where the boys had gone to high school ran a long obituary calling Jeffrey an "awesome guy."[14] A website sprang up in his memory. The Kentucky legislature passed a formal resolution to "pause in silent reverence for his soul."[15] People who had never met him called him a hero. A couple at Fort Sill even named their child after Jeffrey.

The Grahams agreed: Jeffrey was a hero, everything any parent could hope for. But sometimes they felt uneasy about the attention. Where had this outpouring of love been when Kevin died, they wondered? After all, Kevin was just as kind and brave and idealistic. He had been striving to make the world a better place, just like his brother. He had simply been killed by a different enemy—one that was harder for people to comprehend.

Jeffrey came home in a flag-draped coffin and was buried next to his brother in March 2004. The family wept under the bare branches of the stately old trees in the Frankfort cemetery. They had suffered more losses than they ever thought possible. There was nothing really to say that could describe the hole ripped in their lives. On the car ride home from the cemetery, Mark broke the silence. "You know, this is one dark chapter in our lives, but it doesn't have to be the whole book," he told Carol.[16] He did not know how, but they would have to try to find some good in all this.

A few days after the funeral, they returned to Fort Sill. Mark was not sure he could continue serving in the army. The thousands of young soldiers in uniform marching across the grounds of Fort Sill acted as a daily reminder of all the family had lost. Carol asked Melanie to come home to the army post from school for the semester after Jeffrey's death, and she declined. "It's too sad," she said.[17]

On March 10, 2004, Mark told Carol he was quitting. He could not stay in the army anymore. That night they barely slept. In the morning, Mark got up to make coffee and Carol sat down at the kitchen table with an eighty-year-old Christian devotional titled "Streams from the Desert" that she liked to read from every day. She cracked it open to a passage written by a Pennsylvania minister who had cared for soldiers during the Civil War. She started reading. A minute later Mark looked up from his coffee to see tears spilling down his wife's cheeks.

"What's wrong?" He said.

She choked back sobs and began to read the passage out loud.

A distinguished general related this sorrowful story of his experience in time of war. The general's son was a battery officer. An assault was in progress. The father was leading his division in a charge; as he pressed on in the field, suddenly his eye was caught by the sight of a dead battery officer lying just before him. One glance showed him it was his own son.

Carol glanced up at her husband, then continued.

The General's fatherly impulse was to stop beside the loved one and give in to his grief, but the duty of the moment demanded that he should press on in the charge; so quickly snatching one kiss from his son, he hastened away, leading his command in the assault. . . . We never really get over our great griefs; We are never quite the same after we pass through them. . . . But, if we turn away from the gloom and take up the tasks in duties in front of us, the light will come again, and we shall grow stronger.[18]

Carol was much more likely than her husband to say something was a sign from God, but even Mark was struck by the poignancy of the passage. There were thousands of young men just like Kevin and Jeffrey fighting in Iraq and Afghanistan. The devotional was right. However strong the urge, he could not give in to his grief. The moment demanded that he should press on. That day he did not tell the commanding general of Fort Sill that he was quitting. He never thought of it again.

But what was the battle being waged, he wondered. Clearly there was the literal battle for control of Iraq, one that Graham wholeheartedly supported. But as the weeks and months ran on from that day, Graham began to realize the conflict reached deeper. It reached down to the individual challenges of soldiers and their families—soldiers who sometimes were struggling to find a scrap of normalcy after war, families who sometimes had lost a soldier in the battle—whether through physical combat wounds or something like what had claimed Kevin.

He started going to every memorial for fallen soldiers and opening his arms to the families of those who had been lost because he knew what they were going through. But he also took an interest in depression and suicide. In the months after Kevin died, Graham educated himself about how slight changes in chemicals in the brain could make a person fall apart. Sometimes it could not be fixed by telling someone to buck up or go for a jog. It wasn't a way of thinking, it was a matter of molecules. People needed help. They needed to really understand mental illness and the risks of ignoring it. Slowly Graham began to understand that the tragedies that drove him to want to quit the army were the reasons he now had to stay.

Graham and his wife started to speak about suicide prevention all over the country, telling their story to army audiences and civilians. Graham would tell people that his sons died fighting different battles. Depression could be just as deadly as combat in Iraq, especially in the army, where seeking professional help wasn't always seen as an option.

Mark started telling military groups that depression should be treated like "the bleeding of the soul." The army taught every soldier to stop the bleeding if a fellow soldier was wounded by a bullet, he said. If a wound was serious, troops knew they had to get the soldier to a doctor. There was no shame in going to the hospital if you were shot. What if troops could be taught to react the same way to the bleeding of the soul? What if the stigma against seeking help for depression or PTSD could change? What if soldiers learned to see it as the combat injury that it really was?

CHAPTER 3

OPERATION MAD MAX

In August 2004 the Band of Brothers arrived on the same bomb-pocked stretch of desert highway where Jeffrey Graham had been killed six months before. They were given the same mission: drive up and down Route Michigan in search of insurgents. Since Jeffrey's death, his battalion had not made much progress winning the hearts and minds of the Sunni Triangle. If anything, the situation had grown worse. Mosques and homes along the highway stood blackened and burned from the fighting. Dead cars marked the sites of roadside battles and suicide bomb blasts. Because the postapocalyptic desert landscape of burned-out vehicles and craters reminded the Band of Brothers of one of their favorite movies, they called their new mission Operation Mad Max.[1]

The Brothers started the operation with a driving tour of the twenty-seven miles of asphalt that would be their home for the next eleven months. "The road can be dangerous, but most of the time it's OK," the grunts from Graham's unit told the newly arrived Brothers.[2] The biggest enemy, they said, was the roadside bomb. Bombs hit Humvees on the highway almost every day—so regularly that Route Michigan had earned the nickname IED Alley. The explosives were buried in the ground, stashed in tattered boxes or piles of junk, hidden in craters from previous blasts, even stuffed into the carcasses of dead animals. In the trash-strewn streets, they were almost impossible to spot, but the veterans of the Big Red One told the Brothers they had discovered a way to predict their presence. The locals always knew what was going on. If you see people out doing stuff in the street, they said, you know you are safe. "But if you pull through a town and no one is out, pucker your asshole and get ready, you are about to get blown up."[3]

Route Michigan ran west from Baghdad through the province of Al Anbar—an old Persian word meaning "the arsenal." The barren state was almost entirely empty desert. Only a green line of irrigated fields along the Euphrates River colored the endless wasteland. That green line had become the center of the growing resistance to the Americans. The violence came courtesy of two groups: Iraqi nationalists still loyal to Saddam Hussein—who were motivated by some smoldering sense of patriotism—and the mujahideen, or "mooj," as the soldiers called them, a loosely organized band of international Islamic guerillas determined to defend their religion from what they saw as the crusading Americans. Some of the mooj were trained foreign jihadists streaming in over the border from Syria—the same types of organized Muslim hardliners who brought down the World Trade Center. Some were simply the local rednecks fighting just because there was someone to fight. Sometimes the Saddam loyalists, the mujahideen, and the rednecks worked together, sometimes not. Intelligence officers distinguished between different insurgent groups, but the Joes rarely bothered. They referred to anyone shooting at them interchangeably as the mooj, the hajjis—an honorary title Muslims use to denote someone who has made a pilgrimage to Mecca, which the soldiers turned into a derogatory slur for any Arab—or simply "the bad guys."

For two weeks the Big Red One and the Band of Brothers patrolled the highway together. The tours allowed the new guys to learn from the veterans. Every unit in Iraq did the same thing. They called it the "right-seat ride." First the outgoing unit ran the mission from the driver's seat of the Humvee while the new guys sat in the right seat, soaking it all in. Then, near the end of the two weeks, the new guys would drive with the veterans sitting in the right seat, making sure the newbies didn't do anything stupid enough to get themselves killed.

"The guys we were replacing looked the same as us," Kenneth Eastridge said, reflecting on his first days in Iraq. "But at the same time they looked much older. They were quiet. They weren't excited about Iraq at all. They told us it wasn't going to be like we thought."

Route Michigan was so dangerous, the guys from the Big Red One said, because the cities at either end were even worse. Ramadi, at the western end, had a population of perhaps 300,000, though with waves of refugees no one knew for sure anymore. The city was a hive of Al Qaeda fighters from all over the globe who slipped in over the poorly guarded borders, turning the urban maze of flat roofs and narrow alleys into a shooting gallery for mortar gangs and snipers. The pavement was shattered by the repeated blasts of hidden bombs. Looting, corruption, and sabotage had crippled basic city services such as electricity, water, and garbage collection. Sewage pooled in the streets. But, for all the problems, the city was, at least nominally, under the control of coalition troops.

Fallujah, twenty-seven miles down the road on the eastern end of their patrol area was not. The city had around 250,000 people. It was also a hive of insurgents and was infested with snipers and roadside bombs. There too, dependable electricity or water had disappeared. There, too, sewage pooled in the streets. But American troops did not control the city. They did not even dare enter. In March 2004, insurgents had ambushed an American convoy in Fallujah and killed four armed Blackwater contractors. A mob then set fire to their bodies and dragged them through the streets. Photos of the jubilant crowd hanging the charred and mutilated corpses from a bridge in town became glaring proof around the world that the White House's contention that troops would be "greeted as liberators" was dead wrong.

In early April, American jet fighters and helicopter gunships strafed Fallujah and 2,200 marines stormed in to, as one general put it, "pacify that city."[4] After four weeks of fighting, and twenty-seven American deaths, the marines pulled out, leaving the city in the control of the "Fallujah Brigade," a group of Iraqi soldiers armed by the Americans and led by one of Saddam Hussein's former generals. By August, when the Band of Brothers arrived, the Fallujah Brigade had disbanded and its soldiers were increasingly using their weapons against the Americans who had supplied them.

Between the two simmering cities, Route Michigan ran as straight and wide as a Texas interstate. Heat shimmered off the pavement. The average high temperature for August in this corner of Iraq was 111 degrees Fahrenheit. To the soldiers, with boots, helmets, body armor, and fifty pounds of gear, it often felt much hotter.

The highway passed through lifeless desert and green bands of farmland growing dates, wheat, and potatoes along the Euphrates River. Through the blast-proof windows of the Humvees, Al Anbar sometimes looked like little had changed since the cradle of civilization days when loose-knit societies first started farming and building cities. Soldiers would pass bright new houses full of glass and gaudy columns, or guys in shiny track suits talking on cell phones, but just a few seconds down the road the Humvees would near hand-built mud huts and stop for herds of goats clattering across the asphalt followed by weather-beaten old men wearing long, flowing robes as if they had just stepped out of ancient Mesopotamia.

Khalidiya quickly established itself as the main pucker spot on Route Michigan. In the months since Jeffrey Graham had been killed there, attacks and counterattacks had mutilated many of the multistory buildings along the single main road. Walls bore the welts of uncounted bullets. An American F–16 had dropped a laser-guided bomb on the tallest building in town, a five-story concrete structure, reducing it to a charred and skeletal ruin. The mooj had blown up the main police station. Iraqi fighters increasingly used the burned-out shells of buildings to stage attacks. Almost every day a hidden road-side bomb went off within earshot of the little town. "It was just a tiny, nothing town," David "Nasty" Nash, said. "But it had a massive amount of hate. It was just a bomb waiting to happen."

Two miles east of Khalidiya stood the new home of the Band of Brothers, a place called Habbaniyah. Eastridge expected their base to be a mud and cinderblock dustbowl in the desert. Instead, Habbaniyah was beautiful. Palms and trimmed hedges surrounded simple but elegant buildings. Breeze-ways shaded the barracks. Neat, tree-lined streets divided irrigated parade fields and parks. It did not seem like Iraq at all. And, in a way, it wasn't. It was an air base built by the British in the 1930s after the fall of the Ottoman Empire. Over the decades it had grown into an oasis of European civilization. During World War II it served as a vital stop on the route connecting the Western allies to the Soviet Union. Then, in 1958, the base was abandoned after an Iraqi coup overthrew the British-installed monarchy. In 2004, after a half century of neglect, Habbaniyah still retained a timeless air of British civility.

Between missions, Eastridge, Bressler, Barco, and other soldiers sometimes wandered the extensive grounds exploring the ruins. There was a sailing club with the windows smashed out and an Olympic-size swimming pool, now empty except for a few rust-colored puddles reflecting the blue desert sky. At one end of the base, tombstones bearing English names baked in the sun. At the other stood a 1930s movie theater with Art Deco desert murals on the high walls and a tattered, silk curtain still hanging over the stage in front of rows of folding seats under a thick layer of desert dust.

The whole thing was a crumbling monument to the failure of an over-stretched empire. In 2004, as America struggled to support two wars and troops in dozens of countries, while at the same time facing mounting debt and a stalling economy, Habbaniyah might have served as a cautionary marker on the course the United States was taking. But few of the Joes in the Band of Brothers gave it much thought. In the ranks, opinions about the war and its un-

derlying justifications were split roughly three ways between believers, nonbe-
lievers, and those who just did not give a damn.[5] But, soldiers said, almost all
were eager to fight—to prove that they could do the job they were trained to
do. It did not matter who started the fight or why, or whether it was a good
idea. They were going to finish it.

The Brothers—who were overwhelmingly in their late teens and early
twenties—turned their spartan concrete barracks into something resembling a
heavily armed frat house. Soldiers sleeping ten to a room hung ponchos and
sheets for privacy. They ripped pages from girlie magazines and *High Times*
centerfolds and plastered them all over the walls. They built couches out of
old wooden pallets and installed TVs and PlayStations. Cookie wrappers and
Pringles tubes and the debris of countless care packages from home littered the
floor. A bank of four computers gave the soldiers access to email, shopping, and
all the other vices of the World Wide Web. Stereos let them pump themselves
up with bass-heavy rap and death metal before missions. Empty energy drink
cans rattled in their Humvees.

During the first few months of the fall of 2004, the Band of Brothers' lives
fell into a predictable rotation of missions: guard the base, man outposts
along the highway, or pile into Humvees for Mad Max patrol. Platoons went
on Mad Max three days in a row, twelve hours at a time. It usually meant
driving the asphalt road between Ramadi and Fallujah, then setting up traffic checkpoints in the 110-degree sun to search for weapons and would-be
bomb planters.

About once a week, the battalion, acting on intelligence the grunts usually
knew little about, raided neighborhoods at night. They would cordon off
whole blocks and search door to door for fighters and guns. Sometimes they
knocked. Sometimes they didn't. Often they led young men away in zip cuffs
and hoods. About half of the two thousand men they detained during the tour
eventually ended up behind bars. About a quarter ended up fifty miles down
Route Michigan at the notorious Abu Graib prison.[6] But the raids failed to
provide the satisfaction that the soldiers had imagined during training. The
Band of Brothers almost never met resistance. The men they collared on raids
were often not caught red-handed. They were detained on circumstantial evidence and second- or third-hand intelligence. Local tipsters tended to be motivated by old neighborhood grudges and schisms. Worst of all, the families
were there, watching silently as fathers and sons were led away. It was not so
much like a war movie as a confusing international episode of *Cops,* with all

the accompanying pathetic frustration. There were no uniformed enemies or obvious targets. There was just heat and ambiguity. And IEDs.

"Going in, we weren't sure about our mission. We were at first going in to seek and destroy the enemy," Kevin Shields's platoon leader, Lieutenant Matthew Hurley, said, recalling the tour. But the battalion did not find much of an enemy, he said. "So we had to change to counterinsurgency—winning hearts and minds—which we did not really know how to do."

Weeks ran into months with no battles. Just like the raids, going on Mad Max patrol was more like being a very heavily armed small-town police force with little to do but watch the traffic breeze through on the main street. Guys like Eastridge and Bressler—who had pumped themselves up for a fight—soon realized there would be none. At the same time, the Triangle was viciously deadly. At any moment, a well-placed 155 round could kill a guy or, worse, leave him burned and maimed and limbless on a medevac plane back to a hospital in the States.

The same scenario played out again and again: the quiet highway, heat swimming off the asphalt, the sleepy towns with their bizarre foot traffic of modern and ancient, the mind-numbing routine of Mad Max, then *boom!* Usually when the smoke and confusion cleared, the only damage was a tire or an engine and a dozen or so eardrums, but sometimes the mooj got lucky and a soldier was seriously injured or killed. Even so, the mission never changed. The day after a blast, soldiers were expected to go back out on the same stretch of highway. The repeating pattern of mind-numbing patrols and sudden bomb blasts created a contradictory existence that was dull, tragic, and oddly routine, all at the same time.

"That was the thing about Iraq that I was not expecting," Jose Barco said years later. "It was dangerous, but it was also pretty boring."

Free time became just as repetitious as patrol: send emails home, eat some chow, then spend hours playing epic bouts of Halo or some other shooter game on the PlayStation to make up for the fact that there was no real enemy to shoot in Iraq. There was no spot behind the front lines where the soldiers could relax without fear. There was no way to mix peacefully with the locals. There was no way to get a beer or meet a girl. In deference to the Muslim traditions of Iraq, alcohol was forbidden.[7] Even in the relative safety of the barracks, the thud of mortars landing on the base reminded the soldiers that there was no real escape from the war. All their windows were lined with sand bags.

To unwind, the grunts watched the Nature channel. They watched the shopping channel. They watched MTV. They had a mainline to American culture even though they were living in another world. They watched fashion TV to feel like they had at least some contact with women. They even watched the *Band of Brothers* HBO miniseries again. Many of them wanted their war experience to be more like the massive World War II assaults shown on the screen, with the roar of tanks and artillery and hordes of men storming across beaches. Instead they had Mad Max, which did not look like a war at all. There was no enemy, let alone enemy lines. There was just a battalion in the desert, driving up and down a highway full of bombs a year after President Bush announced that major combat operations in Iraq had ended.

The pace of missions never let up. There were few days off, and men could not be spared. In October that year, Louis Bressler found out that his father, Big Lou—the reason he had joined the military—was dying of cancer and only had six months to live, tops. His lieutenant told him to make a hard choice. Fly back to the States to visit for a few days while his father was alive or fly back for the funeral. Bressler chose the visit. Then he sobbed on his lieutenant's shoulder a few months later when he got the news that Big Lou was dead.

With almost no days off and no clear seasons, soldiers found it easy to forget what day of the week it was, then what week of the month it was, or even what time of year. Guys in Iraq called the phenomenon Groundhog Day, after the 1993 film in which Bill Murray is forced to live the same day over and over. The mission was always same. The desert was always brown. Progress was too slow to notice. When soldiers tried to recall the tour, it was hard to say whether something happened in September or in December. The days blurred, so soldiers naturally started marking time by memorable events—mostly bad ones, the split-second tragedies that stood out. Things happened "around the time when." Around the time when an IED blew off Private Noah Nahinu's arm, or around the time when Lieutenant Erwin Godoy's truck was hit by a suicide car, or around the time when a sniper shot Private Michael Garibay in the neck. Someone in the headquarters office got a hold of a big sheet of paper and a Magic Marker and drew a huge copy of the title from the *Band of Brothers* miniseries box—a line of silhouetted young infantry soldiers with their rifles against the words "Band of Brothers." Whenever a brother was killed in the Sunni Triangle, the others taped his photo up on the homemade memorial. It became a kind of calendar of the defining events of the tour.

November 11, 2004, was one of those days. Early that morning Eastridge's sergeant, Sean Huey, said their platoon, 3rd Platoon, Charlie Company, would start its rotation on Mad Max.

As much as Eastridge liked Huey in Korea, he admired him even more by the time they reached Iraq. He thought the sergeant was exactly what a sergeant should be. The man did not play favorites with his squad. Every soldier was expected to be the best he could be and follow orders to the letter. He was a bulldog if soldiers stepped out of line. The exacting level of discipline had turned the nine soldiers in his squad into one of the best-trained urban combat teams in the unit. At the same time, Huey was a serial joker and genuinely nice guy. He would chase soldiers around with a broom and tickle their noses when they tried to sleep. He was happy to wrestle with any of his privates. As long as soldiers lived up to the same high standards he set for himself, he treated them like friends. To many in his squad, he was the strong father figure they never had. No matter how bad things got, Huey always exuded a tough confidence. The guys came to rely on it. As long as Huey was around, they would be OK.

Just after dawn, the platoon walked out into the gravel yard of their barracks and climbed into Humvees for their twelve-hour shift on the highway. On the spectrum of different missions the battalion performed, Mad Max was not considered that bad. It was more exciting than guarding the base's gate, which essentially meant standing in the searing sun watching heat rise off the desert for hours. And it was safer than setting up a roadblock to search cars. At least on Mad Max, if the platoon ran into an IED or sniper attack, they had the protection of the trucks. At a roadblock, the only cover soldiers had was a sharp, thin coil of concertina wire strung across the road.

By that second week of November, cover seemed increasingly vital. What had started in September as a relatively quiet tour with few attacks was increasingly becoming wide-eyed, white-knuckled, and angry. Bomb and mortar attacks went from rare to regular to daily. That week, the Band of Brothers had been attacked multiple times each day. "It was the month of Ramadan," John Duval, a specialist in the platoon said, looking back. "And everything went bat shit crazy like the gates of hell had opened."

At the start of the Muslim holiday of fasting and reflection, the size and boldness of the attacks hit like nothing the soldiers had seen before. On Wednesday, November 8, Louis Bressler's platoon parked on the side of the highway so the soldiers could take a leak when a suicide bomber in a black BMW went airborne over the median and exploded into one of their trucks, pummeling four soldiers with shrapnel and seriously wounding their staff sergeant. On November 9, Kevin Shields's platoon went out on Mad Max and was pelted by rocket-propelled grenades (RPGs) and machine-gun fire from a dozen attackers hiding in houses just outside Khalidiya. On November 10, enemy fighters hit Shields's platoon again, a mile west of Khalidiya, with more machine guns and RPGs. About ten Iraqis popped up from windows and rooftops and began to fire. An RPG whizzed down the street like an oversized bottle rocket and slammed into the side of one of the trucks, knocking the gunner perched in the roof turret unconscious. Shields and the rest of the soldiers chased the gunmen down the narrow streets; they killed or captured a handful before the rest melted into the town.

Eastridge and Barco heard Shields's platoon shooting from just down Route Michigan, where their platoon was about to raid a mosque rumored to have a secret weapons stash. Just as their platoon was rushing through the gates, Shields's platoon radioed that several of the guys who attacked them were jumping over the mosque's back wall. Eastridge's unit scrambled in and caught three of the gunmen as they landed in the courtyard. In the mosque, the platoon uncovered explosives and weapons. In the office of the mosque's leader, the imam, the platoon found how-to pamphlets detailing ways to start an insurgent cell, including what to do if cell leaders were killed or captured.[8]

The Band of Brothers were convinced the week's sudden escalation of hostility could only be caused by one thing: four days prior, on November 6, the United States military had launched a massive assault on Fallujah, just a few miles down the road, in a second attempt to take the city back from insurgents. Fifteen thousand troops surrounded the insurgent stronghold and took several key bridges, blocking any retreat. On November 8, they blasted heavy metal from loud speakers and rocked the city with earth-rumbling air and artillery assaults that damaged an estimated 40,000 homes and destroyed 10,000 completely.[9] Ground troops went in that night. Eventually they took back Fallujah, but for the soldiers patrolling Route Michigan it was as if someone had jabbed a stick in a hornets' nest. Whether the hornets on Route Michigan were swarming out of the nest or flying back to try to protect it, the troops weren't sure. They just knew they were pissed.

By the end of the week, on November 11, when Eastridge learned his platoon was going back on three days of Mad Max, everyone was on edge. They had been trained early on to protect themselves from ambushes by watching for anything out of the ordinary. Problem was, they also learned pretty quickly that almost everything in their corner of Iraq was out of the ordinary. Every day, the soldiers struggled to find meaningful hints of what was normal in their patrol areas. Three people dressed head to toe in black robes, their faces covered except for glaring eyes, was that normal? Seven men in headscarves packed into a tiny taxi, was that normal? A burning mound of trash in the middle of a neighborhood with goats foraging on the smoldering edges, was that normal? And then some of the things that appeared the most normal were the most deadly—a person on a cell phone, a boy on a bicycle, a lone driver in a car, three teenagers in track suits, a clear strip of highway. Any of them could be a sign of an imminent bomb attack. Or not. There was no normal. There was no way to predict the explosions. They felt helpless, like rats in some cruel experiment waiting to get shocked. Many soldiers' minds reeled with silent tension until a grim gallows humor set in.

"The first few weeks you are there, you have a fear of dying. You are hyper-alert," Nasty Nash said, remembering his reaction. "But at some point you just don't care anymore. You accept your fate. You wake up this morning and say, 'Heh, I feel it. This is the day I get my ass whacked.'"

On November 11, Eastridge had that feeling. The highway seemed ominously quiet. Someone had scattered large stones across the pavement overnight, perhaps trying to steer the Humvees toward hidden 155s. But no attacks came.

Several hours into their Mad Max patrol, Charlie Company's captain called on the radio. The battalion had a tip that a group of insurgents in a car packed with explosives was on its way from Ramadi to Fallujah. He wanted to meet 3rd Platoon just west of Khalidiya to set up a roadblock. The platoon rolled toward a stretch of Michigan just blocks down from the mosque it had raided the day before. They parked their three Humvees along the side of the highway at around 1:00 P.M. and began to block off all traffic coming out of Ramadi.

Jose Barco and two other soldiers pulled on leather gloves. They heaved a big coil of razor wire off the hood of one of the trucks and began stringing it across the pavement. Eastridge stood guard a few feet away with his big SAW at the ready. On his side of the street, a few bullet-riddled houses baked in the sun. On the other side, a cluster of pathetic-looking shops rippled in the heat, their owners staring at the soldiers through the windows. Eastridge's job was to stand watch over his platoon sergeant, Tim Stricklin, while the sergeant directed the traffic search. Stricklin was conferring with Sergeant Huey about where to put an observation post so they could see what was coming. The street was full of people and cars. Women in long black hijabs ambled in and out of the shops. A group of children played nearby in the dust. If there was normal, this looked close to it. It was a sign that, despite the previous days of violence, all was well.

The platoon's medic, Ryan Krebbs, walked up next to Eastridge and asked the platoon sergeant if he could smoke a cigarette.

Stricklin replied that Krebbs knew soldiers were not allowed to smoke in public, and since the captain was there, he had to be strict about the rules. He nodded his head toward a Humvee fifty yards up the road where their company commander, Captain William Jones, had just pulled up. Jones was adamant that soldiers present a face of professionalism and respect to the civilians, and that meant, among other things, no smoking, but the platoon had been out on their shift for hours and Doc Krebbs said he really needed a smoke.

"Eastridge," Stricklin said, "go take this guy down the alley to smoke."

Eastridge and Krebbs ducked past the platoon sergeant's Humvee, which was parked at the mouth of a narrow, mud-brick alley, and walked several paces down the corridor to sit on the toppled wall of a half-destroyed house.

On the wide lanes of Michigan, Barco pulled the dancing coil of razor wire across the hot pavement. Other soldiers stood in the waves of heat with hands resting on their rifles. A group of Iraqi men who had been circled in a tense conversation on the far side of the road walked up to Barco and the others stringing the wire and asked them to move the Humvee blocking the alley so the locals could get through to their houses. The platoon sergeant looked at the Iraqis, looked at the Humvee, then told them that they could go around, the truck wasn't moving. The men hurried back across the highway, arguing in Arabic.

"Hey Barco, can I borrow your gloves?" a soldier said. Barco turned his head to answer. It was the last thing he remembers. At that moment, a suicide bomber speeding down Route Michigan veered across the median, aimed at the Humvee blocking the alley, and released his detonation trigger. Instantly, a flash of heat and concussion shattered the shop windows. Soldiers felt it before they heard it as a shockwave slapped them to the ground. Glass and metal flew everywhere. Fire and smoke swallowed the roadblock.

The force rippled up the alley and hurled Krebbs and Eastridge to the dirt. They were hit so hard that at first they thought someone had tossed a grenade at them. Everyone lay dazed in a fog of dust as their shaken brains reset. It lasted only a second or two, but seemed to last for several minutes.

"Are you OK?" Eastridge finally said to the medic as he pulled himself up on his knees.

The medic started patting himself for holes. "I don't know. Am I?" he said.

"Yeah," Eastridge said. "Am I?"

Krebbs scanned Eastridge for wounds and his eyes glanced up over his head to a huge cloud of thick, black smoke rising over the street. "Oh fuck! Oh fuck!" Krebbs shouted.

Eastridge whipped around and saw the oily smoke. He grabbed Krebbs by the shoulder and they sprinted down the alley into the black cloud. It was the first time the platoon had been hit by a real attack. Confusion was as thick as the smoke. The army's combat medic training had drilled the decision-making tools needed to sort through the bloody chaos of war into Krebbs over and over, but nothing prepared him for what he saw.

He followed Eastridge as they squeezed past the mangled, burning wreck of the Humvee. The suicide bomber's car was nowhere to be seen. The blast had destroyed it completely. As Krebbs and Eastridge edged into the street, tiny pieces of metal pelted down through the mist of smoke and dust like scorching rain. Silhouettes of bodies materialized in the haze, some moving, some not. An Iraqi woman appeared through the gloom, weeping as she tried to drag two children out of the road. The limp, ragged bodies had been cut into pieces, limbs left on the asphalt in a sickening slick of oil, fuel, and blood. Krebbs groped past the woman farther into the kill zone. The strict priorities of a combat medic mandated that American soldiers always came first.

From every direction members of the platoon dashed toward the blast site while wailing civilians stumbled away. Krebbs and Eastridge found Sergeant Stricklin yelling for soldiers to get rifles up and ready for another attack. The sergeant sat on the ground with his hands raised in the air. It looked like several of the fingers hung only by strips of skin; blood streamed out of his mouth; shrapnel had torn open his calf, leaving ribbons of red muscle hanging from his blood-soaked fatigues. Spreading blotches of blood on his uniform showed where shards of the now obliterated car shot into his body. To Eastridge the sergeant looked like a goner, but to Krebbs he looked like he would make it. All army medics are trained to divide casualties into three simple categories: those who are going to die no matter what you do, those who are going to live no matter what you do, and those who may live or die depending on what you do. They are told to ignore the first two and focus on the last. Bloody or not, Stricklin was going to live. Krebbs told a nearby soldier to give the sergeant some morphine and bandage his wounds, then he pushed on.

Krebbs passed another soldier whose cheek had been sliced open by shrapnel and hung down, revealing the bloody jaw and teeth. A shard of metal was stuck in his jaw bone. He, too, was going to live. Krebbs kept going to another soldier who was bleeding from his face and eyes and yelling, "I can't see! I can't see!" He was going to live. The medic hurried toward a pile of burning wreckage, where Charlie Company's captain and some other soldiers, half obscured by acrid smoke, were wrestling blistering hot razor wire off a tangle of soldiers.

Krebbs took a half step toward the car, then saw Eastridge's squad leader, Sean Huey, who had been standing, crumple to the ground. The medic hurried over and knelt down. He saw blood spurting from his sergeant's left thigh. Huey was paper white and gulping air like a trout. Krebbs probed along the right thigh. A chunk of car had punched through both legs, right below the pelvis, clipping both femoral arteries. Blood was flooding out in a quickly spreading pool on the ground. If he didn't get care right now, he was going to die. Krebbs tried to apply pressure to stop the bleeding and watched his whole hand sink into the wound. He tried again. Huey's breathing grew shallower. Krebbs yelled for Eastridge's roommate, Specialist Josh Butler, and said. "I need you to breathe for him while I hold pressure!"

Eastridge stood near them, scanning his SAW along the bullet-pocked buildings glaring down on Michigan. He was waiting for the rest of the ambush. His barrel passed over Krebbs and Butler frantically working on his favorite sergeant. It passed over charred, ragged Iraqis bleeding on the road. It passed over the smoking wreckage where a soldier with blood dripping from cuts on his face was yelling, "They're burning! They're burning! Help me, they're burning!"[10]

In the wreckage, Eastridge's eyes fell on his friend Jose Barco. The nineteen-year-old Cuban kid from Miami was pinned by the flaming front end of the suicide car. Eastridge watched Barco heave away the wreckage with the help of two soldiers. The private somehow stood up, wobbling in shock, blood soaking into his uniform from a hundred jagged bits of car that had hit him like a shotgun blast. Eastridge heard Barco start yelling, "I'll kill these motherfuckers. I'll kill these motherfuckers! Give me my weapon! I'll kill these motherfuckers." Half of his uniform was still on fire.

Other soldiers frantically patted out the flames and laid the smoking private on a stretcher. Eastridge could smell the burning flesh. Krebbs and Butler loaded Sergeant Huey into the top rack of a medevac truck that had just arrived. Sergeant Stricklin, with his mangled hands, was stacked right below him. Just before they pulled away, the captain pulled Huey's limp hand down from the stretcher, placing it in Stricklin's hand. "Talk to him the whole way to the hospital," the captain said. "Tell him he is going to be alright."[11]

Eastridge kept his gun leveled on a growing crowd of locals gathering on the scene to collect their dead. Little scraps of flesh that had once been the suicide bomber littered the road. A couple of platoons from Alpha Company arrived and split up, so half could control the crowd while the others scoured the surrounding alleys for the attackers. Eastridge watched his captain walk slowly out into the open dirt median of the highway, oblivious of the danger of the open road, and kneel by a limp body. It was an Iraqi boy who looked to be about six. A pool of blood surrounded his body and the whole right side of his head was smashed in like a flat basketball. The captain searched for a pulse. "Sir, he is dead, I felt him take his last breath," a soldier next to the captain told him.[12] The captain looked at the ground and started to weep.

When he stood up, he told his sergeants that no one in the platoon was leaving until after sundown. They were going to guard the gruesome chunks of the suicide bomber's body now slung all over the block. In the Muslim faith, the captain said, a person must be buried before sundown to go to heaven. He suspected the friends of the bomber were waiting to bury their latest martyr. The Band of Brothers was not going to let that happen. They stayed for hours, guarding the gruesome scene. A few locals tried to collect pieces of the suicide bomber's body in buckets. The soldiers raised their rifles and ordered them to dump their buckets back on the asphalt.

Later, the platoon pieced together what they thought had happened in the moments before the attack. The men arguing on the other side of the highway just before the blast—the ones who asked the platoon to move its Humvee— were probably a mix of terrorists and locals. The terrorists had given the locals a heads-up of the impending attack and the locals objected. It was not necessarily that they minded killing the Americans, but the Humvee was parked in a bad spot, and an explosion would damage their buildings. The groups argued back and forth, then asked the platoon to move the truck. When the platoon refused, the bomber hit anyway.

Sergeant Huey died an hour later at the hospital. The soldiers who accompanied him there choked back tears in the hall. A few lost it and wept openly. Barco had second- and third-degree burns on almost half of his body and Stricklin had several deep wounds. They were put on flights to advanced trauma hospitals in the United States.

Krebbs left the hospital and drove back to the scene of the blast to deliver the news to the platoon. Huey's death had hit him like a 155 round. The sergeant had been a mentor to all of the young grunts and the hub of their squad. It was impossible to think of the unit existing without him. Compounding the loss, Krebbs blamed himself. He saw himself as a trained lifesaver who had failed at his job. Maybe if he had gotten to Huey faster, he thought. Maybe if he had done more. He remembered a piece of advice a medic from the Big Red One had given him the first week in Iraq, "Do yourself a favor. Don't make friends with any of your guys."

After Krebbs broke the news of Huey's death to the rest of the platoon, two Iraqis came up and started complaining in broken English that their windows had been blown out. Krebbs jammed the muzzle of his rifle into one of their chests and yelled, "Shut up! Shut the fuck up!" Other soldiers rushed in to push his weapon down.

As the sun went down, Eastridge tried to keep himself squared away. He was guarding the same alley where the blast had knocked him to the dirt. Now, in the failing light, a spine lay in the narrow passage between the walls—no flesh, no ribs, no explanation, just a human spine. Eastridge's battalion had spent months preparing for Iraq, and here they were, totally unprepared. He was trained to shoot, and had been in an attack that had wounded several soldiers and killed the man whom he counted on most, but he had not been able to fire a shot in defense. He almost yearned to be the speed bump poised against the North Korean army. It would have been a battle to the death, but it would have at least been a battle. Guns were almost useless on Route Michigan. There was no good way to defend against a roadside bomb or a suicide bomber. All the training to outshoot, outmaneuver, and outthink enemy soldiers proved useless because the enemy in Iraq was not a soldier; he was a shadow, a cowardly disease that wafted invisibly through the civilian population. It made Eastridge furious. And it really made him seethe that the locals let the scumbags hide in their midst. He was enraged that they had killed Sergeant Huey—his mentor, his leader, the one he looked to for answers. And now Sergeant Stricklin was out of the picture, too. They still had eight months left in Iraq, Eastridge thought to himself: who would lead the platoon? He felt faint. He put his hand down on a crumbled wall to steady himself and felt something warm and wet in his palm. He had leaned into a piece of lung or liver or something—he didn't know what. "Oh god!" he said, jerking his hand away and wiping the blood in a long smear down the wall. This was not what he had signed up for. He felt even fainter. He went to steady himself and put his hand right back in the liver.

———

At midnight, Captain Jones gathered Eastridge's platoon and told them they were going back to the suicide bomb site the next day. They were almost guaranteed to get in a fight, and the men could expect casualties, he said. But it was crucial to let the insurgents know they would not be pushed out of any town in Iraq. The soldiers yelled and clapped. They shouted "Hoo-ah!" and punched one another in the shoulder, yelling "Stands alone!" psyching themselves up like a high school football team at halftime. It was payback time. Nobody was going to mess with the Band of Brothers.

The next morning, Eastridge's platoon went out on Mad Max again. On the edge of Khalidiya, they stopped at the car bomb site to try to figure out who was responsible. On the street, they found two Iraqis picking up scraps of the suicide bomber. The lieutenant jumped out of the Humvee and ran toward them, yelling and throwing punches.[13] The Iraqis scattered. Everybody in the platoon understood how the lieutenant felt. They were sick of being ambushed and wanted to fight back.

An hour later, as they rolled east on Route Michigan, they were hit by another IED. The explosion blew off part of the engine and threw Nasty Nash against the window so hard that he was out cold for over a minute. The two other Humvees in the platoon searched the surrounding farm fields for the triggerman but didn't find him, so they started to tow the disabled vehicle back to camp. Along the way, they stopped again at the previous day's car-bomb site. The company commander was determined to retain control of the area, so Charlie Company was putting two snipers in a building overlooking the road. The captain ordered the platoon to string out concertina wire and stop traffic while soldiers set up the sniper nest. That day, Eastridge was manning the big .50-caliber machine gun that peeks from the turret on the roof of most Humvees. He was so amped from the attack the day before that as the platoon set up the wire, he crouched down in the turret, jaw clenched, hands gripping the triggers, eyes glued to the sights, ready to light up anything that so much as twitched.

"Check this dude out," one of Eastridge's sergeants said, looking at the wide-eyed private. "Relax," the sergeant said with a laugh. "They ain't going to hit us two days in a row."[14]

After what seemed like hours, the snipers were in place. The platoon recoiled the wire, packed up the Humvees, and headed back to base. Just as they were about to leave, a scratchy message from Delta Company came over the radio. They were taking machine-gun fire from the same mosque the Brothers had searched two days before. Captain Jones radioed that they were less than a mile away and were on the way. The line of Humvees sped east on the highway through Khalidiya, past the bombed-out buildings and the abandoned police station. Eastridge noticed there was no one on the street. Then a massive blast hit.

The convoy rolled to a stop in a cloud of dust, shaking off the blast-induced stupor. The soldiers instinctively patted themselves for injuries and checked the others in the Humvee. The blast had shredded the highway, gouging a pit in the road between two of the trucks. Dirt rained down on their roofs, but except for ringing ears, no one was hurt. After bomb blasts, soldiers were trained to fan out and search for the triggerman, but the Band of Brothers was increasingly aware that the enemy studied their movements and adjusted tactics. "Hold up," Captain Jones said over the radio. "Don't get out of the trucks yet."[15]

Within seconds, five smaller explosions, designed to kill soldiers responding to the first blast, shook the street. Then bullets started to pepper the
Humvees. It was a full-on attack. Soldiers could see muzzle flashes from the
windows of burned-out concrete buildings. They didn't know it at the time,
but a half dozen coordinated ambushes were raging up and down Michigan.
Eastridge's truck sped around to the back of the city to cut off the attackers'
escape. The soldiers in Captain Jones's truck who had been closest to the blast
fanned out and took cover to return fire. The big .50 caliber guns on the other
Humvees pummeled the surrounding buildings with bullets. About two dozen
insurgents disappeared into Khalidiya's maze of courtyards and alleys. Jones
and the soldiers with him spotted four men gripping long RPG tubes running
into an alley.

"Follow me," Jones said, and ran down the alley. But the soldiers never followed because gunfire was still peppering their positions. Bullets and RPGs siz-
zled past just above their heads every time they tried to move.

The captain and a lieutenant ran alone into the alley and emerged into a
wide street where they saw an Iraqi gunman sprinting toward another alley.
Jones lifted his rifle to fire and had his feet knocked out from under him. It
was an ambush. An RPK machine gun—the Russian equivalent of an American SAW—flashed from a third-story window. A bullet shattered Jones's
ankle. Others exploded in the dirt all around. Then two more rounds
punched into his legs. He clawed frantically back into the alley for cover and
yelled, "I'm shot!"

The soldiers behind him edged up the alley, taking cover as bullets bounced
off the walls. An RPG whizzed down the alley in a plume of smoke, skipped
on the ground right by the soldiers, bounced past their heads and exploded in
the street behind them. When the team reached the captain, one of the sergeants nosed his rifle around the corner and took out the RPK gunner in the
window. A Humvee drove around so Doc Krebbs could load the bleeding commander and take him to the hospital. The wounds were enough to send him
home. It was an eerie feeling. In less than twenty-four hours the company had
lost its captain, a platoon sergeant, and a staff sergeant. Much of its command
structure was now gone.

The rest of the platoon plunged into the warren of courtyards. Shots
echoed through the small town. One soldier had his throat slashed open by a
grenade. Nasty Nash and another soldier ducked down an alley, chasing an
Iraqi who had fired at them through the neighborhood, but disappeared
around another corner. In a nearby house, the platoon found six men of fighting age, all tense and out of breath. "We didn't find any weapons on them so

we couldn't do anything to them," Nash said later, still revealing bitter frustration in his voice. "But we knew they were guilty."

Later, a few blocks away, the platoon spotted four armed men running and lit them up with machine guns. They chased one who was shot in the back. The Iraqi ran into a house with the soldiers right behind him and sprinted up three flights of stairs where he jumped off the roof and crashed to the ground. The soldiers peered over the roof and saw the Iraqi sprawled on the ground three stories below with his bones jabbing out of his thighs, howling in pain. "We interrogated the fuck out of him," Nash said. They beat him, as much out of anger and frustration as out of any desire for information. Only a few months into the tour, many of the soldiers had little patience left for the Iraqis. The battalion had literally circled the globe in their journey to Iraq. They were spending a year in the sweltering desert to try to bring a modicum of improvement to what appeared to them to be a dirty, dysfunctional, disgusting place, and the Iraqis showed their gratitude by trying to kill them. Doc Krebbs refused to give the man medical treatment, so another medic stepped in. The man died a few hours later. The platoon did not let anyone take his body before sundown.[16]

The violence on Route Michigan subsided after November, but the situation did not improve much. In January 2005, the 3,900 soldiers in the brigade oversaw the first-ever American-style elections in the Sunni Triangle. Death threats, bombings, and warnings from Al Qaeda that voting was akin to treason echoed through the Triangle in the weeks running up to the big day. The Americans banned all vehicular traffic so suicide car bombers could not obliterate the lines of voters at the polls, but when election day arrived on January 30, the polling places stood mostly empty. In all of Anbar Province, only about 2 percent of Iraqis voted.[17] Of Ramadi's 300,000 residents, fewer than 1,000 cast a ballot.[18] The same month, the Bush administration announced that it was ending its search for weapons of mass destruction, having not found a single ounce of uranium or canister of nerve gas.[19]

These events, taken together, left many soldiers wondering what the hell they were doing in Iraq. The Bush administration had argued for the invasion of Iraq on two grounds: "extensive intelligence" proved Saddam Hussein was stockpiling so-called weapons of mass destruction (WMDs) to use against the United States and its allies, and the Middle East was suffering what President Bush called a "freedom gap."[20] The people of Iraq deserved to be liberated, he said, so democracy could set "a new stage for Middle Eastern peace."[21]

Suddenly there were no WMDs, and no will for democracy, either. And there sure as shit wasn't any peace. There was just a bunch of grunts getting blown up on Route Michigan by a bunch of hajjis who didn't seem to want them there. "It was pointless. I'm all for spreading freedom and democracy," Private Josh Butler said, recalling their frustration, "but they didn't even seem to want it."

The attacks that boiled during Ramadan died down to a scalding simmer for the rest of the tour. Instead of daily attacks, they were weekly. Instead of launching all-out coordinated assaults by a dozen Iraqis, the mooj began to prefer anonymous ambushes—roadside bombs or single sniper shots. A week after Sergeant Huey died, a lieutenant in Alpha Company was ripped apart by a suicide bomber on Route Michigan. The first week of December, a staff sergeant from Delta Company was killed by an IED just a mile down the road. The same day, another IED smoked two guys from Baker Company. Two days later it was another soldier from Delta. In all, during the tour, the Band of Brothers was hit by 298 IEDs.[22] The brigade's territory in Anbar Province was the most dangerous place in Iraq, averaging ten times as many attacks as the rest of the country.[23] The day after an attack, everyone had his guard up, but a person can only stay hyperalert for so long. Eventually they grew complacent, then boom.

No one could be trusted. Not even the Iraqi police. When a buried 155 round on the berm of Michigan went off under Eastridge's Humvee one night in January, the platoon followed the trigger wire through the sand all the way back to a nearby police checkpoint.

"It is hard to explain the frustration. There was no emotional outlet," said Erwin Godoy, the lieutenant in charge of Bressler's platoon. "Late at night I would sometimes shed a few tears."

———

On February 11, 2005, Kenny Eastridge's platoon went out on Mad Max again. It was a quiet, warm day. Rain the day before had turned the air fresh. No one in Charlie Company had been seriously hurt in over two months, so the troops felt like their relentless patrols and raids were finally starting to take a toll on the mooj. Late in the afternoon, the platoon rolled past the spot where Sergeant Huey was killed. A charred axle from the suicide car still lay on one side of the road. A block down, they pulled into a wide, sunken farm field lined with date palms on the side of the highway. The spot, next to an elementary school, was one of Charlie Company's favorite places to keep an eye on Khalidiya. The sunken field allowed most of the Humvee to sit hidden below ground level with only the gun turret peeking above the road. The platoons would sit for hours in that spot, making sure no one planted another 155 round. They knew that while they were watching the neighborhood, the neighborhood was watching them, plotting the next attack.

Usually, the Band of Brothers tried to avoid patterns. Following the same routine every day made it easy for the mooj to predict movements and set a trap. So the soldiers avoided schedules and alternated routes. Parking in the ditch next to the school was one of the few things they did regularly, so they tried to take special precautions. When they drove into the ditch, they only drove on the tire tracks the Humvees had pressed into the dirt the previous day. It protected them from driving over mines. If someone had planted an explosive the night before, they would see the telltale scratches in the dirt.

Eastridge was on the gun turret that afternoon. The late winter rain had pelted the powdery desert earth the night before, erasing the Band of Brothers' Humvee tracks, but Eastridge's truck drove into the field anyway, creeping slowly. The soldiers braced for an impact, their eyes searched for any sign of digging as the wheels crept forward through the dirt. Nothing happened. They were safe. Eastridge let out a sigh of relief and leaned on the machine gun to watch the odd Iraqi traffic of military convoys, junky taxis, herds of sheep, and donkey carts shuttle by for almost two hours. Eventually it was time to move on and the platoon started the trucks to leave. They carefully backed out along the same corrugated set of tracks.

Beneath a few inches of sand in one of the tracks sat a powerful Russian-made mine, about the size and shape of a cheesecake. It was designed to destroy tanks with a concentrated upward blast that would pierce the armored belly. For whatever reason, it had not fired when the Humvee drove over the first time. The second time, it did.

The blast bucked the 2,000-pound Humvee ten feet into the air. Somehow it blew open both driver's side doors and rammed Eastridge down the gun turret and out the back door. It shook the nearby school. Other platoons heard the blast two miles away.

Eastridge woke up a few minutes later in a daze—ears ringing, eyes blurry.

"What the fuck did we hit?" he asked, assuming the Humvee had crashed at high speed. He raised his head and found he was lying in a fallow farm field. Twenty feet away, two soldiers were bandaging up a sergeant who had broken his leg. Others shuffled around aimlessly, still in a daze from the explosion. Twenty feet in the other direction sat the smoking Humvee. "What the fuck did we hit?" Eastridge asked again. He stumbled to his feet and walked toward the Humvee to see for himself. The whole front end was gone—shredded into bits and blasted into the air like confetti. Beyond sat the hot crater of the mine. Eastridge looked down and noticed he was covered in oil and antifreeze from the missing engine.

That night at the aid station, medics bandaging Eastridge up noticed that he had brain fluid leaking into his ear. He was patched up and given a few days rest. He assured his commanders that he was fine. That week, he went back out on Mad Max. His speech had a slight slur. His memory felt like a PlayStation that had been reset, but he insisted he was all right to continue fighting. Whether it was because of the soldier's creed to "never quit" or a heartfelt need to stand by the Band of Brothers, he was not going to give up and go home. And he was not alone. Of the ten soldiers in his platoon who were injured seriously enough to be sent home, five refused to leave Iraq. They did light duty until they were well enough to go back out on Mad Max.

During the first years of the war in Iraq, a saying spread among soldiers that became an unofficial motto of the occupation: "embrace the suck." It was a short way of saying things are going to get bad. Really bad. But embracing the boredom, the fear, the pain, and the loss is better than dwelling on it. So soldiers developed a grim sense of humor. Some took "grip and grin" handshake photos with the scorched and mutilated bodies of insurgents. Some in the brigade crafted "I ♥ IEDs" bumper stickers for their Humvees. Even the battalion's promotion ceremonies stressed triumph over pain.

Eastridge was promoted to specialist—one rank above private first class—on April 4, 2005. That morning his sergeant gathered the platoon in the yard by the barracks for the small ceremony and poked the twin insignia of his new rank through his lapels. Each pin had two half-inch-long metal barbs on the back. Most army units attach clasps to the barbs, give the soldier a quick congratulation, and end the ceremony. They called it "getting pinned." In the Band of Brothers, after the sergeant poked the pins through Eastridge's lapels, he turned to the rest of the platoon and said, "Why don't y'all congratulate Specialist Eastridge." The soldiers clapped and laughed. One at a time they shook Eastridge's hand, then pounded both fists on the pins, digging the barbs into his chest until he bled.

"Take the pain! Don't be a pussy!" one soldier in the crowd shouted as the platoon members took turns punching Eastridge in the pins.[24]

The newly promoted specialist stood stiff as a statue with a grimacing smile on his face. He loved the army. He had decided that if he made it home from Iraq alive he would apply for the army's elite Ranger School and try to become a Green Beret commando. So he would take the pain. It was proof he was a squared-away soldier on his way to better things.

Combat has always had the power to make some men rise to a higher level. The discipline, focus, and intensity of war seem to awaken a more noble inner self that otherwise slumbers. S. L. A. Marshall noted it in his extensive studies of platoons in World War II. "Men who had been consistently bad actors in the training period, marked by the faults of laziness, unruliness, and disorderliness, just as consistently became lions on the battlefield, with all of the virtues of sustained aggressiveness, warm obedience, and thoughtfully planned action," he wrote.[25]

The words penned more than a half century ago seemed to describe Eastridge perfectly. Combat gave him focus. He was calm, brave, and able to think under fire. While in Iraq, he was awarded a medal for good conduct and another for achievement.

At the same time, combat has the power to release some sinister aspects of human nature that civilization tries to keep tethered. At a stage of life when many young men are still discovering who they are, the Joes in the Band of Brothers struggled with the vexing conundrum of protecting a population that was trying to kill them. Be too careful and you could die. Be too aggressive and you might not be able to live with yourself. The impossible tension on Route Michigan began to tear the fabric of their humanity. When Eastridge's platoon was hit by an IED, soldiers said, the men pointed their machine guns in every direction and leveled anything moving. They called it the "death blossom."[26] Soldiers in platoons from Fallujah to Ramadi reported using the same technique. "We didn't start out like that," said Eastridge's friend and platoon mate Marcus Mifflin, recalling the tour where he served as a twenty-year-old private. "But after Sergeant Huey died, we went a little bit mad. There was a lot of killing. A lot of killing. People just ignored the rules. We just wanted to level the whole place and let God sort them out."

The most disturbing aspect of this new aggression was the soldiers' attitude. It was not cruelty. It was utter indifference. One night in May 2005, Eastridge climbed into the big machine gun on top of a Humvee. By that time, eight months into the tour, the specialist who had once been dismissed as a drunken shit bag in Korea had established himself as one of the best soldiers in his platoon—a dead-accurate shot with a cool head who never showed fear during combat. That night, he sat in the lead truck of a convoy pulling out of a small army outpost on the edge of Ramadi. As the truck rolled through the gate, Eastridge spotted a taxi driving toward it down the tight urban street. Because of fears of suicide bombers, cars were not supposed to approach

Humvees. He instinctively swung the machine gun and sprayed bullets into the engine of the car. There was no clear evidence that the taxi was a threat—its only offense was getting a bit too close—but after eight months in Iraq, Eastridge no longer worried whether he was shooting a terrorist or just a cabbie taking a wrong turn. Shooting and being wrong just meant another dead Iraqi. Not shooting and being wrong meant someone in his platoon could die.[27] It was an easy choice.

Bullets shattered the taxi's headlights and the car screeched to a halt. The driver slammed into reverse and peeled away. "I steady lit up the front with a gang of rounds," Eastridge said, recalling that night. He watched a stream of bright tracer rounds slice into the car as it fishtailed up the dark street, bashing into walls in an attempt to escape. A block up, the smoking taxi swerved around a corner and crashed. Eastridge and his platoon waited for a few minutes to make sure the coast was clear, then went to investigate. They found the car door open with blood on the seat but no body. Perhaps the driver had run away, or others had carried him. The platoon was unsure whether the driver was alive or not, or a terrorist or not. It did not matter. They did not care. That was Iraq.

"Killing people isn't like what you think. Even the first guy I killed in Iraq, it just didn't affect me that much," Eastridge said later. He assumed killing would somehow change him, but it didn't. He expected it to be a monumental event, but Groundhog Day just kept repeating. The most striking thing about it was how easy and inconsequential it was. "It doesn't bother you. And then it starts to bother you that it doesn't bother you. But you get over it. It just isn't that big a deal," he said. "Even after some of our biggest firefights I would just get in the truck and fall asleep, or go back and play video games."

In the civilian world, killing is treated as a very serious event. Police officers in many American cities are trained to deal with the psychological fallout of firing their weapons on the job. Many departments require officers to take leave and go to counseling if they shoot someone. But the Band of Brothers never really addressed it, at least not among the lowest ranks, even as killing and watching others get killed became a typical occurrence.

In response to the increased violence, some soldiers grew cold and callous. Because they were not required to deal with the emotions of killing, and did not really know how to, they cut the emotional strings. Many unconsciously stopped seeing the Iraqis as human beings. It made their jobs easier. "One time, we were guarding the gate at the FOB [forward operating base]," Marcus Mifflin said years later. "This car was coming and we were bored so we just shot it with the SAW. We never knew if we killed the driver. It just didn't matter. Guys did stuff like that all the time. People were not just popping people—

I mean, a few did and they got in trouble. But if you had any reason to suspect a threat, you were justified in shooting. It was just a free-for-all. You didn't get blamed unless someone could be absolutely sure you did something wrong. A lot of people got killed for no good reason."

After almost daily bomb attacks and the ensuing sprays of machine-gun fire, packs of dogs would often come to eat the scraps of flesh littering the road. Some soldiers began shooting the dogs, first out of disgust, then just for fun. Mifflin once pulled his gun on a sergeant who was about to shoot one of the neighborhood mutts and said, "If you shoot that dog, I'll fucking kill you."[28]

"It felt so wrong to kill a dog," he said later. "But it felt so right to kill a person. It was a complete void of humanity."

Soldiers started doing things they never thought they would. In the small computer room in the barracks, set up so soldiers could send email home, some guys started ordering 500,000-volt stun guns to carry on patrols. It is unclear whether the soldiers knew stun guns were illegal, but they quickly learned they were handy on missions. By spring of 2005 many carried them.[29] Officially, using a stun gun to shock Iraqis is a war crime. It violates the Geneva conventions' prohibition of torture and inhumane treatment. Beyond that, it subjected the Iraqis to the very type of authoritarian abuses the United States was supposed to have freed the country from. But soldiers often felt like they had little choice.

———

The disintegration of morality was not unique to Eastridge's platoon or the Band of Brothers. The 1st Battalion, 9th Infantry Regiment, was a near mirror image of the Band of Brothers. Both 500-soldier battalions belonged to the 2nd Brigade Combat Team of the 2nd Infantry Division. Both started their journey to Iraq in South Korea. Both were filled with soldiers who left checkered civilian pasts to try to make something of themselves in military service. Both trained relentlessly in reflexive fire until the infantrymen could hit a target without really thinking. Both deployed to the Sunni Triangle. Both took heavy losses from ambushes and IEDs. The only major difference was that the 1–9 had a fleet of Bradley Fighting Vehicles, light armored personnel carriers with room for six infantry soldiers. And because of the armor, the 1–9 was given the deadly, disheartening mission of trying to tame Ramadi.

Anthony Marquez was one of the young grunts in the 1–9. Like Kenneth Eastridge and Louis Bressler, he had grown up loving to play all kinds of shooter video games. Like Eastridge and Bressler, he decided to join the army to fight terrorists shortly after 9/11. Like Eastridge and Bressler, he eagerly signed up for the infantry.

"When guys asked why I joined the infantry, I said I just want to kill people and play with all the good guns and the cool toys," Marquez said later. "It seemed like the perfect job for me."

Marquez distinguished himself as an eager warfighter in Iraq. Other soldiers in Marquez's platoon said he always volunteered for missions and never showed any fear when the bullets were flying. Ramadi made Khalidiya seem relatively tame. In the stinking, garbage-choked streets, snipers videotaped their takedowns of one American soldier after another and passed out DVDs as local entertainment. In twelve months, nineteen soldiers in the battalion were killed.

Marquez's platoon called itself "the Bad Boys." And their tour had started off badly. Four days after arriving in Ramadi from Korea, they parked on an overpass on the edge of the city to go over the mission for the morning. The Bad Boys' lieutenant unfolded a map of the city so he could review their patrol plan. As he shook the creases from the open map, a sniper bullet hit him in the thigh. Marquez and the others scattered for cover behind a guard rail and, unsure where the shot had come from, started firing wildly in all directions. Two soldiers rushed over and tried to tourniquet the officer's leg as he slipped from consciousness. A Bradley that had been idling a few hundred yards away raced to provide cover, but as it barreled onto the bridge, it ran over the lieutenant, crushing him.

The tour did not improve much from there. Marquez was a foot soldier riding in the back of a Bradley, or "Brad," as the troops called it. Twice, suicide car bombers hit Marquez's Brad. He lost track of how many IEDs rocked the armored personnel carrier. At the beginning of the tour the bombs never did any real damage. Grunts who were crouched in the dark, cramped hold of the vehicle would feel the sudden buck of the blast, then watch their compartment fill up with dust, and start laughing. "We would go back to the FOB and brag like, 'Yeah, we got hit today,'" Marquez said. But slowly insurgent bomb makers started honing their craft until they learned how to kill a Brad.

"It got scarier and scarier as time went on," said Daniel Freeman, a private in the Bad Boys and one of Marquez's closest friends, recalling the tour. "You would see Bradleys destroyed with the metal of the floor pushed all the way up to the ceiling."

Even with the increasingly lethal IEDs, Marquez never shied away from going out on a mission. Other Bad Boys described him as "gung ho" and "a hell of a soldier."[30] He was always eager to hunt down the mooj or search house to house for bomb-making supplies. He gained a reputation as one of the guys in the platoon not afraid to "rough up" Iraqis to get information.[31]

He, too, ordered a 500,000-volt stun gun and used it regularly to torture the locals.

"We weren't allowed to just hit the hajjis," a soldier from his platoon, who did not want to be named because he feared retribution, said years later. "I'm not going to say we didn't, but we weren't allowed to. Lots of guys used the stun guns as a way to get around some of the rules. It was a way to make hajji tell you something without leaving a mark. At the same time, it was a way to inflict pain on hajjis just for fun. That happened. I can't say for sure that the officers saw the stun guns and never said anything against it, but I can say we never had orders saying we couldn't use stun guns, and guys carried them all the time. It was a useful tool at times."

At least four times, Marquez and his platoon were investigated by their battalion for beating up Iraqis during vehicle stops and house searches and stealing their money. The platoon sergeant was eventually removed from duty. Perhaps because the battalion always conducted the investigations internally, relying entirely on the word of other soldiers, Marquez was never formally punished.[32] Several in the platoon said they liked having a guy like him around.

"He was like the platoon's pit bull," the soldier said. "We called ourselves the Bad Boys, and we really were bad boys. We had to be, in a city like Ramadi. We did a lot of bad things. Beating. Killing. And for that, Marquez was really good. He would do anything you wanted him to do, but you needed to keep him on a short leash because he would also do what you didn't want him to do."[33]

As the soldiers were drifting into sadistic behaviors, the larger mission in Iraq continued to suffer. Many goodwill projects to rebuild shattered infrastructure were left unfinished after workers came under attack by terrorists. Bombings large enough to kill a hundred people at a time terrorized once-peaceful parts of Baghdad. The yearlong fighting by thousands of troops in Ramadi had decimated buildings and roads without bringing any peace. The whole country just seemed to be sliding toward chaos.

————

In April 2005, Kevin Shields decided he had seen enough of Route Michigan. He had been a dependable SAW gunner and a good soldier for months. Now, something had pushed him to his limit. He locked himself in a washroom with his rifle. After he sat alone crying for some time, another soldier knocked on the door and told him to open up. Shields said he was going to blow his head off. After a standoff of more than an hour, with several members of the platoon trying to talk him out, Shields opened the door and let in a fellow soldier, John

Duval. He said he was tired of it all. Just tired. He did not know what to do. With a few kind words and reassurances, Duval eventually talked him out. After that, soldiers talked behind his back about what a "pussy" and a "coward" Shields was.[34]

Shields was not alone in considering suicide. Though there is no way to gauge the number of other soldiers in the battalion who thought about killing themselves, the number who acted on the impulse was obvious. Omead Razani, Louis Bressler's platoon's nineteen-year-old Iranian American medic, went into a portable toilet next to the barracks with a 9 mm pistol just a few days into the tour. After he had been missing for several hours, Bressler discovered him crumpled in the john with his brains splattered on the walls. The second was Private Samuel Lee, a nineteen-year-old Korean American. Lee, whose friends at home described him as a friendly, quiet guy who liked to play video games, in Iraq started having dreams of kidnapping, raping, and killing Iraqis, or of killing his sergeants. He spoke openly of committing suicide to other soldiers and even went as far as to put his gun to his head three times.[35] On March 28, 2005, while soldiers were cleaning their rifles in the crowded barracks, Lee steadied the butt of his M–4 on a cot, put his mouth over the barrel, and fired.

Battalions are supposed to deploy with a combat stress officer, a medical expert who can monitor and tend to troops' mental health needs, but because of their hasty last-minute deployment from Korea, the Band of Brothers and the 1–9 had none.[36] There was also an unspoken understanding that soldiers should be able to handle anything that is thrown at them. Some quietly started using mind-numbing drugs like OxyContin to quiet their thoughts. Others became increasingly erratic and violent.

It was not just the Band of Brothers who started to fray from stress. Every battalion in the Sunni Triangle started to feel the effects. On the morning of June 21, 2005, thirty days before the Bad Boys were scheduled to go home, they headed out in two Bradleys to search for a wanted terrorist in the patchwork of farms along the Euphrates River northeast of Ramadi. Anthony Marquez and the rest of the platoon cordoned off the area and went door to door for hours, questioning the locals. They never found their man. Like a dozen times before, the target either was no longer there, was never there, or was just hiding in plain sight.

In the noon heat, the platoon leader suggested they cross a fallow field to search another cluster of houses. The platoon filed through the open stretch of dirt on foot, leaving their Bradleys a block away. A single rifle crack echoed across the field and a twenty-three-year-old specialist from Indiana named Nick Idalski collapsed on the ground. A bullet had hit just under the rim of his helmet, in the soft part of skull between his ear and his eye. "He died before he hit the ground," Marquez said, remembering the strike.

Immediately, the Bad Boys circled their guns in a death blossom and fired in all directions, even though there was no obvious target. Part of the idea behind the death blossom was to defend against incoming attacks, part of it was to teach locals a lesson, and part of it, especially if a soldier was wounded, was sheer rage. It was their standard reaction, just as it was with the Band of Brothers. "If anyone was around, that was their fault," Marquez said. "We smoked 'em."

Machine guns pelted the walls and rooflines of the surrounding houses with such a constant roar that it was impossible to tell if anyone was shooting back. Marquez raised a grenade launcher and lobbed one fist-sized bomb after another into the surrounding neighborhood.

Then the Bradleys rolled in, each armed with a stunningly lethal 25 mm chain gun capable of firing two hundred high explosive tank-killing rounds per minute. Their turrets came alive with an ominous whir, and the heavy pounding of their big guns thundered over the field as shells shattered the neighborhood, crumbling walls and setting cars on fire. Each Bradley typically carries nine hundred rounds for its big guns. In a matter of minutes, both had exhausted all their ammunition pummeling the tiny village. "I can't tell you how many civilians were in the area," a soldier in the platoon said. "But we leveled it. Totally."

The platoon loaded the limp body of their comrade into the Bradley. Back at Camp Ramadi, they took his body to the aid station, then hosed the blood out of the back of the vehicle. Later, as they cleaned their weapons, the platoon talked about how they were going to go back that night to get more payback. Instead, the company commander sent them on a mission to pick up some soldiers at an outpost in downtown Ramadi. The two Bradleys rolled out of Camp Ramadi around 10:30 P.M. and rumbled through the dark, stinking city on Route Michigan. Marquez sat in the windowless troop compartment in the back of the lead Bradley with three other soldiers. Their faces were illuminated only by a single green cabin light. The roar of the engine and the treads made it too loud to talk, so they just sat there, gripping their rifles.

They felt the Bradley slow down for a sharp corner and pick up speed again. Then, in a flash, a blast tore through the floor between the driver and Marquez. A buried IED had punched up from the road. Fuel spewed everywhere in a plume of fire. Marquez saw flames spread over the driver's back and head. Acrid black smoke filled the tight troop compartment. The driver popped the hatch above and scrambled out, screaming as flames leaped from his back. The four soldiers in the back shoved open an escape hatch and clambered choking into the street. The whole block was dark except for the flames feeding the oily plume of smoke rising from the dead Brad. Marquez scanned the rooftops for the dark silhouettes of insurgents, waiting for an ambush.

Boom! A second IED blew thirty feet away and slammed the soldiers to the ground. Marquez felt a sharp shard of shrapnel burning in his leg. A soldier right next to him lay facedown, unconscious. From the ground, Marquez lifted his eyes to the rooftops again. Then came a flurry of bullets spitting across the dirt. Marquez could hear the sick thump of rounds hitting the soldier next to him. Then he felt a hot numbness as four bullets ripped through his own leg. Blood spurted from his femoral artery. He instinctively raised his grenade launcher to return fire and realized the storm of bullets had come from the heavy machine gun on the second Bradley, which had just come around the corner.

"They must have seen our Bradley on fire, figured it was an attack, and thought we were all dead," Marquez said later, shaking his head, "then just started shooting."

The machine-gun burst only lasted about ten seconds, but it hit five of the six soldiers in the road. The platoon's medic, twenty-three-year-old Brian Vaughn from Alabama, was hit four times in the chest, and a twenty-two-year-old specialist from Connecticut named Christopher Hoskins was hit fifteen times. Both died. When the army notified their families, officials told them the men had been killed by Iraqis.[37]

As blood pumped from Marquez's leg, he started to fade out. He grunted, "I'm hit." A friend from the second Bradley rushed in and pulled the cord from the hand mike on his radio to use as a tourniquet on Marquez's leg. Watching the cord cinch down on his bloody uniform was the last thing Marquez really remembered. From there he was evacuated to a hospital in the United States, but he only remembers pieces of the dark insides of a Bradley and a helicopter and glimpses of a black, ugly place inside his head he thought was hell.[38]

———

As dreary and horrifying as the Sunni Triangle was, some soldiers grew to like it; they developed a perverse affection for the war zone. They feared it, they hated it, but they became oddly attached to it until they were uncomfortable with anything else. Eastridge, who for months had been yearning to go home, started to grow paranoid in the last weeks of June 2005 about what home would really be like. Others felt the same way. The brigade had not been to the United States in two years. After a year in Korea and a year in the Sunni Triangle, most of the grunts had changed dramatically. They had not just grown up; many had had their core beliefs about life and death and politics and morality and God torn down by the realities of war. They were different people. Eastridge decided he did not want to go back. Even though photos of ten of his dead brothers now hung on the memorial wall and sixty-one had been wounded in fighting, he and a handful of soldiers volunteered to stay for another tour.

"It was the oddest feeling," said Mifflin, who also was afraid of returning to civilian life. "The only way to describe that kind of combat is that it is like being raped, but really enjoying it. It scars you, it's horrible, but at the same time, you start to like it."

In the end, their request to stay in Iraq for another tour was turned down by the battalion. Like it or not, they were going back to the United States.

In the spring of 2005, the Band of Brothers learned that the whole brigade would be moving to Fort Carson, Colorado, when their tour was up in July. It would hardly be a homecoming. Few of the troops had ever set foot in Colorado Springs. Fort Carson was fundamentally unprepared to deal with the mental health needs of a brigade of 3,900 war-tattered soldiers. Still, many in the brigade were anxious to leave the Sunni Triangle behind. There was a growing sense, despite upbeat pronouncements from Washington, that Iraq was getting worse, not better. The cities the brigade had seen from their right-seat ride eleven months before were still hives of insurgents with sewage in the streets and no electricity. Bomb attacks still rocked the highway daily. Iraqi Army units that were supposed to take over from American troops were still a tangle of corruption and disarray. Hostility was spreading from the Triangle into once calm areas such as Baghdad. It seemed hopeless.

A scrawl of graffiti in a toilet at Camp Ramadi, the largest army base in the Triangle, summed up the feelings of many. It was a line—incorrectly attributed to Plato, but actually written by the Spanish-American poet George Santayana—that all grunts knew from the opening credits of the 2001 movie *Black Hawk Down:* "Only the dead have seen the end of war."

Beneath it a soldier had added: "You said it brother. But we're still standing. And we're outta here."[39]

CHAPTER 4

CASUALTIES OF WAR

Something happens to the human brain after long-term exposure to the stress and horrors of war—something on top of the conscious stabs of regret or anger or the black-humored fatalism that feeds on young soldiers' idealism. It is something people have recognized for thousands of years but are only now beginning to understand.

Societies have spoken of the changes in men returning from battle since the days of ancient Greece when Homer told of Odysseus's epic struggles to go back home after the Trojan War, even though it is a part of war usually left out of the history books. It has gone by a host of different names: "nostalgia" in eighteenth-century Europe, "war excitement," "exposure," or "soldier's heart" in the Civil War, "war neurosis" or "shell shock" in World War I, "battle fatigue" in World War II. Today it is widely known as post-traumatic stress disorder.

We tend to think of PTSD as a modern disorder, but it is only a modern label. It is neither a new phenomenon nor one only present in some wars. The widely held belief, for example, that World War II did not produce significant psychological casualties is simply false. In 1943, a total of 438,000 troops were discharged from the army for psychiatric reasons—eclipsing the total number of enlistees recruited that year.

"I hear Vietnam vets say they suffer from flashbacks and I think, 'Hey, I've been having them since 1944, I have seniority!'" Edward "Babe" Heffron, an infantry private in the original Band of Brothers during World War II, wrote in his 2007 memoir, *Brothers in Battle, Best of Friends*. "Any soldier who lived through combat, whether it was in 1776, 1861, 1918, 1944, any war, will never be entirely free of the war he fought. Some are just able to brush it off better than others."[1]

Even so, every generation that goes to war seems to forget or at least ignore the threat of psychological breakdown until it discovers it again for itself. The extent of the problem makes it surprising that this consequence of war is so often brushed aside. After the Civil War, thousands of veterans filled state mental asylums and prisons. After World War I, the British discharged at least 200,000 soldiers stricken by shell shock and had to commandeer public hospitals, spas, and resorts to treat the casualties.[2] At the onset of World War II, the U.S. military decided that strict screening for mental and moral defects in recruits could nip the problem in the bud. The army rejected 94 men per 1,000 for not meeting the standards—a total of 1.6 million. Even so, vast numbers of soldiers broke down in combat. By the end of the war in 1946, 454,699 veterans of World War II were receiving disability benefits for neuropsychiatric diseases. In addition, in the mid-1940s, veterans hospitals still housed an estimated 33,000 psychiatric patients from World War I.[3]

These casualties are a long-term and costly aspect of waging war. Studies suggest the total number of PTSD cases from Vietnam is around 479,000. As of 2009, nearly 390,000 veterans were receiving Veterans Administration benefits for PTSD, making it the fourth most prevalent service-related disability.[4] Technology has evolved, but the human threshold for horror has not, and without taking into account the widespread casualties it produces, no accurate tally of the cost of war can be made.

Just as prevalent and long-lived as the psychological injuries of war is the suspicion by commanders that these invisible wounds aren't real. It is hard to fake a broken arm or a gunshot wound. It is relatively easy to fake a psychological wound, so commanders have always been faced with the conundrum of judging who is really injured and who just wants out of the fight. In the first years of the Civil War and World War I, many soldiers stricken by psychological breakdowns from the artillery bombardment were treated as deserters and jailed or shot. It was only after years of conflict and mounting psychological casualties from both wars that the military learned to treat soldiers, offering them rest, and often morphine, to ease their nerves. For a hundred years, the formula for treating soldiers on the battlefield has basically remained the same. Soldiers were offered a break from combat, good food, and sometimes narcotics. They were usually not allowed to return home. Instead, they were kept close to the front lines and encouraged to return to battle in three to ten days. Those who would not return were given menial, distasteful jobs, such as digging latrines.

Using this approach, the army found it could get up to 90 percent of soldiers to return to duty.[5]

Dealing with long-term psychological effects after the battle has proved much more difficult and costly. World War I veteran Willard Waller wrote this stern warning in 1944 of what society could expect from the latest batch of returning veterans: "There is a core of anger in the soul of almost every veteran. . . . In one man it becomes a consuming flame that sears his soul and burns his body. In another it is barely traceable. It leads one man to outbursts of temper, another to social radicalism, a third to excesses of conservatism."[6] The fallout can last for decades and ripples through society. A study tracking a group of World War II veterans over a twenty-year period after the war found they showed persistent symptoms of insomnia, irritability, depression, and nightmares.[7]

Even within the Band of Brothers, who are widely known for their World War II heroics but not for what happened afterward, many men struggled with how combat changed them. "Babe" Heffron, who joined the unit in 1942, wrote that he had flashbacks for decades. "What you don't know going in," he wrote, "is that when you come out, you will be scarred for life. Whether you were in for a week, a month, or a year—even if you come home without a scratch—you are never, ever going to be the same. . . . Living with it can be hell. It's like the devil presides in you."[8]

Even though the human reaction to war has changed little since ancient times, its effects, on a microscopic level, have only recently come to light. Recognizing the cause of PTSD is common sense—trauma creates mental scars that can be permanent. But how and why those scars appear are only now starting to be explained through advances in neuroscience and brain-imaging technologies such as magnetic resonance imaging (MRI) that actually show researchers the physical effects of war on the mind.

—————

"In Vietnam there was still a struggle," Kateri Koverman said. "People did not really understand what PTSD was. I would have guys come talk to me, trying to get this load off their chest, but we had no awareness of what was going on with them. It was only after the war that we learned, and continue to learn."

Koverman, sixty-seven, is a nun—but not one of the stern, habit-wearing women of popular imagination. She is partial to trousers and bright blazers and wears a simple brass cross on a chain. Her hair is short and her smile is broad and wise. She has a habit of letting it slowly spread across her face as she takes a long, thoughtful breath before speaking. On a clear, cold spring afternoon in

Colorado Springs in 2010, she took a rare break from near constant meetings with veterans and their families to explain what is now called PTSD.

Sister Kateri spent much of her life as a nun in war zones, ministering to soldiers and refugees in Vietnam, Cambodia, Ethiopia, Sierra Leone, and El Salvador. "Anywhere there was a conflict, I went," she said. By the time she was fifty, she had spent so much time in war zones that she started to notice she was suffering from the same problems soldiers had talked to her about: anger, numbness, nightmares, flashbacks.

"Here I was, this little old nun with this explosive rage," she said with a gentle chuckle.

At that time, in the mid 1990s, she started working with homeless Vietnam veterans near her home in Cleveland, Ohio. Many of them still seemed to be suffering from problems they picked up in the war decades before. One by one, she started trying to get them help at the local VA hospital. That led her to slowly develop an understanding of PTSD. Soon she recognized it in herself. Before long she was speaking to veterans' groups and small gatherings of the National Guard, explaining in plain talk what she had learned. Eventually, she heard that soldiers at Fort Carson were struggling with PTSD. Her order had a convent in Colorado Springs, so she packed her bags and came to the city. In a small office in the local hospital, she focuses on therapy groups for the most overlooked veterans—those with dishonorable discharges and those behind bars.

"These young guys today," she explained, "these guys coming back from Iraq and Afghanistan, are going through the same stuff guys went through coming home from Vietnam. War has not changed very much. But our understanding of PTSD has. We know so much more now."

That dynamic changed radically in the last decade, as technology progressed to a point where researchers could finally confirm that PTSD—or shell shock, or whatever you want to call it—is not just a subjective bundle of feelings. It is not just pop psychology or the invention of an overindulgent political agenda. It is a physical wound of war. And in veterans from the wars in Iraq and Afghanistan, unlike those in previous conflicts, it can finally be quantitatively measured.

Kateri, who is a licensed social worker and holds regular therapy sessions with a number of vets, finds that the best way to start is by explaining the biology behind the wound. "These guys have to know what is going on with them. Once they see that it is normal, it becomes less scary," she said. So she begins by explaining how a healthy brain is put together before the constant stress of war starts to tear it down.

Some neuroscientists divide the human brain into three distinct parts, based on when those parts developed during human evolution: the R complex, the limbic system, and the neocortex. In fact, the brain is much more complex, but in terms of understanding stress injuries, the three-part model is a good place to start. The R complex sits in the core of the brain, closest to the connection with the spine. It controls all unconscious bodily functions, from breathing and digesting to balance and body temperature. In terms of evolution, the R complex is the oldest and most primitive part of the brain. It is sometimes called the "reptilian brain" because the R complex is similar to the primitive brains of reptiles.

Wrapped around the R complex is the limbic system. It inhabits a thin margin between the R complex and the neocortex. It is a more recently evolved part of the brain, developing in the 300 million years since mammals branched off from reptiles. The limbic system is sometimes called the "emotional brain"—where values such as fear or pleasure are attached to stimuli flowing in through the senses. These value judgments are then passed on to the neocortex and R complex, which react in their own ways.

On top of the limbic system is the most advanced part of the brain, the neocortex, a Latin word meaning "new rind." It is the most recently evolved part of the brain and covers the older sections like a helmet. It is the part of the brain that most people think of as their brain—the part that actually thinks. The folded gray matter is where the brain houses logic, complex planning, personality, manners, idealism, appreciation of beauty, art, humor—in short, all the things that make human beings human.

In a healthy brain, all three parts work together in harmony, but deep in the limbic system sit two sections that seem to short-circuit during the prolonged stress of war. They are called the amygdala and the hippocampus—both named for what they resemble. Amygdala is Greek for "almond." Hippocampus is Latin for "seahorse." Two small, nut-shaped amygdalae sit at the head of the long, crenulated curve of the hippocampi. Both sets lie just beneath the neocortex, snug against either side of the center of the brain. Put your finger a half-inch in front of your ear and the tip will sit very close to the amygdala.

The job of the amygdala is to attach emotional value to information coming in from the senses. It decides whether what you see, hear, smell, taste, or touch is good or bad, safe or dangerous. If something is dangerous, the amygdala can signal a neural alarm that tells the R complex to jump-start the body's natural defenses. It is what causes people to flinch at a loud noise even before they know what they've heard. Throwing the alarm switch floods the body with adrenaline, endorphins, and other steroids. The heart starts pumping faster. The lungs open to maximum, and the rate of breathing increases. Muscles are flooded with energy. The alertness of both the R complex and neocortex crank up.

Neuroscientists have learned much of what is known about the functions of different sections of the brain by studying people with damage to those specific parts. Subjects with damaged amygdalae show little concept of risk or fear. In one experiment, some of these people were shown photos of frightening faces and displayed no rise in pulse or breathing, even though, consciously, they could explain that the faces were frightening. In another experiment, they repeatedly gambled away large sums of play money even though the odds were clearly against them.[10] They were unable to attach the "danger" value of adverse risk to the bets they were making.

The hippocampus acts as an emotional adviser to the amygdala. Though the range of its functions is not fully understood, it is known to be vital to recording, organizing, and storing memories—especially memories with strong emotional weight. In a sense, it is the wise consigliere that uses lessons from the past to let the amygdala know when to sound the alarm. In laboratory tests, healthy rats and other mammals that were repeatedly given an electric shock every time they heard a bell naturally began to fear the sound of bell. They flinched and got a jolt of adrenaline every time a bell chimed, even if the bell was no longer accompanied by a shock. Animals with a damaged hippocampus would experience the bell and the shock over and over without ever developing the same reaction.[11] They could not attach value, good or bad, to memories of past events.

Humans have more neural connections between the emotional duo of the amygdala and hippocampus and the logical part of the brain than any other species. The connections are strongest at a spot just behind the forehead, called the medial prefrontal cortex. This part of the cortex is believed to play a role in the awareness of manners and accepted social behavior, among other things. In studies where healthy subjects were asked to consider complex moral decisions, such as whether it is acceptable to throw one person out of a lifeboat to save five, the medial prefrontal cortex lit up on neuroimaging scans that showed where brain activity was greatest.[12] When researchers asked subjects to consider whether several phrases expressing social traits—I have a quick temper, I forget important things, I am a good friend—applied to them, the same spot lit up, suggesting the medial prefrontal cortex is where we define who we think we are.[13]

"Those millions of connections between the center of the self and morality and the emotional brain act kind of like the reins a horserider holds when perched on a wild stallion," Sister Koverman said. The stallion—wild, quick to startle, ruled by emotions—represents the amygdala and hippocampus. The rider—logical, calm, and calculating—is the cortex.

Just as a rider can pull the reins to calm a startled horse if there is no reason to gallop, the logical mind can send calming "false alarm" messages to a startled amygdala if it does not perceive a real threat. The amygdala often responds faster than the cortex, which is why if someone jumps out and yells "Boo!" you will jump and your heart will start racing a split second before you realize it is a joke, not a threat, and your cortex sends a "whoa" message to your amygdala.

During long bouts of extreme stress, the hierarchy of horse and rider can break down. At first, everything works as it is designed to. During a real threat, the cortex will not rein in the amygdala. The amygdala will signal the R complex that there is an emergency and the body will go into full "fight or flight" mode. The R complex will prepare for an attack by spiking the blood with performance-enhancing adrenaline and endorphins that boost energy and act as natural painkillers. In small doses, these chemicals help the body respond to the threatening situation of the moment, but over time, they become toxic and start to damage parts of the brain.[14] They can literally cause cells to burst and connections between parts of the brain to wither and die.

Researchers studying PTSD using MRI scans have found that the prefrontal cortex and hippocampus in combat veterans seem to shrink. Blood flow to both parts of the brain during threatening situations is decreased. That means the amygdala does not have as much logic or memory to help it decide whether to throw the emergency switch. The amygdalae itself, in contrast, can become enlarged and hyperactive,[15] making them more likely to sound the alarm. At the same time, the neurons connecting the cortex and the amygdalae—the calming reins—shrink in number and size. Severing the connection between the amygdala and prefrontal lobes purposefully through surgery is called a lobotomy. This infamous brain surgery often rendered patients so disastrously vacant and disabled that it was all but abandoned in the twentieth century. Prolonged combat stress is not as severe or irreversible as a lobotomy, but to some degree, it has some of the same effect.

The understanding of the relationship between the cortex, the limbic system, and combat is far from perfect. Researchers are not sure whether the poor connections between the frontal lobe and amygdalae found in PTSD sufferers is a preexisting condition that caused the stress reaction or a result of the stress. Additionally, not every combat veteran seems to have a breakdown in balance between the neocortex and the amygdala, and the factors controlling who does and who does not are far from clear. But this much seems to be true: in some troops, as stress takes its toll, the wild stallion gets stronger, the logical rider gets weaker, and the reins begin to fray. In a real, measurable way, on a cellular level, humanity dissolves, soldiers lose themselves, and the primitive, bestial part of the brain starts to take over.

———

When people think of post-traumatic stress disorder they generally think of the Vietnam War. Government studies suggest somewhere between 15 and 30 percent of the 2.9 million troops who fought in the conflict returned with some form of psychological damage.[16] At the time, psychiatrists knew about combat fatigue but there was no official diagnosis for the group of symptoms many veterans experienced long after they had left the war zone. It was through the lobbying of veterans' groups that their generation's term for this wound of war was officially accepted in 1980 and listed in the American Psychiatric Association's Diagnostic and Statistical Manual—the bible of psychiatric disorders.

PTSD, like all the labels before it, comes with its own limitations. Foremost is that it is so narrowly defined that it does not embrace the full psychological trauma of war.[17] Though the public now uses the term PTSD to refer to the whole range of psychological problems caused by trauma, the diagnosis only covers one specific area. It is literally a checklist of symptoms of easily identifiable symptoms.

To fit the American Psychiatric Associations definition of PTSD, the manual says doctors must recognize the following in a patient:

A.   The person has been exposed to a traumatic event in which both of the following have been present: (1) The person experienced, witnessed, or was confronted with an event that involved actual or threatened death or serious injury, AND (2) the person's response involved intense fear, helplessness, or horror.

B.   The person persistently reexperiences the event in one (or more) of the following ways: (1) recurrent and intrusive distressing recollections of the event; (2) recurrent distressing dreams of the event; (3) acting or feeling as if the traumatic event were recurring (illusions, hallucinations, and dissociative flashback episodes, including those that occur upon awakening or when intoxicated); (4) intense psychological distress at exposure to internal or external cues that symbolize or resemble an aspect of the event; (5) physiological reactivity on exposure to internal or external cues that symbolize or resemble an aspect of the traumatic event.

C. The person exhibits persistant avoidance of stimuli associated with the trauma and numbing of general responsiveness as indicated by three (or more) of the following: (1) efforts to avoid thoughts, feelings, or conversations associated with the trauma; (2) efforts to avoid activities, places, or people that arouse recollections of the trauma; (3) inability to recall an important aspect of the trauma; (4) markedly diminished interest or participation in significant activities; (5) feeling of detachment or estrangement from others; (6) restricted range of affect (i.e., unable to have loving feelings); (7) sense of a foreshortened future (e.g., does not expect to have a career, marriage, children, or a normal life span).

D. The person has persistent symptoms of increased arousal, as indicated by two (or more) of the following: (1) difficulty falling or staying asleep; (2) irritability or outbursts of anger; (3) difficulty concentrating; (4) hyper vigilance; (5) exaggerated startle response.

E. The duration of the disturbance (symptoms in Criteria B, C, and D) is more than one month.

F. The disturbance causes clinically significant distress or impairment in social, occupational, or other important areas of functioning.

This list of symptoms is thought to be caused by the breakdown in the hierarchy between the neocortex and the amygdalae. When a returning Iraq vet's amygdalae startle over something that reminds them of trauma—a pile of trash on the side an American highway for a soldier who has been hit by IEDs placed in similar piles in Iraq, for example—they will throw the alarm switch. The logical brain is supposed to tell the amygdalae that a pile of trash in the United States does not contain a bomb. But the atrophied connections cannot relay the calming message, so the vet will get a jolt of anxiety and often suddenly, almost involuntarily, change lanes to avoid the trash. Flashbacks of Iraq can erupt out of the withered hippocampus, causing more alarms. The constant flood of adrenaline can make veterans hyperalert and cause problems with sleep.

"We like to tell veterans that PTSD is a normal reaction to an abnormal situation," Sister Kateri said. It is not a defect or a weakness, it is the body's natural coping mechanisms responding to a bad situation—not so different from a fever or swelling. Given that, she said, some people treating these veterans have started to take issue with the term post-traumatic stress disorder. How can something be both a normal reaction and a disorder?

"These guys coming home don't want to be told they have a disorder, and they don't," she said. Instead, she prefers to use a term coined by Dr. William Nash, a navy psychiatrist who was in the Sunni Triangle at the same time as the Band of Brothers, and who has been working since then with the marines to craft a better mental health program for combat veterans. He calls the psychological wounds of returning vets "combat stress injuries."

Like sports injuries, Nash argues, combat stress injuries vary widely in type and severity.[9] Many can heal on their own, with a little rest. Others require rehabilitation. If the injury is serious enough, it can necessitate extensive care and treatment. No matter the severity, classifying what happens to soldiers as an injury instead of a disorder is an important first step toward healing because it lets soldiers know there is a path to recovery. The fault does not lie in them.

PTSD, while potentially debilitating, does not touch on all of the problems associated with combat trauma. PTSD often blows in with a storm of other issues that don't show up on the diagnostic list: depression, anxiety, substance abuse, guilt, shame, anger, and a loss of faith in self, society, and the very institutions, such as the army, that may be extending offers of treatment.

Dr. Jonathan Shay, a clinical psychiatrist at the Department of Veteran Affairs Outpatient Clinic in Boston who has worked for decades with combat veterans and is considered one of the preeminent thinkers on PTSD, calls these other problems "moral injuries." He argues that the disorder should really be classified in two forms, simple and complex. The best way to explain simple PTSD, he says, is as "the persistence in civilian life of valid adaptations to survive lethal danger. So the infantryman's caution about bunching up and making a target for enemy snipers and mortarmen may persist into civilian life as a non-negotiable aversion to crowds and open spaces. Likewise, shutting down all emotions that do not contribute directly to survival in a fight may persist into civilian life as a cold emotional distance that makes family life so much harder."[18]

Most people with simple PTSD, he says, can recover or at least adapt to live normal and productive lives in spite of their injuries. But if part of what is damaged by the trauma is a soldier's character, what Shay calls "the capacity for social trust," then the natural coping and healing process can be crushed. The stimuli that soldiers can form an aversion to and try to avoid can be the bonds of humanity itself. These soldiers, Shay says, become infected by "virulent cynicism, the constant expectancy of exploitation and harm, and propensity for violence."

Treatment for simple PTSD comes in a variety of different forms—everything from traditional psychotherapy to relatively recent virtual reality simulators. Almost all of them are built on the same principle: allow the patient to reexperience some facets of their traumatic event little by little until the event no longer causes the panic and anxiety that it once did. Through talking about, writing about, or somehow reexperiencing the stimuli that the patient has been avoiding, therapy can force the brain to reestablish the proper relationship between the logical rider and the startled stallion.

Treating complex PTSD is, not surprisingly, more complex. There are no clinically proven treatments to heal the moral injuries that often accompany returning veterans. In fact, a team of psychiatrists led by Dr. Bret T. Litz, one of the leading researchers in the field, noted in a 2009 paper that, in large part, "questions about moral injury are not being addressed" and that there is a "clinical care vacuum."[19] He suggested a possible model of treatment that Sister Koverman had used in her own way for years: creating a strong relationship between veteran and caregiver to gradually let the veterans explore, accept, and forgive those involved in the trauma, including themselves, then forge new trust-building relationships.

Koverman has had some luck getting troubled veterans back on their feet, but she said it is a labor-intensive process. "These things take time. Years. Years," she said, shaking her head. "It is a difficult road and the first part is the hardest, gaining a guy's trust."

She paused, as if remembering a certain veteran she had counseled, or maybe her own experiences in Vietnam, which eventually led her to get counseling for PTSD. "Most of these guys are in denial," she continued. "And why not? It is a scary road to go down. Vietnam. Or Iraq. To talk about what happened. To *really* talk about it, the floodgates will open and you'll just dissolve. It is just so vast. . . . So vast."

Simple PTSD, complex PTSD, and their accompanying moral injuries all fit under Dr. Nash's broader, more accurate combat-stress-injury label. This injury is not dependent first and foremost on a traumatic event, like PTSD, he explains. Instead, there are three types of combat stress injuries troops can experience: trauma, fatigue, and grief.[20]

Trauma is an injury of impact: fearing death, witnessing an attack with mass casualties, seeing women and children killed, handling dead bodies, witnessing or committing atrocities, being injured in an attack, feeling helpless or unable to counterattack, and killing—each can cause a traumatic combat stress injury.

Fatigue is an injury of wear and tear. Heat, exhaustion, heavy loads, poor food, relentless missions, lack of sleep, and long-term exposure to situations that are stressful, but not necessarily traumatic, still take their toll and can eventually lead to breakdown.

Grief perhaps needs no explanation. As Nash notes, soldiers forge relationships "infused with an intensity that has few parallels in civilian life, coming closer to the attachment a parent has for a child than the bonds of siblings or mere friends."[21] So experiencing repeated loss can exact a debilitating price. But it is more than that. War can cause the obliteration of cherished core beliefs—grief for the loss of one's own self.

Everyone has a specific capacity for stress. Think of it like a bathtub. Some people may have bigger tubs, some smaller. All of the stresses of war—traumatic or merely grueling, grief and killing, fear and gore—pour into the tub. Stresses from home pour in along with stresses from the war zone. If the tub overflows, it results in a combat stress injury. The intensity of the flow of stress and the time exposed, as well as each person's ways to cope (the drain) control whose tub overflows. No one has yet figured out how to gauge the size of each person's tub, the speed of their drain, or how well or quickly each individual can recover from a spill.

To further complicate things, many soldiers in modern conflicts suffer from traumatic brain injuries, or TBIs. A major IED blast sends out a shock wave traveling at 1,600 feet per second—about 1,000 miles per hour. A ridge of pressure up to 1,000 times atmospheric pressure shoots right through armor, helmets, skulls, and brains. The brain not only gets knocked around in the skull by the pulse, but the quick changes in pressure seem to cause tiny gas bubbles to rip small holes in the brain. Multiple blasts can compound the injuries. Over 150,000 troops have been diagnosed with mild TBIs, and studies suggest many thousands more suffer without a diagnosis. Some of the symptoms of TBIs seem obvious: slurred speech, decreased motor skills, and problems with memory. But TBIs can also cause soldiers to be irritable, aggressive, and overly emotional. These symptoms overlap almost entirely with PTSD, and they can linger years after the injury.[22] Complicating the injuries, it is not uncommon for soldiers who have been in combat to have both, which can make it hard for medical staffs to know what to treat.

It is easy to see that many of the Band of Brothers suffered almost every stressor in the book. They feared death and felt helpless against IED blasts. Some killed and witnessed killing. Some participated in atrocities. Many lost long-valued beliefs. They also lost dear friends and mentors. They were taxed by heat and long hours and heavy loads. They may have had moral injuries caused by the lack of a clear enemy. Many were physically injured as well. Many had traumatic brain injuries. While many miraculously shouldered this burden when they returned home, a number succumbed to the normal reaction to an abnormal situation that is PTSD.

By the time the Band of Brothers returned to the United States in August 2005, PTSD as a label was almost twenty-five years old. There were hundreds of studies of its symptoms, clinically proven treatments, and army-wide plans to deal with the psychological casualties.

The army knew it was facing a tide of cases coming back from Iraq. An army study published in 2004 showed that up to a fifth of soldiers could return from Iraq with symptoms of PTSD and that the greater a unit's combat exposure, the greater the numbers would be.[23] The study, led by Charles Hoge, a top psychiatrist at Walter Reed Army Institute of Research, also suggested that treating these soldiers would be a challenge. Of those veterans reporting mental health problems in the study, about 40 percent said they did not want professional help, mostly because they feared they would be stigmatized or would hurt their careers.[24] Other studies had documented that PTSD's symptoms could include drug and alcohol abuse, irritability, and poor performance on the job. All the information needed to predict the problems that the Band of Brothers would bring home from Iraq and the difficulties in treating them was in the army's hands. But no one passed this information effectively to the people who really needed it: the company commanders, the sergeants and lieutenants in charge of soldiers, and the grunts themselves.

Sister Kateri has encountered severe combat stress injuries among army vets who ended up in jail in Colorado Springs. She also works with veterans in Kentucky and Montana, as well as her home state of Ohio. She sees increasing numbers of soldiers struggling with the very same issues she did. "Think about how long we have been at war," she said as she got up from a seat in her office to go to talk to chaplains at Fort Carson about returning veterans' needs. "Think about how many people there are now across the country like this. And how many people are really doing anything to help them?"

CHAPTER 5

STANDS ALONE

In the summer of 2005, when jets loaded with thousands of soldiers from the Band of Brothers brigade touched down on the high, treeless prairie of the Colorado Springs airport, lines of men in desert camouflage filed out through the summer sun toward a tent with two tables. At the first table, soldiers handed in the rifles they had carried everywhere for twelve months. At the second, McDonald's handed them free cheeseburgers to welcome them back to America.

Beyond the burger table gathered crowds of soldiers from the unit already in Colorado Springs. Eastridge saw Jose Barco, who had been flown to a special burn treatment center at Brooke Army Medical Center in Texas, where his dead, charred skin was scrubbed off and replaced by new skin grafts. When he came to greet his friends, he still had to wrap his legs in special tights under his uniform to hold the grafts in place. Their injured platoon sergeant, Tim Stricklin, was there, too. Eastridge strode across the tarmac and greeted both, exchanging giddy smiles and slaps on the back with them and everyone from Charlie Company. They were happy to be home safe and in one piece.

Beyond the waiting soldiers, a small crowd of Vietnam veterans stood applauding, giving the troops a welcome home they had never received. After passing through the Vietnam vets, the Brothers packed into buses for a twenty-minute ride across town to Fort Carson. Because they deployed from Korea and many had never been to Colorado Springs, they were seeing their new home for the first time. The convoy rolled west toward the green, craggy mountains on the other side of the city. Along the route, intermittent crowds waved signs and painted sheets that proclaimed THANK YOU! and WELCOME HOME!

The buses were greeted by more signs and more crowds at the gates of Fort Carson. Finally, they stopped at a gymnasium, where the soldiers' families waited. Hundreds of families—both longtime stateside wives and newlywed drinky girls—had moved to Colorado Springs and set up homes during the year their soldiers fought for Route Michigan. Their kids, dressed in their best outfits, fidgeted in the bleachers as they waited for their fathers. A military band began to play, and the precise files of infantry soldiers marched through the main door under an enormous flag with an eagle spreading its wings above the slogan WELCOME HOME OUR HEROES. Parents and children cheered and shook homemade banners. Svetlana Shields held her almost one-year-old son on her hip as she looked for Kevin in the ranks.

The Band of Brothers formed perfect ranks and stood motionless at attention while the brigade commander, the post commander, the mayor of Colorado Springs, and other brass made a few short remarks. Then, with a knowing smile, the commander said, "You are dismissed," and the crowd swarmed down from the bleachers and into the ranks of uniforms. Husbands and wives locked in embraces, trying to make up for months of absence. Fathers hoisted babies they were meeting for the first time. Ryan Krebbs, the medic, was surrounded by his parents and fiancée. Kenneth Eastridge, David Nash, Marcus Mifflin, and Josh Butler piled together arm in arm, laughing as they took one group photo after another. It was good to be home.

Colorado Springs rolled out the welcome mat. Since the start of the war, the town had thrown repeated parades on the town's main drag, Tejon Street, to "thank our troops." The celebrations attracted as many as 80,000 people. Yellow SUPPORT OUR TROOPS ribbons were almost as ubiquitous on local cars as license plates. Area businesses offered soldiers everything from free hotel stays and zoo passes to free facials and massages. It was not uncommon in the city for a soldier to go out to lunch and have a stranger pick up the tab.

The flood of kindness and gratitude and the big welcome-home ceremonies were, in part, an attempt to correct the mistakes of Vietnam. During that war, soldiers did not come home as a unit. They usually came home one or two at a time when their tours were finished, often with no fanfare. Many of the returning veterans of that war had been forced into service by the draft. Sometimes they felt like the country that had compelled them to fight showed little gratitude in return. The sullen veteran—burdened with despair and doubt—is one of the most enduring images of the Vietnam War era. It is usually paired with a bitterly ungrateful American public, spitting on the veterans who returned. Like the low World War II firing rates proposed by S. L. A. Marshall, research has shown that these images are perhaps exaggerated. The vast majority of Vietnam vets were treated with kindness when they returned and went on to lead normal lives, but the image, valid or not, of society's disdain for the downtrodden vet and the alienation it caused was the driving force behind the exhuberant celebrations soldiers received when returning to Colorado Springs from the war in Iraq.

Unlike Vietnam, battalions came home en masse after a tour in Iraq. At the same time, Colorado Springs police showed little tolerance for the type of public antiwar demonstrations that raged during Vietnam. In February 2003, just a month before the invasion of Iraq, Colorado Springs police showed up with riot gear and dogs at a peace demonstration of about a thousand people. When a few dozen of the demonstrators tried to march down a main road, slowing traffic, the police fired tear gas, pepper spray, and rubber bullets.[1] The protest was one of dozens of large rallies across the country that day, but it was the only one where police used force to disperse the crowd.[2]

Early in the Iraq War, the city and the army seemed to think the boisterous welcome and lack of serious dissent had successfully nipped the problems that plagued the previous generations of veterans in the bud. In 2004, an optimistic local police spokesman told the *Colorado Springs Gazette* that his department had not seen any problems with soldiers getting in trouble with the law once they returned from war. He suggested the reason was the city's warm reception.[3] The community seemed to think that all that was needed to diffuse the explosive emotions of war and save a new generation of soldiers from alcoholism, drugs, despondency, and post-traumatic stress disorder was a really emphatic "thank you."

The army, and society as a whole, failed to prepare for the real effects of combat and educate soldiers, their leaders, and their families about the road ahead. Decades of studies since Vietnam had documented the psychological fallout of war. Researchers had written at length about the symptoms, treatments, and dangers of prolonged combat stress. But the army and the government, for the most part, had not listened. Fort Carson was understaffed, and what staff it had was undertrained. It did not have the forces in place for the ordeal ahead. In many ways, preparations for the fallout on the home front mirrored preparations for the invasion: they were wildly optimistic and, as it turned out, totally inadequate.

Before long, the rates of drug use and drunk driving soared. So did the number of soldiers being booked at the county jail. If the unruliness of the returning veterans surprised civilian and army authorities, it was only because they had not studied history. The same struggles had been documented again

and again at least as far back as World War I. Philip Gibbs, a British war journalist, wrote extensively about it in his 1920 memoir *Now It Can Be Told*.
"All was not right with the spirit of the men who came back," he wrote. "They
put on civilian clothes again and looked to their mothers and wives very much
like the young men who had gone . . . but they had not come back the same
men. Something had altered in them. They were subject to queer moods, queer
tempers, fits of profound depression alternating with a restless desire for pleasure. Many of them were easily moved to passion when they lost control of
themselves. Many were bitter in speech, violent in opinion, frightening."

Every soldier in the Band of Brothers brigade got a monthlong "block break"
vacation after coming home from Iraq, but before going on leave the troops
went through three days of mandatory Soldier Readiness Processing, which included reentry classes on managing personal finances and family relationships.
The training included a quick discussion of how to turn a "battle mind" into
a "peacetime mind," including the commonsense advice that soldiers no longer
needed to carry a gun around all the time. It was the same reintegration every
soldier in the army went through. Every soldier also had to go through a screening process in which the whole battalion shuffled through a vast, three-story
building, getting everything from their teeth to their blood checked, to make
sure they were healthy. Near the end of the screening process, each one sat
down across from an army technician who asked a two-page list of questions
known as the Post-Deployment Health Assessment (PDHA). The idea was to
quickly document war wounds and potential for PTSD. Soldiers answered yes
or no. Toward the end of the PDHA, questions centered on invisible wounds
to the psyche:

> *Did you see anyone wounded, killed, or dead during this deployment?*
> *(mark all that apply)*
>   Yes—coalition
>   Yes—enemy
>   Yes—civilian
>   No
>
> *Did you ever feel that you were in great danger of being killed?*
>   Yes
>   No

Have you ever had any experience that was so frightening, horrible, or
upsetting that, IN THE PAST MONTH, *you . . .*
> *Have had any nightmares about it or thought about it when you did*
> *not want to?*
> *Tried hard not to think about it or went out of your way to avoid*
> *situations that remind you of it?*
> *Were constantly on guard, watchful, or easily startled?*
> *Felt numb or detached from others, activities, or your surroundings?*

Over the LAST 2 WEEKS, *how often have you been bothered by any of the*
following problems?
> *Little interest or pleasure in doing things*
> *Feeling down, depressed, or hopeless*
> *Thoughts that you would be better off dead*

The grunts waited on long rows of chairs in the hall to go through the
screening a few at a time. Sergeants had told them that the process would move
faster, and that they would get to go home sooner if they kept their mouths
shut. When it was Eastridge's turn to answer the questions, he did what others told him to do—he lied. He had watched his favorite sergeant die. He had
been through multiple bomb blasts. He had shot and killed an estimated twenty
people. He had helped bag mutilated and dismembered bodies. He had nightmares. He avoided crowds. He felt numb and detached. But he said no to every
question. Any problems he had, he could handle. Like the battalion motto said,
"Stands alone!"

Rumors in the ranks held that answering honestly would guarantee a trip
to the army shrink instead of block break. So Eastridge said he had not seen
any combat. He said he had not fired his weapon. He said he was not constantly on guard. When the technician came to one of the final questions, *"Are*
you currently interested in receiving help for a stress, emotional, alcohol or
family problem?," he said no.

Every grunt Eastridge knew did the same. So did thousands of soldiers in
the brigade. No one had truly educated them about combat stress injuries or
the physical breakdown between the thinking brain and the emotional brain.
There was no Sister Kateri to sit down with them. They did not know post-
traumatic stress disorder was a legitimate war wound. The soldier's creed said,
"I am disciplined, physically and mentally tough." The infantry grunts had
come to equate combat stress injuries with weakness. The army had trained

them to think they were capable of overcoming any hardship. Admitting to emotional problems from the war was the same as admitting they had no business in the Band of Brothers. And Eastridge and the other guys loved the Band of Brothers.

"We all thought PTSD was just a bunch of bullshit guys would use to get out of the army. None of us thought it was real," said Eastridge's friend Josh Butler. The young specialist had breathed for Sergeant Sean Huey in the minutes before he died. Huey had been his friend and his hero. Years later, the medic Ryan Krebbs shook his head and said he never should have asked Butler to breathe for the sergeant; it fucked him up for life. "He and the sergeant were too close, and the experience really messed Butler up. He wasn't ready for it. He couldn't handle it."

Butler started secretly taking OxyContin in Iraq to quiet the memories of the dying squad leader. At home he started doing cocaine. He, Eastridge, and Krebbs went out and got big tattoos on their arms in memory of Sean Huey. After coming home, Butler started shouting at his wife and hitting her. But when he sat down to fill out the PDHA, he swore he was fine.

Private Marcus Mifflin lied during the PDHA screening, too, even though he had started smoking pot to numb his nerves—a serious offense in the military. Kevin Shields and Louis Bressler both said they were fine, too. Ryan Krebbs said there was little choice. He was afraid of crowds. He would only drive in the middle lane on the highway out of an instinctive fear of IEDS. But, he said later, "If you say yes to any of the questions, you are automatically a shit bag because then you have doctor's appointments so you can't train. That just doesn't fly in the infantry."

The soldiers of the 2nd Brigade had seen some of the worst fighting in the war. The brigade claimed almost half of all Fort Carson's casualties, even though it made up only a fifth of the post's population. Hundreds of soldiers were haunted by the tour. Even the colonel in charge of the brigade, Gary Patton, later said he continuously relived nightmares of Ramadi, but few soldiers admitted they had problems.[4] They were all, in a way, like General Graham's son Kevin, who did not disclose his depression to the army because he did not want to hurt his career. Of the 3,800 soldiers who filled out the PDHA in the brigade, only 80 were recorded as high risk. The rest said nothing and went on block break.

Two weeks later, on August 3, 2005, a thirty-five-year-old private named Stephen Sherwood started arguing with his wife. Sherwood was part of the brigade's field artillery unit in Ramadi, but because the fight against shadowy insurgents in the city had little need for artillery, the battalion was given infantry-

style missions, such as guarding the highway. A rocket attack had killed everyone in his squad while he was on leave, leaving him the sole survivor. Longtime
friends said Sherwood came back from Iraq a changed man. After a few days,
he took down the American flag in front of his house and scraped the SUPPORT
OUR TROOPS sticker off his car. On the day of the argument, Sherwood's wife
had told him about an affair she had started while he was in Iraq. Hours later,
he shot her five times in the face and neck, then killed himself with a single
shotgun blast. In his pocket, police found a newspaper clipping stating that 30
percent of troops returning from Iraq developed mental-health problems.[5] Fort
Carson assured the media it carefully screens every soldier and Sherwood's
postdeployment health assessment did not indicate he was "high risk."[6]

———

Along with the emotional baggage they brought back from Iraq, Eastridge,
Bressler, and most of the other Joes returned with more than $25,000 in their
pockets. Like thousands of soldiers from the brigade, they had spent little of
their pay while in Korea and Iraq, but now they swarmed the city's malls and
drove hundreds of new cars out of local dealerships. They packed a string of
bars on Tejon Street every weekend. Before long, many of them had blown all
their money.

Eastridge burned through $27,000 in little more than six weeks, buying
booze, drugs, clothes, CDs, and other junk. He had set aside $5,000 because
his wife, who was still living in Korea, needed back surgery. But when he exhausted his other $22,000, he broke into the surgery fund and spent it all. She
never spoke to him again. Years later, he said it was one of the great regrets
of his life, but at the time he had no control. Some of the first things he bought
were guns: six pistols, a shotgun, and an AR–15—the civilian version of the
assault rifle he carried for twelve months in Iraq. He carried a pistol on him
all the time. "You've got to have a gun, because you think everybody that
looks at you on the street is out to get you," he said later. "It feels like everyone is the enemy. The people that were in Iraq with you are the only ones you
can trust."

His friend Butler had $17,000 in savings, but he also had a wife, a baby,
and a cocaine habit. Soon all of the money was gone. Like Eastridge, he bought
two pistols and carried one constantly, even when playing with his daughter in
their little apartment.

Mifflin spent most of his $20,000 on clothes and traveling, but he also
spent a lot on drugs. Like many, he found the parades and being referred to as
a hero infuriating. He needed to get high just to feel normal. "I felt deprived

of something. I couldn't feel that much anymore for anything. After the rush of combat there was nothing to come back to. There was no point, you are just kind of there."

David Nash, still too young to buy a beer, eventually spent a lot of his savings on cocaine to fill the cold, hollow ruts Iraq had left. The first few months after getting back he felt pretty good, but then he started feeling sad for no reason and he couldn't shake it. Many soldiers become so used to the high of naturally produced adrenaline in combat that they can go through something like withdrawal when they return home, leaving them numb and depressed. The feeling makes many especially susceptible to abusing chemically similar drugs such as cocaine, crystal meth, and heroin. "After feeling so down and low for so long," Nash said, "cocaine was the perfect upper." But even cocaine did not help the paranoia that followed him home, so he bought a .45 and slept with it under his pillow. "I felt I needed protection," he said. "You don't want to survive Iraq only to get jumped at home."

Some soldiers appeared to be fine. Bressler went to the bars occasionally, but he spent much of his free time hunting and fishing in the Rockies. He met a nursing student named Tira Brown at a Tejon Street bar; they got married and went on a honeymoon to Aruba. It seemed to his family that, if anything, Iraq had made him more squared away than ever.

Shields, too, seemed proud to have served his country and happy to have his new family around him. He applied to join the Band of Brothers' elite scout platoon and reveled in the fact he was stationed in Colorado, where he could snowboard almost every weekend.

Other soldiers seemed helplessly lost and out of control. One night, Ryan Krebbs blew $5,000 at a great new bar the soldiers had discovered on Tejon Street called Rum Bay. It became the soldiers' new Ville. Huge crowds from the brigade hit Rum Bay every weekend, burning through their quickly dwindling cash. "The whole idea was to go out, get as drunk as possible, and get in a fight," Krebbs said later. "We were pissed off and angry and doing coke and drinking. There was just a period when I was totally depressed and I didn't even know why. I couldn't think for five minutes without picturing someone who got killed over there, and it was like that every fucking day. The idea was to drink and forget."

The thousands of quiet struggles of individual soldiers grew to a roar in the city. The cops had to break up melees at Rum Bay and a club called the Vue, directly across Tejon Street, 580 times in 2006.[7] They started parking patrol cars in the middle of the street in anticipation of violence, riot gear stowed in the trunks. Arrests of military personnel in the city shot up 65 percent between

2005 and 2006. Arrests for assault in the city doubled. Alcoholism in the returning soldiers reached astonishing levels, even by army standards. By March
2006, the rate of DUI arrests at Fort Carson was triple that of two much larger
posts, Fort Lewis in Washington and Fort Bragg in North Carolina.[8] Fort
Carson officials blamed the spike in drunk driving on one factor: the Band of
Brothers' brigade. The base commander put up signs shaped like thermometers
by the front gate to show the alarming rise in DUIs. Soldiers darkly joked that
the rising levels of drunk-driving arrests were a point of pride.

The low-level commanders of the Band of Brothers were getting called to
pick up soldiers in jail all the time. "Good soldiers who were never a problem in
Iraq started getting into trouble, getting into meth and cocaine. It was new for
us, we did not know how to deal with it," said Lieutenant Erwin Godoy, who
left the army shortly thereafter. "These guys never got a chance to really decompress. The combination of the drugs and drinking and the pressure of being
back home and the PTSD—it all played a factor in these guys going crazy."

Drug and alcohol abuse in the brigade increased 1,400 percent.[9] At the
same time, young officers like Godoy did not have the training or resources to
effectively address the widespread problems in their troops. Charlie Company's
commanders started calling mandatory formations every night at 10:00 P.M. at
which soldiers who lived in the barracks would line up so officers could see that
they were sober. Lieutenants and senior sergeants patrolled the barracks to try
to keep the soldiers clean and under control. The battalion commander ordered increased drug screening, and dozens of soldiers were caught with illegal substances in their urine. "We had to rein them in, and in many cases that
just made them worse," Godoy said. "You want to show compassion, but with
the drugs and crime, there have to be consequences."

Among Eastridge's friends, everyone seemed to be falling apart. Josh
Butler was downing more and more drugs and booze, but was still haunted by
visions of Iraq. One night he decided he could not handle going back for the
next deployment. He called up Eastridge and Barco and asked them to come
over and shoot him in the leg. Then he could be medically discharged out of
the Army. Both Eastridge and Barco were excited to get to shoot him. They
picked him up at his house and drove to a dark parking lot, psyching themselves up by yelling, "We're going to do this!"[10]

In the lot, Butler chickened out. He said he couldn't go through with it, but
Barco got angry and started yelling. "You called me to come over here in the
fucking middle of the night saying I get to shoot you and now you're going to
bitch out?" he yelled. "Fuck it! I'm shooting your ass whether you like it or
not." He shot a round right through his friend's calf. Butler screamed. Blood

splashed everywhere. Bulter later told authorities that the gun had accidentally gone off while he was handling it.[11]

"It was hilarious," said Mifflin, who saw him shortly afterward. "He only ended up getting out of duty for a few days, but that's only part of why he did it. He also wanted the Percocets they prescribed him at the hospital."

Any drug use in the army, even occasional marijuana, is grounds for dismissal. By the spring of 2006, there were so many soldiers getting kicked out of Charlie Company for drugs and other disciplinary infractions that the company commander created a new platoon, called 5th platoon, just for them. Soldiers called it "the shit bag brigade." Soon it was the biggest platoon in the company. Butler, Nash, and dozens of others were caught with cocaine and put in the platoon until they were officially kicked out of the army. Soldiers in the platoon would have to do menial tasks, such as picking up trash, painting rocks, or pulling weeds.

After he was kicked out in the spring of 2006, Butler moved to Texas, where his symptoms grew worse. There was no one to help him understand and deal with his combat stress injuries. He was eventually arrested for beating his wife. After he got out of jail, he moved into a small RV along a busy highway. In Iraq, Butler had been decorated for capturing the fifth-most-wanted person in the country—Saddam's half brother—but when he got home he felt like he could do nothing right. "It was like somebody flipped a light switch, turned me into this super-asshole," he said.[12]

In December 2005, four months after returning from Iraq, all the soldiers in the battalion were given the PDHA survey again. This time David "Nasty" Nash was truthful. He said he was having nightmares and flashbacks. He was depressed. It was affecting his work. He said he thought about taking his own life. The medical technician giving the assessment noted he was a danger to himself and others. She referred him to Evans Army Community Hospital, where he was prescribed two antidepressants.[13] But, he said later, the medication "made me feel like a drone and I stopped taking it." He went back to cocaine. No one—not a doctor, not a sergeant, not an officer—ever followed up on his treatment. Nash was caught doing drugs a second time. With his PTSD diagnosis, he should have been medically retired with benefits, but instead he was "other-than-honorably" discharged. That meant he was ineligible for benefits or treatment by the Veterans Administration unless he applied for reconsideration.

Soldiers like Nash ultimately bear responsibility for what happened, but so should the army's failed mental health and substance abuse programs and the commanders who let them slip through the cracks. Instead of taking responsibility, the army tossed Nash and many like him aside like damaged goods. Because of the way they were dismissed, they were not eligible for benefits that could help them heal. Nash was lucky enough to get a union job fixing gas pipelines, but he is still far from normal. He cannot go to bars without getting into fights. He keeps to himself most of the time, and in his car, Nash said, he still carries "enough guns for World War III."

"That's the shady thing," Nash said years later. "The army neglected their responsibility to take care of soldiers they trained to be this way. Most of them were ordinary people put in shitty situations. The side effect is you turn ordinary people into ravenous beasts."

Spikes in crime and antisocial behavior among veterans are nothing new. There is a popular perception that, with the exception of the Vietnam War, which is still etched in living memory, returning war veterans have always taken off their uniforms and easily slipped back into the contented norms of civilian life. In fact, soldiers who have operated for months or years outside the normal restraints of society—killing, beating, and contending with levels of horror, honor, terror, bravery, and regret rarely glimpsed in civilian life—have often chafed on returning to society and many have reacted with violence.

In his book *Shook Over Hell: Post-Traumatic Stress, Vietnam, and the Civil War,* historian Eric T. Dean, Jr. notes that the years immediately after the Civil War were marked by shocking levels of turmoil. Two-thirds of all men sentenced to prison in the North were war vets, and in some states the number of men in prison increased 400 percent. Murder and armed robbery soared. Newspapers in the South reported a "frightening increase in crime." One article noted that "Murder stalks abroad and crime of every character and grade is rife everywhere." The *New York Times* surmised in 1866 that the sharp increase in crime in New York City was caused by "rough material turned loose upon society by the close of the war."[14] In many ways, the Band of Brothers were not acting out. They were just acting in ways soldiers returning from war always have.

By poring through yellowed documents from one insane asylum in Indiana, Dean found hundreds of former Union soldiers who had been committed. Of them, five percent were drug addicts. Twenty percent were drunks. Many kept loaded weapons with them at all times. Over forty percent had turned violent.[15]

After the Civil War, many disillusioned veterans went west. Several of the men who became the West's most notorious outlaws, including Jesse James and the Farrington Brothers, got their first taste of blood in the Civil War. It is entirely possible that the legendary gunfights of the Wild West, which peaked in the 1870s, were in part a result of the war between the states.

A major difference between the Iraq War and past wars was that with the Iraq War, the homecoming celebrations and struggles with disillusionment did not come at the end of the war. They came in the middle. Then the soldiers were asked to go back again and again. They could not focus on fitting back into society. They could not focus on healing combat stress wounds. They had to focus on preparing again for war.

In November 2005, the Band of Brothers was ordered to gather on a sunny parade ground at Fort Carson. They lined up platoon by platoon until all five companies of the battalion stood at attention in neat rows. The outgoing commander, Colonel Dave Clark, stood at the head of the battalion next to the flags representing the Band of Brothers and their 506th Infantry Regiment. Then another group of soldiers marched solemnly in with a new set of flags bearing the name 2nd Battalion, 12th Infantry Regiment. The army was "reflagging" the infantry battalion. For reasons none of the soldiers really understood, and that ultimately had to do with a an army-wide restructuring that had nothing to do with them, the designation of 1st Battalion, 506th Infantry Regiment was being moved to another unit at Fort Campbell, Kentucky, and the soldiers who had carried the flag of the regiment through Korea and Iraq were being renamed. Most of them were deeply disappointed. They had never heard of the 2–12. Their identity, their traditions, their pride, even their grail forged from Hitler's pilfered silverware, were being taken away. As the color guard bearing the new flags marched toward the front of the battalion, a few soldiers started to quietly boo. Then more troops started to boo.[16]

The grunts had just learned they would go back to Iraq in eleven months. At first the army had told the Band of Brothers they would get two years to refit at Fort Carson. Then eighteen months. Army guidelines recommend that units take at least two years to recover and retrain. But with the situation in Iraq continuing to deteriorate, time for recovery was a luxury the army could not afford.

To compound problems, almost all of the battalion's officers were leaving the unit for new assignments. It was an army-wide pattern. After the deployment, a round of promotions and reassignments scattered the unit. The soldiers soon learned that the new captains, majors, and lieutenant colonels were focused on the mission ahead and had little interest in or tolerance for dealing with the problems of the past. The new captain of Charlie Company even changed the name to "Chosen Company" to make a break with what he called its "troubled past."[17] When Colonel Jeffrey Bannister took command of the 3,900-soldier brigade that included the Band of Brothers, he said the priority was to prepare to go back to war. "My No. 1 charter," he told the *Colorado Springs Gazette*, "is to reset this brigade."[18]

By that time, morale was as scarred and pitted as Route Michigan. The color guard marched through the quietly booing ranks and reached the front of the battalion. The flags of the Band of Brothers were rolled up and cased. Then the new flags of the 2nd Battalion, 12th Infantry Regiment were uncased, and they waved in the November breeze. The men would no longer use the nickname the Band of Brothers. From now on, their commander said, they would call themselves "the Warriors."

———

Post-traumatic stress disorder is a lot like an IED on Route Michigan. It is hard to spot until it hits. The symptoms can lie in wait, covered by the jubilant glitter of homecoming for months, then explode. Like an IED blast, PTSD can cripple some soldiers and leave others in the platoon untouched. And just like an IED, PTSD can look like something else. In many cases, it looks like a bad soldier. In addition to flashbacks and nightmares often associated with combat stress, army studies say, symptoms can include heavy drinking, drug use, emotional numbness, aggression, slacking off at work, and disobeying orders.

As a wave of combat stress injuries hit Fort Carson, the system in place to care for them failed at almost every level. The first failure was in the barracks, where sergeants had little training to deal with combat stress injuries. Many had not been told how to spot the warning signs or to address them. Some reasoned that if they could deal with what they saw in the Sunni Triangle, others should be able to as well. When young soldiers started abusing drugs, not showing up for formation, or ending up in jail, they were usually punished instead of helped. If they tried to say they were screwed up in the head, and needed mental health counseling, superiors often accused them of faking it. "People are trying to say they have problems who don't," a sergeant from the unit named Travis Platt told National Public Radio in 2006. "Just because people are, you know, getting in trouble and they're just blaming it on PTSD." [19]

Most of the grunts agreed with their sergeants. They also had next to no training concerning combat stress injuries. Most tended to believe a vast majority of PTSD cases were fake and the few legitimate cases were soldiers who could not hack it. To them, having PTSD meant one of two things: you were either a pussy or a liar. So the soldiers who were experiencing nightmares and paranoia generally kept it to themselves.

Marcus Mifflin was one of the few in Eastridge's platoon who tried to get help. He could not sleep most nights, and when he closed his eyes he often had nightmares about Iraq. He was paranoid and would lash out, hitting his fiancée. He had flashbacks to Route Michigan, as if he were dreaming, even though he was awake. He would often hear someone yelling his name in the distance and turn around and find no one there. His platoon sergeant tried to discourage him and others from going to seek treatment at Fort Carson's hospital. Mifflin had also seen other soldiers come back from the counseling center only to be called cowards behind their backs and assigned to menial details such as cleaning trash cans. But he went anyway.

At the hospital, a counselor asked standard questions about whether Mifflin was planning to hurt himself and others. He said he wasn't suicidal, but he did want to kill other people. "No one in particular, just anyone, everyone, guys who acted tough and looked at me wrong and women in fancy-ass cars smiling as they drove down the road," he recalled saying. He felt like a slave to his own rage. The army psychiatrist immediately checked him into Cedar Springs, a civilian mental hospital in Colorado Springs, for a week. When he got out, he was ordered to go before his first sergeant.

"He bitched me out, telling me what a liar I was. He said I was just trying to fake my way out of the army," Mifflin said. Many soldiers, seeing how Mifflin and others were treated, chose to keep quiet.

The second failure in the system occurred at Evans Army Community Hospital. The hospital serving Fort Carson was a sleek, relatively new facility with an airy glass atrium leading to a comfortable, inviting waiting room. For years it had acted as the peacetime community medical center for the post, handling everything from broken bones to births. Since serious trauma cases from Iraq and Afghanistan went to larger medical centers, Evans at first changed little during the war. It continued to act as a small-town hospital serving a base with 18,000 active-duty soldiers. It was totally unprepared when a wave of casualties started arriving with deep, invisible wounds to their psyches.

"It was a total shit storm," said a licensed social worker who worked at the hospital at the time. The fourth floor, which housed all behavioral health and substance abuse counseling, was flooded with new cases. Often when he did morning triage, it took three hours just to sort through the crowd of soldiers in the waiting room. Most of them had been sent by commanders because the once squared-away soldiers were now in trouble. In his brief meeting with each soldier, he would try to assess who was an immediate risk. Did they have a plan to kill themselves? Were they planning to kill someone else? If so, they were sent directly to Cedar Springs. If not, they were told to make an appointment for treatment at Evans. A backlog of cases meant getting an appointment took three or four weeks. After waiting a month, soldiers would often only see a psychiatrist for a few minutes. Frequently the doctor would prescribe a few antidepressants and sleeping pills and send them on their way. One-on-one counseling was extremely rare. Soldiers were encouraged to go to group therapy sessions, but many felt like they were ineffective. "It was just a bunch of guys dealing with the same shit I was dealing with, and that never gave me any kind of hope," one soldier in the brigade said. "I knew those other guys had watched their friends die just like I had. They had seen all the terrible things I had. There was no answer, we were all lost, just sitting there rehashing the events over and over. That never helped me."

The problem was not unique to Fort Carson. The entire army was short of trained psychiatric staff at the time. A quarter of behavioral health jobs in the army sat vacant in 2006.[20] At Fort Carson, the rate was one third. In Fort Carson's substance abuse counseling office, half the positions were empty.[21] Cases of drug and alcohol abuse literally piled up. Many were tossed aside. In the Band of Brothers' brigade, only one in five soldiers who tested positive for drugs was given a required screening a month after getting caught. Many never received follow-up treatment. Instead, soldiers at Fort Carson were often kicked out of the army using a loophole. It was called being "chaptered out."

The army requires soldiers who were going to be kicked out for disciplinary infractions to first get a medical screening for wounds, including PTSD. Many in the Band of Brothers' brigade could easily meet the checklist requirements for the disorder, but diagnosing a soldier with PTSD posed a problem for Fort Carson and the army as a whole. Soldiers who had diminished ability to perform their duties because of PTSD or other psychological war wounds were required to be medically retired from the army. But by 2005 the medical retirement process was as swamped as the waiting room at Evans Army Hospital. It often took six months to a year or longer to medically retire a soldier. Commanders could not fill spots in their units with fresh soldiers until their combat stress casualties passed through the slow bureaucratic process. In order to prepare to deploy again, commanders needed to get damaged troops out and fresh troops in as soon as possible. So someone came up with the idea to just chapter soldiers out.

"Chaptering" was the fast way to get rid of undesirable soldiers. The term "chaptered out" draws its name from the chapters of Army Regulation 635–200, which spell out how soldiers can be separated from the army for any number of reasons (misconduct, drug addiction, homosexuality, poor physical fitness, etc.). Soldiers whom the command wanted to get rid of for using drugs, disobeying orders, showing up late for formation, or doing any number of things that army studies showed were symptoms of PTSD could be chaptered out under chapter 5–13, which allowed soldiers to be kicked out if they had a preexisting personality disorder.

"It was called Anxiety Disorder NOS. That means Not Otherwise Specified. We used it all the time," said the Evans social worker. The psychiatry staff was warned not to give soldiers PTSD diagnoses and encouraged staff to instead probe their pasts for any hints of other mental health problems, then diagnose them with an anxiety disorder or personality disorder.[22] "Then we could blame a soldier's problems on a preexisting condition. It was not the army's problem," he said. "Then we could chapter them out. Treating a soldier and medically retiring them took months. Chaptering took a few days."

The questionable practice was not unique to Fort Carson, but the base used it at an exceedingly high rate. The explosion in chaptering at Fort Carson was driven in part by commanders, who pressured the hospital to not diagnose troops with PTSD so they could clear them out of their units, and in part by the head of psychiatry, Colonel Stephen Knorr, who readily cooperated with them. In one memo, he warned commanders that the hospital could not be treated as a reform school that could help soldiers who "break barracks restriction and go get drunk, or get in fights, or engage in similar misconduct." He encouraged commanders to kick soldiers out of the army before they become bigger problems, concluding, "get rid of dead wood."[23]

According to the social worker, under Knorr's leadership Fort Carson led the army in diagnosing personality disorders. One month, the staff chaptered out 170 soldiers. Knorr would pressure his staff to chapter out soldiers that unit commanders wanted gone. "I argued with him once about a soldier who had been a sniper and had seen a lot of things," he said. "I said, 'I just don't think this is right.' He said the unit wanted him out, so get him out. And I did."

Between 2005 and 2007, the army chaptered out about one thousand soldiers a year with personality disorders. Chaptering soldiers out does not just rob them of a proper diagnosis and the potential benefits of medical retirement, it often bars soldiers from getting treatment at VA hospitals, meaning the soldiers who need help the most often don't get it.

———

Troops who made it past the stigma and resistance in the battalion and the loopholes in the hospital stumbled into additional failures when they got treatment. Because the fourth floor of Evans was so overwhelmed, many soldiers said doctors' first course of action usually involved mixes of prescription drugs. Doctors routinely prescribed soldiers antidepressants such as Paxil or Lexapro, paired with sleep aids such as Ambien. For more serious cases, doctors started using strong psychotropic drugs in ways not officially approved by the Food and Drug Administration. They gave soldiers the antiseizure drug Neurontin and the bipolar drug Seroquel to calm PTSD, and Prazosin, a potent blood-pressure drug, to silence nightmares. But the medicines often made the young soldiers groggy, despondent, and unable to do their jobs, which sometimes led to disciplinary actions and chaptering out.

One day, six months after returning from Iraq, Kenneth Eastridge went to Evans Army Hospital to get a checkup on the brain injury caused by the anti-tank mine in Khalidiya. A doctor sat him down in her office and started talking to him about how he was doing. For no reason, Eastridge found himself silently weeping. She asked what was wrong.

"I don't know," he said. "Every day I wake up is the worst day of my entire life. Every day."

The soldier clearly needed help. The doctor sent him to the fourth floor where he told a counselor he was depressed, almost suicidal. The counselor said he wanted to send Eastridge to Cedar Springs. Eastridge, remembering how Mifflin had been treated when he got back from the civilian psychiatric hospital, quickly talked the doctor out of it. Instead he was put on the antidepressant Lexapro and sent to group therapy.

He hated the pills. They made him yawn all the time. And he saw no point in the group therapy, so he abandoned both and went back to treating his depression and PTSD with alcohol. No one from his battalion or the hospital ever followed up with him. On March 11, 2006, he got drunk at a bar near his apartment and got in a fight with his girlfriend, whom he had met a few months after returning from Iraq. Back at his apartment, he pulled out the pistol he always kept in his waistband and pointed it at her face. A friend standing in the doorway called the police, and Eastridge was taken away in handcuffs and charged with a felony.

Eastridge had received medals for good conduct and commendation for his first Iraq tour. He was about to be promoted to sergeant and had applied to the army's elite Ranger School. He saw the army as his life career, but after his arrest, his commanders stopped all his promotions. They did not have time to deal with problem soldiers like him. They put him in the shit bag brigade and told him he was going to be chaptered out.

CHAPTER 6

"A WALKING TIME BOMB"

In September 2005, an ex-army Special Forces interrogator named Georg-Andreas "Andrew" Pogany walked into the office of the mayor of Colorado Springs to warn him about the growing storm of mental health problems at Fort Carson.

Pogany, a thirty-four-year-old former staff sergeant with close-cropped brown hair, had been out of the army for two years but was still thick-armed and muscular. He spoke with an almost imperceivable accent that remained from a childhood in Germany. In the years since being medically retired from Fort Carson, he had become a local expert on the inner workings and nonworkings of Carson's behavioral health system, and he had begun acting as a sort of underground combat stress injury Harriet Tubman—a guide to bring suffering soldiers through the vexing system, past chaptering to medical retirement.

After sitting down in the mayor's office, Pogany laid out the situation he saw brewing. The number of soldiers with PTSD and other mental problems at Fort Carson was growing, he said, and the post hospital was overwhelmed. At the same time, many soldiers struggling with PTSD were not seeking help because they did not want their commanders to find out and did not trust the post hospital to keep their treatment confidential. These issues together, he warned, had the potential to create a psychiatric perfect storm, leaving a path of drug use, assaults, domestic violence, rape, and maybe even murder that would spill out of Fort Carson and into the city. Pogany handed the mayor a packet of research, much of it produced by the Department of Veterans Affairs, that lent weight to his predictions. He was basically saying, "This is the big one, and it is headed your way."

At first, the mayor, a forty-eight-year-old native of El Paso, Texas, named Lionel Rivera, was receptive. Rivera had come to Colorado Springs in the early 1980s as a young army captain at Fort Carson, and since being elected mayor in 2003 he had championed the city's passionate support of the troops. He asked Pogany what he, as mayor, could do to help. Pogany explained that for months he had worked to put together a network of civilian therapists willing to donate their services to local soldiers. He called it Operation Just One. He asked the mayor to officially endorse Operation Just One and declare a local "Combat Operational Stress/PTSD Awareness Day" to bring attention to the problem. Rivera said he would be happy to help. A few days later, his office issued a press release saying the mayor would sign a proclamation announcing PTSD Awareness Day.

A day later, the mayor changed his mind. He canceled the proclamation and tried to wash his hands of any association with Andrew Pogany. The mayor said he took issue with some of Pogany's claims that ongoing wars would contribute to mental health problems and lead to a rise in crime and sexual assault. "This is personal for me, being the child of a three-war veteran," Rivera told the *Denver Post* a few days later. "My father was a fine father. I don't recall this description fitting my family."[1] It was a moment that showed, perhaps better than any other, that it was not just the army that was unwilling to accept the psychological casualties of the war, it was society as a whole.

Pogany offered to amend the wording but the mayor still refused. Pogany began to suspect that the problem was not the proclamation but who had written it. Pogany was one of the least popular people at Fort Carson. He had been assigned to Fort Carson's 10th Special Forces Group at the beginning of the Iraq War in 2003. With five years in the service and a criminology degree, he served as an interrogator and counterintelligence specialist. His job was to accompany the Green Berets on raids in and around the city of Samarra and question their captives. On his second night in Iraq, in September 2003, Pogany stepped out of his barracks and saw passing soldiers dragging the dead body of an Iraqi killed in a firefight. The limp man had been ripped in half by a machine gun. The two halves of his torso were connected only by a spine. Pogany turned away in disgust and retreated to his room. He started to feel sick and began trembling. An all-encompassing, uncontrollable terror enveloped him. His head and heart pounded. He felt dizzy. He tried to sleep but was plagued by nightmares. At one point he woke to the room exploding. A mortar had hit and the ceiling was coming down. He jumped up to escape and realized it was all a hallucination. Something was seriously wrong.

The next day he told his superiors that he was having a mental breakdown. He was sent to an army psychologist who wrote, "Soldier reported signs of symptoms consistent with those of a normal combat-stress reaction."[2] After a few days of rest, Pogany was sent back out with the Green Berets, but he told his unit he was still too addled to function in his job and needed more time. The unit's commanders, apparently convinced that he was faking his illness, sent him back to Colorado Springs. A week after he arrived, the army charged him with cowardice—a charge that had not been leveled against a soldier since 1968. Pogany was infuriated that the army was targeting him when he felt he had done nothing wrong. He immediately hired civilian lawyers and took his case to the media. The story made headlines across the country. In November, the army reduced the charge against Pogany to dereliction of duty. Still, Pogany fought the accusation. "What am I derelict of?" he told the *New York Times.* "I got sick. I asked for help. But I never said I wouldn't do my job. I requested to stay and work through my problem. I always planned to return to duty."[3]

Pogany had been a volunteer firefighter before joining the army and had seen mangled bodies pulled from car wrecks. He had never shied away from scenes like that before. He could not understand what had induced the crippling dread he experienced in Iraq until six months later, when an air force doctor told him the panic attack may have been caused by an antimalarial drug called mefloquine. His Special Forces unit required all soldiers to take the drug weekly. It has several side effects, which, according to the manufacturer, can include anxiety, confusion, depression, hallucinations, mood changes, paranoia, and suicidal thoughts or attempts. Travelers to third world countries often call the drug, which also tends to cause disturbing dreams, "the nightmare pill."

Pogany had taken the pill regularly in the weeks leading up to his panic attack. He took his findings to the press and the army dropped all charges against him in July 2004. Instead of being punished, he was eventually medically retired.

But the army was not happy with Pogany. Many felt he was a bad soldier who had avoided the punishment he deserved by playing the overly sympathetic liberal media. He says the commander of Fort Carson even wrote him a letter of reprimand saying he was a disgrace. But by trying to punish Georg-Andreas Pogany, the army unwittingly created an insurgent in its midst—a trained intelligence agent whose main target was now the arcane workings of the army medical system. As he went through the long, slow medical-boarding process on his way to retirement, he started learning all he could about the proper procedures for treating soldiers with combat stress injuries. He learned about the benefit structures and what regulations allowed commanders to do and not do. Then he started sharing what he had learned.

"It was all word of mouth," he said, looking back years later. "I was going through the process of getting medically retired, which meant being at the hospital all day long, having to go to appointments. I saw other guys there going through the same thing, or I would overhear them in the waiting room, and I started answering their questions. I would say, 'What your sergeant is telling you is not true. Here is the regulation.' I would give them my phone number. Guys quickly realized I was the only one who had some of these answers. I would get calls from other soldiers. The word spread that there was a guy named Pogany who knew his shit."

Pogany was finally medically retired from the army in April 2005 and left Fort Carson, but the phone calls from soldiers and their families kept coming. They told him stories of overmedication, harassment, and lack of treatment. They told him about the long waits at the hospital and the stigma that kept soldiers away. They told him about getting chaptered out. He continued to help soldiers free of charge, working on nights and weekends. To some in the Fort Carson command, he seemed like the worst kind of soldier—a coward who had cheated the system with the help of the civilian press and lawyers, and who was now teaching other shit bags to do the same. But Pogany thought he was finally living up to the Special Forces motto: "De oppresso liber"—"to free the oppressed." Pogany got a job in the summer of 2005 with the National Gulf War Resource Center in Washington, D.C., and started getting paid for the advocacy work he had been doing for free. Early that fall he went to the mayor of Colorado Springs with his plan to help soldiers connect with local therapists.

After the mayor said yes and then no, Pogany and a small crowd of local peace activists packed the city council meeting on October 11, 2005, to voice their disappointment. After sitting silently through several comments, the mayor accused them of being "antiwar" and "antiarmy," saying, "I'm not in the business of criticizing the Army for the programs that they have set up, and I can tell by what I have read in the press from some members who support this operation that there seems to be a second agenda, and that's to criticize the Army, their programs, and the way they handle soldiers coming back from combat."[4]

No one can be sure why the mayor initially agreed to help Pogany then pulled his support. Maybe he really did not believe that war would bring the plague of crime and drug abuse the ex-sergeant predicted. Maybe it was political. At the time, the mayor was preparing a run for Congress in Colorado's overwhelmingly Republican Fifth Congressional District, and making a public statement about the corrosive psychological effects of war would have almost surely been used as a weapon against him in the campaign.[5] Or maybe, as Pogany believes, influential brass at Fort Carson, the city's largest employer, got to the mayor, told him the ex-sergeant was "a disgruntled shit bag out to give the army a black eye," and warned the mayor keep his distance.[6]

If the mayor had listened to Pogany, the civilian population that surrounds and overwhelmingly supports Fort Carson could have shouldered some of the burden of Evans Army Hospital. But ignorance of combat stress injuries was as widespread in the civilian population as it was in the army. Instead of helping, the city stood by and let the problem grow worse. In the next twelve months, arrests of military personnel in Colorado Springs increased 65 percent. After being steady for years, rapes at Fort Carson doubled in 2007, then tripled in 2008.[7] And slowly, without anyone noticing the pattern, the murders continued.

That September 2005, just a week before Pogany warned Mayor Rivera about the coming violence, Anthony Marquez arrived at Fort Carson, limping with the help of a cane. The twenty-one-year-old specialist once had the springy, muscular frame of a high school fullback, but after being shot four times while on patrol with the Bad Boys of the 1st Battalion, 9th Infantry Regiment on the edge of Ramadi, he was crippled and gaunt.

The night he was shot, three and a half months before, Marquez was given a strong sedative by an army doctor. He woke up four days later in an airplane literally stacked with other casualties on his way to Walter Reed Army Medical Center in Washington, D.C. At Walter Reed, Marquez went through seventeen surgeries to save his now scarred and withered left leg. He was still bleary on morphine when someone from the hospital told him that President George W. Bush planned to visit the ward over the Fourth of July weekend and wanted to personally award Marquez a Purple Heart. The hospital encouraged him to invite his family so they could meet the president too. Marquez's mom was excited, but his older sister refused to see the president because she was so angry about the war and her brother's wounds. Marquez was indifferent. "I had gotten hurt, but it is part of the job," he said. "I wasn't mad at nobody."

The president, wearing a black suit, glossy bronze tie, and ever-present flag pin, visited forty wounded soldiers that day.[8] When he came to Marquez's bed, he told the soldier that he appreciated his service and his sacrifice, and that his friends in the platoon had not died in vain. He was not aware that Marquez and his friends had been hit by friendly fire.[9]

In the next two and a half months, Marquez pushed himself through grueling physical therapy at Walter Reed. The care was good, but Marquez could not stand the hospital. Being surrounded by other soldiers who were paralyzed or missing arms and legs, or even faces, depressed him. They were a constant reminder of his own trauma, and he often had flashbacks. He once woke up in a rage, tearing away the tubes going into his body until nurses came to hold him down. He wanted to leave as soon as possible. More than anything, he craved the comfort and security of the Bad Boys. In September 2005, even though his leg was still withered and weak and he walked unsteadily with a cane, he convinced the army he was well enough to go back to his unit. He was transferred to Fort Carson. Twelve months later, he was arrested for murder.

———

Marquez worked hard to learn to walk without a cane. He was determined to prove he was healthy enough to deploy again. He yearned to be back in Iraq with his friends. He wanted a chance to come back as a hero, not a casualty, but after a few months the army told him it was no use. He was going to be medically retired.

His invisible wounds proved just as hard to heal. He kept having nightmares about the war. He felt worthless, crippled, and depressed. He could not imagine what he was going to do with the rest of his life. After Iraq, nothing really mattered. On a visit home to California at Christmas, he asked his mom to put away all his high school sports trophies and photos of dead army friends. He did not want to see any reminders of his past life.

For his injuries, he said, doctors at Evans prescribed him a bevy of narcotics: 90 morphine pills, 90 Percocets, and 5 fentanyl patches every three weeks. "They were for pain," he said. "And I still had pain. But, mostly, I was using them to get high."

As the months went on, Marquez watched his once tight-knit platoon dissolve. Several of his close friends from the Bad Boys were kicked out for drugs or other problems while others moved on to new assignments. One of his best friends from the platoon was arrested in Colorado Springs for attempted murder after shooting a man during a bar fight. The few who were left were in the process of being medically retired for physical wounds or PTSD.

As fellow soldiers dropped out of the Bad Boys one by one, Marquez started to lose his direction. During a visit home in January 2006, his mother saw that he was deeply troubled. He would have thrashing nightmares, then get violently angry when she woke him up. He would sit in his room for days doing nothing but eating pain pills the army had given him. Then he attempted to take old Vicodin in his mother's medicine cabinet. When his mother tried to get him out of the house by taking him to a local convenience store, he became tense and angry when he saw three Arab men. It was just not like her son.[10]

His mother called his company in February 2006 and asked for his commander. She had been following the healing of his leg so closely that she had never thought to watch out for PTSD. A sergeant answered and she told him her son needed help. He was abusing his medication and drinking heavily. She said he had nightmares and anger issues. "That's a bad combination," she said. "He's a walking time bomb."

The sergeant told her there was nothing he could do. There were no army rules that instructed sergeants to intervene in soldiers' personal lives.

That didn't make sense to Marquez's mom. She was a cop in Los Angeles, and as a cop, if she ever so much as shot at someone she was required to go to counseling. Her twenty-one-year-old son had been through God knows what in Iraq and killed who knows how many people, but he had no similar requirement.

A few days later Marquez called his mom, annoyed that she had talked to his sergeant. Now the platoon was taunting him, saying, "Your mommy called. She says you're going crazy."[11]

So many soldiers in the 1st Battalion, 9th Infantry Regiment, were in the process of being medically retired, chaptered out, or otherwise separated from the army that the battalion created a whole new company for them in the spring of 2006. Officially it was known as Echo Company, but, just as in Eastridge's battalion, all the soldiers called it "the shit bag brigade." Marquez was assigned to the unit even though his only offense was being too injured to train with his platoon. Occasionally the troops of Echo Company were required to do menial jobs, but much of the time the soldiers were required to just sit together in a room. Many of them were injured or suffering from PTSD; others were getting kicked out for drug abuse or disciplinary problems. And they all started feeding on each other.

"It was the biggest mistake you could make," said a sergeant who was assigned to Echo Company because he had been diagnosed with PTSD. "We had nothing to do. Most of the guys in there were heavily medicated or should have been. They were bored out of their skulls. They are going to start doing other guys' drugs. It became a fucking candy store."

Soldiers like Marquez who had morphine and Percocet for injuries started trading for antipsychotic drugs like quetiapine and clonazepam. Improper use of either can cause psychotic reactions, anxiety, panic attacks, aggressiveness, and suicidal behavior, but injured soldiers traded them like children in a lunch-room swapping desserts. Marquez said later, "It was real common among guys who were getting hurt."

As Marquez sank deeper into despair and paranoia, he bought a small ar-senal of guns, including three pistols, a riot-style shotgun, and an assault rifle like the one he carried in Iraq. He stored them all in his car even though army rules required he keep them at the Fort Carson armory. Though he said his ser-geants knew about the guns, they did nothing to intervene. He carried a pistol constantly, even when he went to church. He also dug out a battered 500,000-volt stun gun he brought home from Iraq and tucked it next to his driver's seat. He drifted away from his friends in the army, who said he was starting to "turn gangster."[12]

Marquez was planning to move back to his mother's house in California when he got out of the army. On October 22, 2006, three days before Mar-quez was scheduled to be honorably discharged for his wounded leg, his mother sent him gas money for the drive home. At 4:30 that afternoon, Mar-quez took the money and drove to a working-class suburb of Colorado Springs called Widefield. In the maze of cul-de-sacs and aging split-level ranch houses lived a small-time, nineteen-year-old pot dealer named Johnathan Smith. Marquez had never met Smith, but his girlfriend's cousin was a regu-lar customer, and the cousin and a friend took Marquez to the dealer's house to buy an ounce of weed. On the drive over, Marquez smiled and said instead of buying the weed, they should just take it. The cousin laughed. He didn't think Marquez was serious.[13]

At the house, one of the dealer's friends said only one person was allowed in and the cousin and his friend would have to wait in the car. Marquez fol-lowed the kid through the door and limped down into a messy basement, where, in a bedroom at the end of the hall, Smith and a seventeen-year-old friend were sitting on a futon playing video games. Marquez came in, closed the door, and said he wanted to buy an ounce of weed. Smith put down his game controller and pulled out a scale and an open lockbox. He said it would cost $375. Marquez said that sounded like a lot, and that he wanted a lower price. They haggled back and forth until the bargaining became heated.[14]

Marquez said he did not want to get ripped off. Smith stood up and told him to leave. Marquez pulled his ever-present pistol from his waistband and pointed it at the dealer, saying, "Give me the weed!"

Smith said no.

Marquez had encountered this kind of stubbornness many times in Iraq. He whipped out the stun gun he had used in Ramadi and sent a two-inch bolt of electricity dancing between the metal probes. He jabbed it at Smith, who winced in pain. Still holding a gun to the dealer's face, Marquez said, "Give me the weed and your money!"

The dealer again said no.

Marquez shocked him again.

At that moment, the dealer's brother's nineteen-year-old girlfriend, oblivious to what was going on in the room, walked down the hall and tried to open the door. Marquez slammed it in her face and leaned against it to hold it closed. Suddenly things had started to go wrong for him. He was trapped. His infantry training had told him never to become cornered. His heart began to pound. His battle-scarred amygdalae, sounded the alarm in his brain. Then, he said, his instincts took over.

The girlfriend, wondering why someone had just slammed the door in her face, shoved the door open about six inches and heard someone say, "He has a gun! Get out!" Through the closing door, she saw Smith rush Marquez. She heard two quick shots.[15]

Marquez fired using a technique for close combat that infantry soldiers are taught over and over until it is a reflex: put two shots, known as a "double tap," into the center of mass. Smith was shot square through the heart and collapsed back onto the futon. The teenagers on the couch sat stunned. Marquez quietly collected his two shell casings and the containers of weed and walked out. That night he went out to a bar with his girlfriend but never mentioned the shooting. The next day, he surrendered peacefully to the police at his house. Later, in prison, after pleading guilty and being sentenced to thirty years, he said he never planned to rob or kill the dealer but his infantry reflexes took over.

"When someone grabs you or something in Iraq, you're going to light 'em up. It probably won't even be that hard because it's not like it's your first time," he said. "I should not have had a gun. I was on way too much medication. But when he rushed me, I just reacted. If that was a military training exercise, I would have passed."

———

Marquez is chilling evidence of what can happen when reflexive fire training and the corrosive effects of war, poor leadership, and substance abuse are combined. In Iraq he was allowed to run wild. He was allowed to steal from civilians, beat them, and shock them, according to soldiers in his platoon. He may even have been allowed to murder them. He was certainly allowed to kill perceived combatants, even when they were unarmed. From the platoon's point of view, he was useful in that role—a "pit bull" they could use against the locals.

But once he was wounded he was no longer needed, and he was let loose in Echo Company.

The army had spent over a year preparing Marquez for war; they didn't spend more than a day preparing him for peace. In the months he waited for medical discharge, he did not receive any beneficial reintegration classes or job training that might have eased the passage from Iraq to civilian life and given him some prospects for the future. Young soldiers live a strictly regimented life. They are trained to let superiors tell them what is right, but Marquez was left to navigate the terrain of his despair without real guidance. He just sat around in the shit bag brigade, doing drugs and buying guns. The people who were supposed to be in charge of him did nothing to point him in the right direction. Ultimately, no one but Anthony Marquez is responsible for the murder of Johnathan Smith, but there are dozens of people who could have steered him down a better path and never did.

A week after the murder, sheriff's deputies questioned his commanders at Fort Carson in search of a motive. Just as the mayor of Colorado Springs was reluctant to admit that crime, especially a serious crime like murder, could be a consequence of war, the commanders in charge of Echo Company dismissed Marquez's crime as his problem, not the army's. They said they knew Marquez was edgy and moody and talked about wanting to rob people. They said they knew he abused his medication and showed them his car full of guns. They did not mention ever trying to get him help. Captain David Larimer, the company commander, told detectives that Marquez had been diagnosed with PTSD, but the captain didn't believe it. He said he thought the wounded soldier who had been personally decorated by the president was just a "whiny bitch."[16]

CHAPTER 7

"THIS ALMOST PAINFUL STILLNESS"

After the police arrested Kenny Eastridge for pointing a gun in his girlfriend's face in March 2006, he went AWOL—absent without leave. He bailed himself out of jail the morning after the arrest, but he did not want to go back to Fort Carson to be yelled at by his commanders for getting arrested. He was eligible for promotion to sergeant, and he knew he had just blown his chance and would likely end up in the shit bag brigade. So he stayed home that Monday, figuring he would deal with the fallout on Tuesday. Then Tuesday he decided to wait until Wednesday. After skipping two days of formation, he knew he was in even bigger trouble than before, so he stayed home Wednesday. After that it seemed pointless to show up the rest of the week. The next week went the same, and the week after. Eastridge did not show up at Fort Carson for about six months.

In the meantime, Louis Bressler, Kevin Shields, and the rest of the battalion tackled the relentless training that the new leadership had scheduled to whip hundreds of new soldiers into shape for the impending tour. The battalion had only six months left to prepare for another yearlong bout of combat. At the same time, soldiers and officers were leaving for new assignments and new men were arriving to take their places.

It was a tumultuous time in the unit, full of comings and goings. The rush to get soldiers in place and trained helped contribute to later problems with violence. The battalion did not have time to tend to festering combat stress injuries from the first tour. It barely had time to adequately train healthy soldiers for the next tour. And so some men who should have gotten help, like Kenny Eastridge and his friends, were lost in the triage of obligations. With the war on, the battalion simply did not have time to do things right.

In the influx of new recruits were four who would later end up like Eastridge and Bressler: Jomar Vives, Rudy Torres, John Needham, and Bruce Bastien.

Bruce Bastien was the one who got to know Eastridge and Bressler best. In April 2006, the baby-faced twenty-year-old medic from Fairfield, Connecticut showed up in Chosen Company. He was tall, with red cheeks, wide eyes, and a wholesome, goofy appearance that made him look like he was right out of a Norman Rockwell painting. After graduating from high school in 2004, Bastien had worked at a bar in his affluent hometown, but after a year had joined the army. He signed up to be a medic because he did not want to go to war and thought that, as a medic, he would just end up working in a hospital somewhere. When he was assigned as a combat-line medic to the Warriors, he tried to pretend that he was a tough guy from New York who had cut his teeth in a street gang. He showed up in Chosen Company using a slang-laced ghetto drawl. He talked about fighting his way up through the Bronx and robbing people on the street, but it was an act he could turn off as soon as he saw his mother's number on his cell phone. "He always tried to pretend he was a kid from the wrong side of the tracks, but really, he was just a kid," his roommate, Robert Forsythe, said, recalling meeting Bastien. "He would get expensive gifts from his parents and, being excited, would tell me about them right away, like a kid at Christmas." Then he would play himself off as if he, like many of the other soldiers, was trying to escape a rough childhood.

It didn't take long for the soldiers in the battalion who really had joined the army to get away from gang life to spot Bastien as a phony. A new staff sergeant named Michael Cardenaz, who had grown up just outside Los Angeles and transferred to the unit after two tours in Iraq with another brigade, put his chest in Bastien's face and offered to fight him. Bastien backed down in a flurry of excuses and the rest of the soldiers watching rolled their eyes. Some gangster. Soldiers noticed Bastien was constantly making up stories—even lying when he had no reason to lie. He was the ultimate poseur—a shape-shifter who would do anything to try to fit in. Few were able to maintain any respect for him. Before long, most treated him as the platoon bitch—the beta dog of the pack that the other males pushed around.

Rudy Torres, in a way, was a Mexican version of Bruce Bastien—a stocky nineteen-year-old who grew up in the urban sprawl of East Los Angeles. When he arrived at the headquarters of the Warriors, he wore a thin vato mustache, flashed gang signs, and wore a "Southsider 13" jersey that he claimed marked him as a member of the Sureños Hispanic prison gang. He talked about getting into fights so often that soldiers stopped calling him Rudy and started calling him Rowdy, but the unit quickly realized it was an act. In fact, Torres was a poor immigrant whose writing skills were so clumsy that he had to get other soldiers to help him pen letters. He was assigned at the last minute to fill a spot in the elite scout platoon.

"Torres was an alright cat, but he always wanted to live the thug life," Paris Taylor, a soldier in his platoon, said later. "He was a follower. He always wanted to be in a gang. It is like he craved it."

Under normal circumstances, soldiers have to try out for the elite scout platoon and only the best qualify, but with deployment looming the Warriors had no time. They rounded up a few top soldiers from the Band of Brothers days and filled the rest of the slots with fresh newbies. Torres did not have the gung-ho attitude to shine in the elite unit. Soldiers noticed that while he talked like a tough guy, he was prone to whining and quit when he was tired. Once, during training, a downpour threatened to flood the platoon's tent. While the others ran out in the rain to dig trenches around the tent, Torres just pulled his feet up on his cot. Because he was the lowest-ranking new guy and an obvious wannabe, he was given most of the worst chores in the platoon. If something needed picking up, Torres got the job. If a Humvee was dirty, Torres was going to wash it.

Jomar Vives arrived in the Warriors in July 2006, just a few months before shipping to Iraq, and was also assigned to the scout platoon. He eventually became good friends with Torres, though the two were almost polar opposites. The twenty-one-year-old Puerto Rican was six foot four and 235 pounds. He was so big and round that the other scouts started calling him Baloo, after the big brown bear in Rudyard Kipling's *The Jungle Book*. But behind his bearlike bulk was a friendly, considerate man who called his mother almost every day. Unlike Torres, Vives exuded a tough but easygoing cool that quickly won him respect.

Vives had grown up the son of an army nurse named Marta who had risen to the rank of lieutenant colonel. Like the Graham family, they moved from post to post every few years, and the constant relocating had forged an especially strong family bond. They spent his high school years at a base in Hawaii. When Jomar turned sixteen, Marta devised a scavenger hunt for him that took him from clue to clue, all over the island of Oahu, finally ending at a new, green Chevy Camaro. In school, Jomar loved football, and his size made him a natural at center and lineman. After graduating in 2002, he got married to a woman named Johlea and they had a son. He worked as a security guard and took classes toward an associate's degree in computers at a local community college. In his spare time he liked to play war video games like Halo and Call of Duty or to work on the massive sound system he had installed in his Camaro.

Vives got his degree in 2005 and was thinking about going into law enforcement—maybe border patrol, since his Puerto Rican upbringing made him fluent in Spanish. That year, his mother learned she was deploying to Iraq. Jomar and his wife and child were living with his mother at the time, and he decided he was not going to let his mother go to war alone. She encouraged him, saying joining the army would give him a career to provide for his family. When he signed up, he said he only wanted to do one thing: infantry. A year later, he landed in the Warriors, bound for Iraq.

John Needham, like Vives, wanted nothing other than to join the infantry. He was a six-foot-four surfer with sun-bleached, wavy long hair and a perpetual tan from practically living on the beach in his hometown of San Clemente, California. He had spent most of his life in a house just steps from the Pacific. He and his father and two brothers would have raucous games of football on the beach and go for long walks along the frothy surf. "The ocean was like the blood in our veins, it brought us peace and harmony and fun. It is a landscape of possibilities," his father, Mike Needham, said years later.

Needham's father was an electrical engineer who worked on sophisticated microprocessors for a military contractor, but John had never showed much interest in school. "It wasn't his thing," his father said. "He was more of a doer."

Throughout high school John surfed competitively and played on the golf team. He loved to paint, play guitar, and sing. The tall, good-looking kid always drove cool cars and had plenty of luck with girls. After graduating, he stuck around San Clemente, working at local surf shops, painting houses, and doing other odd jobs that gave him the flexibility to watch the surf reports and throw his board on his car when the breaks looked just right. He lived a life so monastically devoted to surfing that his father called him "Five Buck John." "He would spend all day at the beach and then spend five bucks on a burrito. That was all he needed to be happy," his father said.

After high school, Needham became a sponsored surfer and tried to go pro, but in 2002, at a competition in Ventura, he stumbled on a massive wave that pitched him ten feet in the air. His father, watching from the beach, saw him plummet down the face of the wave and land on his board, snapping it in two. When John bobbed up in the churning foam almost a minute later, he was waving his arms frantically. His ankle was shattered. After that, John realized surfing would always be his passion, but never his career. He started casting around for something else that would provide the same action and intensity, and he decided on the military.

San Clemente is a military town just a few miles north of Camp Pendleton, which is home to more than 37,000 active-duty marines. Since September 11, 2001, Needham had felt a deep patriotic tug to do something for his country. He watched the invasion of Iraq on TV in 2003 and watched his hometown welcome home thousands of marines. By 2006 the TV was showing that security in Iraq was crumbling. It looked to Needham like his country really needed him. One day he told his father he had talked to a recruiter and was thinking about joining the army.

Mike had been an army intelligence officer during the Vietnam War. He knew war was something he did not want his son mixed up in. Politically, he was also dead set against the invasion of Iraq. "John," he said, "let's look at other options. Let's look at ways to develop your other interests. Maybe you could go to art school or do something with your guitar playing." He argued with his son that Iraq, like Vietnam, was a misguided war, but his son wouldn't listen. John wanted to be a Green Beret—the elite of the elite war fighters, and there was only one place to start. He was going into the infantry. He signed up early in 2006 and started training on his own by going out on long runs every day on the beach with a rucksack full of stones. He lifted weights until his long, lanky surfer body bulked up by forty pounds. He breezed through basic training. In August 2006, not quite two months before shipping out to Iraq, he arrived in the barracks of the Warriors. He stood out among the privates in his platoon in Baker Company because he was taller, stronger, and, at twenty-three, older and more confident. When he arrived, his sergeant took the new privates out to a sand pit on the edge of Fort Carson and had them wrestle to establish a pecking order. Needham won. After that, the platoon nicknamed him Needhammer.

In late August 2006, as the new recruits were training to go to Iraq, Kenny Eastridge knocked on the apartment door of his buddy Jose Barco. Eastridge liked Barco because he was mellow and charming most of the time, but could change into "a total badass." Nothing phased him. Like Eastridge, Barco never seemed to loose his cool in a shoot-out. Eastridge viewed him as a real warrior. After Barco was pinned by a flaming suicide car bomb in Khaladiya in 2004, he had spent months recuperating at Brooke Army Medical Center before being sent to Fort Carson. He still had to wrap his burned legs in special bandages every day and officially was not fit for combat, but he felt like an idiot sitting at home while the Band of Brothers was still on Route Michigan, so he snuck into a replacement platoon headed back to Iraq. An officer reviewing medical records yanked Barco from the deploying platoon at the last minute. "He called me an imposter," Barco later said with a sly grin when he told other Brothers the story. He ended up working at the Fort Carson gymnasium instead while his papers crept through the long, slow medical retirement process.

That day in 2006, Eastridge sat down in Barco's living room and they talked about everything and nothing. Eastridge told his friend about his court case and how he had been AWOL for months. He said he would probably get kicked out if he ever went back. Barco talked about the medical disability process and how he would soon be out of the army. Both discussed what they might do when they got out. Neither had any very good ideas. Barco said that, lately, he had started to wish he could go back to Iraq.

"You know they're deploying again in, like, a month," he said as they sat drinking beers in front of the TV.

"Damn, I guess I better show up, then," Eastridge said with a smile.

"Why, are you trying to go?" Barco said. He thought Eastridge was done with the army.

"Hell yeah, I'm trying to go," Eastridge said. "Iraq is the only place I've felt sane for a while." It was so simple, so intense. He turned and looked at Barco. "Besides, wouldn't you feel terrible if you didn't go and something happened to one of the guys because you weren't there?"

Barco nodded. He hadn't felt good since the last deployment either, but he had another reason for going. His older brother had joined the army just months before him and made it through a tour in Iraq unscathed, returning with a healthy supply of cool war stories and medals. Barco wanted another chance to prove himself.

"Fuck it," Barco said. If Eastridge was going, then he was going.

"Man, they're not going to let you go," said Eastridge. Barco was so scarred that he couldn't sweat in several places. He was in no shape for Iraq. And he was only months from retirement.

Barco replied that there was no way the battalion would let Eastridge go either, with his court case and his long absence. But they decided it was worth a try. They made a pact that afternoon to somehow get back into the Warriors.[1]

To a military outsider, it may seem crazy that either man wanted to return. Both had almost been killed by explosions. Both had seen friends die. Both knew first hand that any glory in war is far outweighed by boredom, discomfort, and grief. But there is a timeless, paradoxical pull that draws some soldiers back to combat even when they have seen the worst.

"Despite its hardships and dangers," James W. Willette, a young Union soldier, wrote in his diary in 1864, "there is a strong fascination about war life, and when a heart, especially a young heart, has once been fired by the peal of the cannon, roar of musketry and shouts of contending forces it soon chafes under the monotonous quiet of home. It appears very lonely & dull. I shall go back just as soon as my feet will allow for with all the horror and danger of war, I prefer it to this almost painful stillness that broods over one here."[2]

During World War II, William "Wild Bill" Guarnere, one of the original Band of Brothers, was shot in the leg by a German sniper and was sent to England to recuperate, only to paint his cast black with shoe polish so he could sneak out of the hospital, jump a supply ship, and make his way back to his beloved unit on the front lines. "I couldn't even walk," he said in a 2007 memoir. "But I walked anyway."[3]

In part, a soldier's urge to remain with his unit may be a way to cope with stress and heal. Soldiers naturally equate their unit with safety and strength. When struggling with the fear and uncertainty of combat stress injuries, it is understandable that they will seek out that comfort.[4]

A few days after Eastridge visited Barco, he drove to Fort Carson for the first time in months and walked into Chosen Company's command building. In his absence the chain of command had changed. There was a new platoon sergeant Eastridge had never met. Eastridge knocked on his door and said, "Are you busy?"

The sergeant looked up and asked him who he was.

"I'm sure you've heard of me," he said with a grin. "I'm Eastridge." He paused to let the first sergeant flip through his mental files until he landed on one that said, "Eastridge: Specialist. AWOL since March. Pending felony." Then he told the sergeant he wanted to come back. He wanted to deploy to Iraq. He not only wanted to go, he needed to. He was a good soldier with experience in combat, and he had to deploy with them to protect his friends. He was sorry for being gone for so long, but now it was time to make amends.

The sergeant listened. Then he sighed and put his fingertips against his temples. He pulled a blank form called an Article 15 from his desk. An Article 15 is for "nonjudicial punishment." It is a way for commanders to punish soldiers for minor offenses without going through the formal court-martial process. The commander, acting as judge, jury, and jailer, writes up the charges and the punishment on the form, then the soldier signs at the bottom as an admission of guilt. Punishment can include extra duty, restriction to post, forfeiture of a few weeks' pay, and reduction in rank.

The sergeant slid the blank Article 15, with no charges or punishment yet filled out, over to Eastridge and asked Eastridge how much he trusted him.

Eastridge looked at the blank sheet. The sergeant was asking him to sign it without knowing what he was signing. "Well, I don't know you, so I have no reason to think you are trying to screw me over," Eastridge said. He knew if he signed the paper, the sergeant could add any crime and punishment he wanted, but he had nothing to lose. So he signed.

The sergeant smiled and said, "At least you have faith in me. Come back tomorrow and we'll see what we can do."[5]

There were a number of reasons not to give Eastridge a second shot. He had a traumatic brain injury from the first tour. He obviously had developed an aversion to taking orders. And the signs that he was troubled within were literally written all over him. He had gotten a number of tattoos since his first tour. Most of his forearm held a memorial to Sergeant Huey. On his wrists were dotted red "cut lines" to show where, if needed, he could slit his wrists. On his other arm were the twin bolts of the Nazi SS. Ringed around his neck were thick black letters that read BORN TO KILL READY TO DIE.

Still, there was one major reason to give Eastridge a second shot. In 2005, the army had missed its recruiting goals by the biggest margin since 1979. In the months it took to get recruits through screening and training, the drought had worked its way through to the ranks. At the same time, the battalion had hemorrhaged hundreds of soldiers through injuries, natural attrition, and chaptering. Commanders did not have as many men as they needed. They were preparing to deploy "understrength." They also did not have as much time as they needed to train the new recruits they had. Raw young privates were still trickling in just weeks before heading to Iraq. At the same time, the situation in Iraq was growing worse every day. The annual casualty rate for U.S. forces has climbed from 486 in the first year of the war to 846 in 2006. Eastridge was a well-liked, almost fearless specialist who had qualified as an expert on every weapon. He had experience with buried 155 rounds, suicide bombers, and everything else Iraq could unleash. He knew how to handle himself in a firefight. In all, he seemed like a real asset.

It is a dynamic that commanders have always struggled with. Major Dick Winters, who commanded the Band of Brothers company during much of World War II, said he kept a few guys around that he knew were shooting captives and doing other illegal things because there was little choice. "You needed every man you had. Those guys that goofed up, didn't measure up, you couldn't just get rid of them. You needed the body, because if you lose that body, then somebody else has to shoulder twice the burden. You needed every body you could get."[6]

The next morning, Eastridge walked into the sergeant's office not knowing his fate. Maybe the sergeant had asked guys from the first tour about him. Maybe they had said good things. Maybe not. Maybe the sergeant had decided the Warriors needed him either way. When Eastridge sat down and the sergeant slid the Article 15 across the desk, there was a long list of charges, including disobeying orders and being absent without leave. Under the charges the sergeant had listed the punishment. Eastridge looked at the small handwriting. It said, "No punishment."

The sergeant asked if it looked fair.

Eastridge smiled, then started to laugh. "No," he said. "But I appreciate it."

Because of the lack of soldiers, Jose Barco was able to talk his way back into the unit too, just a week later. It didn't matter that he was slated for medical retirement. If he wanted to go, that was good enough for the Warriors.

Eastridge still had the matter of his pending felony case. Army rules barred any soldier from deploying with a pending felony. Each soldier had a checklist for deployment in which commanders checked off criteria—everything from dental exams to emergency contacts—to make sure he was ready to go to war. One box they had to check read "Pending civil[ian] felony court case (if so may not deploy)."

Someone in the unit decided to deploy Eastridge anyway. His company commander knew about the felony but later told a reporter he let him deploy because he thought the charges were going to be dropped.[7] Eastridge's was not an isolated case. There were a handful of other Warriors who also illegally deployed with pending felonies. Sergeant Michael Cardenas, who became Eastridge's squad leader just before they deployed, said the command told Eastridge that he could stay home and sort his case out or man up and deal with it when he came back.

He manned up.

CHAPTER 8

HEART OF DARKNESS

"**Y**ou may think this is no big deal—you've already done this . . ." a hard-jawed sergeant said, gazing out at a sea of soldiers dressed in drab desert-colored uniforms. They sat in a massive tent in the Kuwaiti desert. It was October 2006 and the five hundred Warriors were just days into their second combat tour. Outside the tent, the dust-covered terrain and dust-filled sky of the Arabian Desert fused in a seamless horizon of more dust. Inside the tent, army experts on the deteriorating situation in Iraq were briefing the Warriors on what the tour ahead promised. For the first time, the Joes learned where they would spend the next year: Baghdad. And it was not going to be pretty.[1]

"You may think you are old hands, real hard asses . . . combat veterans . . . but you've never seen anything like this," the sergeant said as he paced at the front of the crowd. "Even you guys who were in the Sunni Triangle, and I know a lot of you were, that was nothing compared to this; you guys are all cherries."

Sitting in the uniformed ranks were Kenny Eastridge, Louis Bressler, Jose Barco, and their new medic Bruce Bastien. On that sweltering day in October, they were all still considered squared-away soldiers, guys no one should have to worry about.

In the tent they were told they would be spending the next several months in a little neighborhood of Iraq's capital city, a few miles south of the Green Zone. When Eastridge heard they were heading to Baghdad, he thought to himself, "Cool, this will be easy." During the previous tour, Baghdad was where the Band of Brothers sent soldiers when they needed a break from the bloody Sunni Triangle. Huge bases in the city offered not only security, but a hint of normal American life. "It was a place where guys could chill for a week, swim in the pool, go to Burger King," Eastridge said, recalling his reaction. "But we found out this was not the same Baghdad."

In the fifteen months since the unit had left the Sunni Triangle, violence in Iraq had intensified to unforeseen levels. The war was worse than it had ever been. And the center of the storm had drifted away from Fallujah and Ramadi and the other towns along Route Michigan. It was now squarely centered on Baghdad.

The explosion of violence in the capital city was triggered by one event. In February 2006, terrorists had blown the famous golden dome off one of the holiest sites of Shia Islam, the al-Askari Mosque in Samarra, sixty miles north of Baghdad. The attack tore open long-festering wounds between the country's Sunni and Shia Muslim sects and threw the country into near civil war. Saddam Hussein had been a Sunni Muslim. Under his rule, other Sunnis tended to get the best jobs and benefit the most from government projects, while Shia Muslims, who made up a majority of Iraq's population, were largely treated as second-class citizens. After coalition forces toppled Saddam, the Shia, with their superior numbers, dominated the government, including the army and police. The disenfranchised Sunnis grew angry and increasingly aligned themselves with terrorists attacking the Americans and the Iraqi government. Tension grew between the sects. When one of the Shia's holiest mosques was destroyed, it was the last straw. Decades of bad blood bubbled to the surface and chaos ripped across the country as enraged Shia took revenge.

Baghdad became the center of the feud, the sergeant briefing the Warriors said. What had once been a cosmopolitan city where Sunnis and Shia mixed freely had turned into a mass-murder spree that set neighbor against neighbor. After the dome was bombed, Shia mobs burned and bombed Sunni mosques and shot up Sunni homes and businesses. Sunnis retaliated with car bombs at crowded markets and mosques. Reprisal killings begot more reprisal killings, turning Baghdad into the murder capital of the world. In March 2006, eighty bodies—either strangled or bound and shot in the head—were found in the city in a single thirty-hour period. Baghdad was a city with about as many people as the state of Maryland, but in May of that year it had about as many murders as the entire United States.

At the same time, Sunnis and Shia were battling in the streets, fighters targeting American forces were growing more sophisticated.

It isn't going to be some mooj farmer shooting an AK at you then running away anymore, the sergeant said. "These guys are trained, they have been doing this for years."[2]

On a screen at the front of the tent, the sergeant flipped through slides showing the latest insurgent weaponry and devastation in Baghdad. The most alarming was a new kind of IED called an explosively formed projectile, or EFP. It was a small bomb, usually packed with only a few pounds of explosives, but it could shred all but the best armor. The EFP was essentially a foot-long section of pipe filled with explosives and sealed at one end with a heavy concave copper plate. When the explosives detonated, the plate turned into a dagger of molten metal traveling at 6,000 feet per second. It could easily burn through the armor of a Humvee, and through everyone inside. The sergeant flipped through slides of the small bombs, slides showing how they were often disguised as trash or blocks of concrete along the road, and slides showing how an EFP could mangle a Humvee.

Then a map of the city of Baghdad popped up on the screen with the Tigris River snaking through the middle. The sergeant pointed to a swath of the city on the southwestern edge. This, he said, was the very worst area—a grid of bombed-out neighborhoods that Sunni terrorists had decided to claim as their last stand, their Alamo.

The neighborhood was called Al Dora. Locals had once called it the Vatican of Iraq because the tidy, middle-class streets of concrete two- and three-story town houses were home to a vibrant Christian population that peacefully worshipped among the majority Sunnis. Churches and monasteries stood on the same blocks with mosques and madrassas, tucked among bakeries, cafes, and palm-shaded gardens. A thriving commercial district that the army called as the Dora Market teemed with more than seven hundred shops and innumerable stands and sidewalk peddlers, attracting shoppers from around Baghdad.

But in the aftermath of the invasion, looters had ravaged the markets and shops. Electricity and sewage systems grew spotty and then stopped working altogether. Because the new government was overwhelmingly Shia, the crippled municipal services of the Sunni majority in Al Dora got little attention. The Iraqi police in the neighborhood were almost entirely Shia and often killed or kidnapped local Sunnis only to ransom them back to their families.[3] For protection, the Sunnis increasingly offered refuge to groups such as Al Qaeda. It brought with it a fundamentalist hard-line brand of Islam that not only had no tolerance for the American occupiers and their puppet Shia government, but also for anyone who did not follow the strict beliefs of Sunni Islam. They burned the neighborhood's churches and raided its monasteries. They bombed the neighborhood police stations. Then the terrorists leveled their sights on the Al Dora market, where throngs of shoppers still packed the streets buying everything from fruit and vegetables to pirated DVDs. One car bomb after another ripped through the crowds, slaughtering dozens at a time and leaving an aftermath of burning vehicles, shattered shop windows, and smashed produce soaking in the street in pools of blood.[4]

Non-Sunnis started fleeing the area. Others were thrown out violently, under threat of death. The insurgents in Al Dora blew up oil pipelines in the neighborhood and assassinated judges and civil servants. They killed shop owners, teachers, and imams—all Shia. Anyone hired by the Iraqi government or the Americans to repair the neighborhood's crippled streets and sewers was either shot, targeted with IEDs, or co-opted to work for the terrorists by planting explosives beneath the pavement. Al Qaeda increasingly used Al Dora as a springboard for suicide attacks all over the city. As Shia residents fled the neighborhood, their houses were often taken over by displaced hard-line Sunnis driven from Shia neighborhoods. The once mixed blocks became almost entirely Sunni.

After the bombing of the golden dome in Samarra, Shia murder squads targeted Al Dora. In a single week in July of 2006, death squads produced 425 bodies there—more murders than Colorado Springs saw in ten years. To defend against the superior numbers of Shia surrounding Al Dora, the local Sunni's laced nearly every intersection in their tight neighborhood streets with hidden IEDs or EFPs, creating a de facto fortress—their Alamo—and daring anyone to come get them.

Because Al Dora was a launching point for insurgent attacks, the U.S. military had decided that reclaiming it was a priority. They expected the terrorists to fight to the death. It was the Warriors' mission to give them that opportunity.

The Warriors first saw Al Dora at night, from the air, at high speed. They were loaded into the back of a fleet of Black Hawk helicopters racing a few hundred feet over the packed urban rooftops of Baghdad on their way to the battalion's new home, Forward Operating Base Falcon. Insurgents in the city liked to aim rocket-propelled grenades skyward to try to take down America's big helicopters, and on occasion had tasted success, so pilots always flew fast and low, giving pedestrians on the street just a few seconds warning before the aircraft swept across the narrow gap of sky between rooftops.

Eastridge looked down from the open side of the Black Hawk. Below him the dim, crooked grid of urban blocks stretched like an endless concrete labyrinth to the horizon. Buildings crowded right up to the edge of dangerously narrow streets. Fused jumbles of flat roofs created a whole other terrain that looked down at the sidewalks. There was no empty desert to act as a buffer, only houses and more houses packed with more than 5 million people.

It looked nothing like the tiny farm towns strung along Route Michigan where the battalion only needed to patrol one road. "How are we going to patrol this many roads?" Eastridge wondered to himself. "How are we going to find anyone in this mess?"

By the time the Warriors hit the streets of Baghdad in November 2006 for their introductory right-seat ride, Al Dora was, for all practical purposes, a no-go zone. The hidden bombs were too big and too numerous. The U.S. Army would patrol the edges of Al Dora but avoid going into the heart of certain neighborhoods. "The guys we were taking over from, who had been in charge of Al Dora for a year, were driving us around saying 'Don't go down that road. Don't go down that road. Stay out of there,'" said Eastridge's squad leader, Sergeant Michael Cardenaz.

Garbage mounds choked the streets, often spilling into fetid green sewage that ran down the gutters and pooled at intersections. The market that once held seven hundred shops now had just three. Unemployment was almost total. Crowds of houses stood abandoned, their windows shot out, their doors ajar, and furniture emptied by looting and fire, leaving only dust and broken glass. The neighborhood's once-lush gardens had mostly wilted and died. The streets were often devoid of life, except for filthy prides of stray dogs and cats abandoned when families fled or were murdered

The rattle of AK–47 fire echoed through the neighborhood several times a day. The commander of the Warriors, Lieutenant Colonel Stephen Michael, a stoic, battled-hardened man who had grown up in Guyana and done tours in Kosovo and Iraq before coming to Al Dora, had never seen anything like it. There was no hope. There was no functioning anything. The only things that thrived in the burned-out blocks were mistrust and hatred. He called Al Dora "the heart of darkness."

"It was the most contested area in Baghdad. We were attacked every day. Every day. Sometimes multiple times a day," he said, recalling the tour.

As was true in the Sunni Triangle, the enemy wore no uniform and hid in the civilian population, which meant even though attacks were constant, soldiers' chances to retaliate against a known, armed insurgent were frustratingly rare. The battalion's mission was simple but seemingly impossible: root out the terrorists, win back the locals, and bring peace. Several units before them had failed. In fact, the situation had only grown worse with every attempt.

———

Kenneth Eastridge was glad to be back in Iraq. It was worth whatever consequences skipping court in Colorado Springs might bring later. The presentations in Kuwait had not scared him. If anything, they had only gotten him fired up. He had learned to thrive on the simple intensity of life at war. The most vivid moments of his first tour in Iraq had been when he was fighting. It was so pure and powerful and such a rush that it verged on transcendental.

"It's almost like a religious experience to be on a battlefield," he said years later. "To hear the explosions, to see a person bleed out and die and see the inside of them. To see everything on fire and smell the smoke and burning. It seriously makes you think about what life is all about. It's the most extreme sport there is. Combat. It is the biggest rush. There is nothing like it. It's better than sex to me."

His closest friends—guys like Louis Bressler and Jose Barco—felt the same. None of them shied away from the prospect of a fight. None of them were afraid of Al Dora. At least, not at first.

"The first thing my platoon did when we got there was learn the way to the hospital," Eastridge said. "Everyone had to know the way because you never knew—after a fight the lowest private could suddenly be in charge and have to find his way."

That morning in early November 2006, the platoon left FOB Falcon, a sprawling high-security compound that housed thousands of troops, and cruised up a four-lane highway called Route Jackson in Humvees that showed how far the war had progressed since their first tour. The vehicles, which were originally conceived as light replacements for the army jeep, now weighed five tons. A solid inch of armor and blast-proof windows encased the passengers. A ring of bulletproof glass that soldiers called a Pope Shield protected the gun turret. The trucks boasted sophisticated recorders that could decipher the range and direction of rifle fire and powerful cell phone and infrared jammers to foil increasingly sophisticated trigger devices for roadside bombs. This new generation of "up-armored" Humvees was designed to survive almost anything the insurgents could throw at them. But the insurgents had studied those designs in the bomb laboratory that was Baghdad and learned to defeat them.

Eastridge's convoy rolled north and turned east onto a highway called Route Sonics and veered onto a ramp for another four-lane highway called Route Senators. To the left stood a sprawling landscape of date farms along the river, where the first cruise missiles of the war had hit almost four years before. Next to them sat a power plant, heavily guarded and still, miraculously, operational. On the right sat the sinister concrete maze of Al Dora.

As he drove, Eastridge watched the Humvee in front of him turn onto the on ramp. Suddenly there was a loud pop and a puff of smoke on the side of the road. The Humvee in front of Eastridge swayed just slightly from the blast. It was an IED, but a pitifully small one compared to the ground-shaking 155 rounds of the Sunni Triangle. The guys in Eastridge's truck started laughing. Was that the best Baghdad could do?

Then the truck in front of them veered to the shoulder. "Casualties! We have casualties!" a voice crackled over the radio. What appeared to be a tiny puff of smoke was actually an EFP, carefully aimed with a laser trigger to hit a Humvee right at the height of a soldier's head. The molten spear of copper formed by the explosion had melted right through the truck's blast-proof glass, passing through an empty backseat where a soldier's head might have been and slamming into the gunner's hip. The other soldiers pulled the bleeding man out of his sling and raced to the hospital.

"That was our first mission. It was only to go to the hospital, and we got hit," Eastridge said years later. "I knew right then that this tour was going to be a lot worse."

From that day forward, the tour started to lapse into a gruesome routine. First thing in the morning, soldiers would pick up bodies from the sectarian murders the night before. They usually found them scattered around the edges of Al Dora—the no-man's land between Shia and Sunni turf. Sometimes they appeared in piles. Usually they were bound with zip cuffs and shot in the head. Some bore the grizzly marks of torture—nails driven into their heads or a drill bit through the eye.[5]

"That really got to you," Paris Taylor, a private in the scout platoon with Jomar Vives, said later. "They would even kill pregnant women or women with babies and just hurl the baby against the wall."

The ethnic strife created a war within a war. One night early in the tour, Louis Bressler was ten stories up on the power plant at the edge of Al Dora as a part of a sniper team watching the main road for IED planters. They heard the rattle of an automatic weapon ring out from the neighborhood, then several more. It grew into a full-on fire fight. Bressler's team radioed battalion headquarters to report the shots and get updated on the status of American soldiers in the area. The radio man on the other end said there were no American soldiers in the area. It was just Iraqi against Iraqi, killing each other.

The standard operating procedure for soldiers on body detail was to bag them, throw them in the trunk, and dump them at an Iraqi police station. The soldiers thought it was fair turnabout since they theorized that the police were doing much of the killing. "The bodies' hands were almost always zip-cuffed," Eastridge said later. "Who else but the police would have those?"

The terrorists were always watching what the soldiers did and soon realized a dead body was an easy way to bait U.S. soldiers. They started wiring some corpses with explosives. One officer in the brigade was killed when he went to inspect a body and it exploded. One morning Eastridge's platoon found eight dead Iraqis, zip-cuffed, lined up, blindfolded, and shot in the back of the head. When one of the new privates got out to bag them, Sergeant Cardenaz said, "Whoa, hey, what are you doing? They could be booby trapped." He had learned anything out of the ordinary—eight bodies in a row instead of the usual one or two—could be a trap set to draw a large number of soldiers. Instead of picking up the bodies, the platoon called in the bomb squad to bring a remote-controlled robot to blow the bodies to pieces.

The second part of the almost daily routine was setting up what soldiers called "block parties." Warriors cordoned off streets and searched every house on the block. In order to break the insurgency, the army first had to know who was an enemy and who was merely a local. While some soldiers guarded the block, others went door to door compiling a detailed census, mapping every house and recording the names, ages, and occupations of each resident. The grunts on guard in Humvee turrets and on rooftops often waited for hours. Like patrolling Route Michigan, it was hot, dusty, and usually boring work that hid a lurking lethality in the tedium. A platoon could search all day and find nothing, then drive home toward the FOB only to be hit by a sniper's bullet or a hidden IED.

"At first you are jumpy," Jose Barco said, recalling the day-to-day reality of Al Dora. "But after a while you become numb to it. You can't maintain that high state of vigilance that long. You just accept it. You are going to get hit or you are not, and there is not much you can do about it."

In laboratory experiments, the condition of accepting that there is no way to avoid a horrific fate is called "learned helplessness."[6] In the studies that established this condition in the 1960s, groups of caged animals were often subjected to random electric shocks. Some of the animals were given ways to escape the shock, such as pushing a lever or jumping over a low divider to escape an electrified floor. Others were given no escape. Most of the animals not given a way to avoid the shocks eventually stopped even trying and fell into a state of helpless depression. IED blasts in Al Dora were so random and inescapable that few soldiers thought they had any control over them. Many just accepted their fate and drove on.

———

The scout platoon often had to do normal infantry missions as well as set up small kill teams of snipers to watch problem roads for IED planters, which meant they shared the same stresses of the ordinary line troops. In one partic-

Army portrait of Kevin Shields taken in South Korea before he deployed to Iraq in 2004. (Courtesy Deborah Shields)

Kevin and Svetlana Shields in 2004 in Korea, where they met. They married and had two children. (Courtesy Deborah Shields)

Kenneth Eastridge's Humvee after it hit an antitank mine in Al Anbar province in 2005. Eastridge was blown out of the gun turret and had cerebral fluid leaking out of one of his ears. He went back to doing missions a few days later. (Courtesy Leann Eastridge)

Josh Butler, Kenneth Eastridge, and David "Nasty" Nash (left to right, front row) pose with other soldiers at a welcome home ceremony in July 2005 after spending a year in the Sunni Triangle of Iraq. Butler and Nash both suffered from the mental toll of combat and were eventually kicked out for drug use. (Courtesy Leann Eastridge)

Kenneth Eastridge and Louis Bressler in the barracks in Iraq, 2007. The two would hang out regularly together after missions, and even had a contest to see who could get the most kills. (Courtesy Leann Eastridge)

Louis Bressler (left) and Jose Barco wrestle at temporary quarters in Kuwait, just before landing in Bagdad in the fall of 2006. Both were later arrested for shooting civilians in Colorado Springs. Barco returned to Iraq even though burns from the previous tour made it difficult for him to sweat. (Courtesy Leann Eastridge)

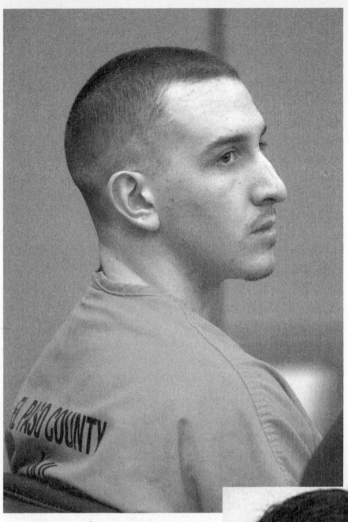

Bruce Bastien at his arraignment in April 2008, four months after he was put in jail, charged with conspiracy to commit murder and attempted murder. (Courtesy Mark Reis, The Colorado Springs Gazette)

Kenneth Eastridge's mug shot from December 2007, when he was arrested for the killing of Kevin Shields. (Courtesy El Paso County Sheriff's Office)

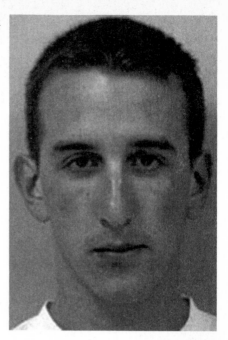

Bruce Bastien's mug shot in December 2007, after he was arrested for the killings of Kevin Shields and Robert James. (Courtesy El Paso County Sheriff's Office)

Jose Barco in 2007, posing next to the sniper shot that came inches from hitting his head. Barco survived Iraq only to fall apart at home. He was eventually convicted of attempted murder and sentenced to fifty-two years in prison. (Courtesy Leann Eastridge)

John Needham poses with friend Christopher Smith and another soldier at Ft. Carson in the summer of 2006, shortly before deploying to Iraq. When he came home after trying to commit suicide, his father said he no longer smiled. (Courtesy Michael Needham).

John Needham in San Clemente, home on leave, January 2007. He was once a sponsored surfer, but after being injured in Iraq, he could no longer catch a wave without pain. (Courtesy Michael Needham)

John Needham with his grandmother, Mary Celaya, at Fort Carson in the summer of 2006, just before he deployed to Iraq. "He was never the same," she said. (Courtesy Michael Needham)

John Needham's mug shot, September 1, 2008, after he beat nineteen-year-old Jacqwelyn Villagomez to death in his family's Southern California home. (Courtesy El Paso County Sheriff's Office)

Kenneth Eastridge in prison, March 2009, after being sentenced to ten years for accessory to murder in the killing of Kevin Shields. (Courtesy David Philipps)

General Mark Graham, in his Fort Carson office in March, 2009, with photos of his sons Kevin (left) and Jeffrey. (Courtesy Hellen Richardson, The Denver Post*)*

ularly bad run of luck, Humvees from the platoon were hit by IEDs four times in two days.[7]

Jomar Vives was picked as the SAW gunner in a sniper team because his big frame allowed him to carry the thirty-pound gun and lots of ammo. His job was to pull security for the snipers with his machine gun in case something went wrong. In several instances, something did.

"He saved our asses a number of times," said Paris Taylor. "He did some shit. Nothing illegal, but he grabbed his balls and did his job."

The insurgency was just as vicious as it had been in the Sunni Triangle, but the American response was much more controlled. Since the beginning of the war, the U.S. military's rules of engagement—the conditions under which soldiers can use deadly force—had tightened considerably, even if Al Qaeda's had not. In Al Anbar in 2004, the Band of Brothers could legitimately shoot anyone they perceived as a threat, even if the target was armed with nothing more than binoculars. Under the new rules in Baghdad in 2006 and 2007, an Iraqi had to be holding a weapon in a threatening manner. Otherwise soldiers were required to detain the suspect, collect witness statements and photo evidence, and draw up lengthy reports with sketches of what happened. Basically, they were required to behave as police. The command saw the tightened regulations as the vital first step in winning over the locals. After all, soldiers can't establish trust with a family whose son they have just killed.

But many grunts in the Warriors felt hamstrung. The enemy they faced intentionally avoided direct attacks and focused on surreptitious sniper fire, surprise grenades, and concealed IEDs. The terrorists employed young unarmed "watchers" to report on the Americans' positions from rooftops so they could coordinate the attacks. They often hired kids to throw grenades. Everyone in the city, armed or not, seemed to be in on the attacks. Locals even sold each other DVD copies of insurgents detonating IEDs on the Americans.[8] This left the Warriors with a feeling that the whole town was targeting them when they had no way to respond or even defend themselves. Some soldiers felt like they had no recourse but to start breaking the rules.

"I believed, and still do, in the war, that we need to be there and there are a lot of Iraqis there that need to be killed," Robert Forsythe, a medic newly assigned to Eastridge's platoon, said after the tour. "We also believed no one there was innocent; they were all guilty of either helping the enemy or staying out of their way. I was happy to make up for their lack of will, their lack of fight."

Forsythe had already been through one combat tour. He had started out as idealistic and interested in Iraqi culture, but by the second tour he viewed the Iraqis as vile people. The medic soon became good friends with Barco and

Eastridge because they all felt the same way: some people just needed killing, rules or no rules. All three would shoot watchers and other unarmed but suspicious locals, then say they had taken fire and returned fire in self-defense. They would beat detainees to get information.[9] Whenever they were attacked, they would fire their guns in every direction. Anyone that was around, armed or not, was killed.[10]

"The three of us felt like we were the last real warriors," Forsythe said. "And everyone else was just playing games."

Sometime early in the tour, Eastridge had a dark self-revelation. Given the things he had done in his life, from shooting his best friend when he was twelve to killing dozens of people in Iraq, he was probably going to hell. It depressed him, but he also found it liberating. He was already damned, so he could do what he wanted.

Every day he grew to increasingly despise the locals. Since Eastridge did not care about the Iraqis, or his eventual fate, he started quietly stealing guns and money from houses during block-party searches.[11]

"I would rob them fucking blind. I hated the Iraqis," he said later.

He would stockpile the guns—mostly AK–47s—and sell duffel bags of them back to the Iraqi police. "I knew they were Shia militia—basically terrorists—but I did not care," he explained. He also built a false-bottom crate so he could bring stolen guns back to the United States.

The platoon kept a number of the confiscated Iraqi rifles stashed in its Humvees.[12] Forsythe and others said soldiers would use them as "drop weapons." "If we killed someone who was unarmed, we would drop the AK next to the body for the pictures to prove his guilt. We would also use them to start contact. The sound of an Iraqi AK firing is so different from an American M–16 or M–4 that no one would question why we were firing as long as the AK was the first to go off."

The "drop weapons" were not limited to one platoon or one company. John Needham said his unit in Baker Company used them, too. When a soldier in Jomar Vives's unit was asked if his elite scout platoon used drop weapons, he would only say, "You have to protect yourself. That is all I am going to say. You got to do what you got to do. Whether it is Vietnam or Iraq, the rules of war don't change. The only rule that matters is it is either you or them."[13]

Early in the tour, Bruce Bastien started tagging along behind Eastridge in Al Dora like a little brother. As people, they were worlds apart. Eastridge was a poor kid from a broken home in Louisville, Kentucky. Bastien was from a solidly middle-class family in a tony Connecticut suburb that sent him lavish care packages in Iraq, including 1000-thread-count Egyptian cotton sheets for his cheap foam mattress in the barracks. But Bastien imagined himself as a hard-core gangster and hanging out with the nihilistic gunner with the most kills in the company gave him instant credibility.

Most of the platoon disliked Bastien. He was lazy and full of excuses. He refused to help clean the Humvees and do other small duties. When sergeants like Cardenas told him to do something as minor as get water for the other troops, he would tell them to get someone else to do it. To teach him a lesson, sergeants repeatedly smoked him, making him do push-ups in the sewage-laced mud of Al Dora until his knuckles bled.

Eastridge never joined in on the abuse. He always protected the twenty-year-old medic and kept him close. Eastridge used to razz the sergeants when they smoked Bastien, saying, "You'll wish you hadn't done that shit to your medic when you are bleeding out on the street."

For all Bastien's faults—and even Eastridge readily admitted they were many—he never hesitated to perform his duty as a medic. One afternoon, the platoon's convoy drove right into an ambush. What seemed like a dozen Iraqis suddenly swarmed out on a narrow street with AK–47s and machine guns. The driver and gunner in the lead truck in the platoon froze up, trapping the convoy. Eastridge was driving the second truck when his gunner suddenly fell out of his sling with blood pouring from his mouth. He had been shot in the face. Eastridge jumped out of his Humvee and raced to get a medic from the front truck. Bullets whizzed by, popping and exploding off the Humvees. One hit so close to Eastridge that shards of the shattered round peppered his cheek.

When he got to the first Humvee, Eastridge shouted for a medic.

Without a word, Bastien jumped out into the steady sizzle of bullets and sprinted back to patch up the gunner. Bastien made some beginner's mistakes. He once treated the entry wound on a gunshot to the chest but forgot to turn the patient over and treat the exit wound.[14] But other soldiers never saw him shy away from his duty. Even when it came to treating Iraqis, he was eager to help.

Despite Eastridge's dark side, he continued to be a favorite of the platoon. He was brave, calculating, and full of funny stories that made him popular on boring but perilous patrols. The command even reconsidered promoting him to sergeant. But he had deployed to Iraq with problems, and as the months went on, his problems grew worse and worse. As his bathtub of stress filled, he grew increasingly nihilistic and erratic.

One afternoon, when a cat-and-mouse firefight with insurgents in a particularly bad corner of Al Dora stretched on for hours, Eastridge decided to go get some lunch for the three soldiers pinned by gunfire in his Humvee. About fifty meters away stood a falafel store that had just had its windows shot out.

"Who wants a pita?" he asked the guys in his truck with a wry grin.

"You can't be serious," his sergeant said. Bullets were literally whizzing past. From the Humvee they could see the puffs of dust from rounds hitting the buildings.

"I'm serious," Eastridge said, opening the door of the truck. He told the gunner to cover him, then sprinted with his head low for the falafel shop. As he ran through the door, he could hear glass flying everywhere as a machine gun strafed the block. He ducked behind a counter. The owner was nowhere to be found but the restaurant was still fully stocked. Eastridge reached up, feeling for supplies on the counter as bullets thumped into the walls. He grabbed a big bag of pita and a bowl of falafel that had been fried that morning. He started to get up, then turned back and grabbed an armload of sauces. He clicked a radio clipped to his lapel and said, "Cover me, I'm coming out!" The gunner lit up the street with his big .50 cal and Eastridge sprinted for the truck, fumbling with an armload of food.[15]

"I had already decided I was going to die on that tour, I didn't expect to come out alive," Eastridge said later. "I did not worry about it. Once you are already dead you lose all fear. I decided if the hajjis were going to get me, they were going to get me. But I was going to make them pay dearly for it."

Eastridge started to occasionally fire down streets on missions without warning or reason.[16] He was assigned as a gunner on the big .240 machine gun on top of the Humvee, and he earned a reputation as a guy who would shoot first and ask questions later. Even gung-ho shooters like Barco and Forsythe started to question his sanity.

Louis Bressler was a gunner just like Eastridge.

They were in separate platoons and usually went on separate missions, but they hung out religiously back at the barracks. Bressler had been the epitome of the squared-away soldier after the first tour, but the gore of Al Dora started to get to him. He was in several close calls with IEDs. And yet, time after time, his platoon would go out the next day and do it all over again. It was as maddening as the random shocks of the learned helplessness experiments. After his father died during his first tour in Iraq, Bressler got a tattoo on his back of the grim reaper standing over his father's tombstone. During his second tour, he got a tattoo on his arm of his own grave. He asked his buddies to fill in the date when he finally got killed. As far as he was concerned, he was already dead. He would call home, seeking solace. "He was jittery all the time," his wife, Tira Bressler, recalled. "I tried to calm him down, but a few hours later, he would call back in a total panic."[17]

As the tour stretched on, Bressler and Eastridge grew closer and closer. Between missions, they would play video games and trade tales of how many Iraqis they had shot.

"We got to be friends in Iraq because we were both going through the same thing, both losing it," Eastridge said later. "When you start breaking down over there, one of two things happen; either you become a coward and don't want to leave the wire, or you become super aggressive and decide 'I am going to kill everyone.' Bressler was one of those. He got a lot of kills. He would hear about our kills and be jealous. We had a contest going. Him, Barco, me—all the killers."

Kevin Shields went the other way. The constant threat of IEDs terrified him. So did the idea of killing people. Once, while Shields was manning a checkpoint, a car did not heed his commands to stop. He got orders to fire warning shots over the car, then kill shots. "His bullets hit a child," his grandfather said. "He carried that child to first aid. I know it devastated him."

Shields eventually refused to go out on missions in Al Dora. The command took him off the line and sent him to the relative safety of the Green Zone to train Iraqi troops. That is where all soldiers went when they refused to go out anymore. Shields's greatest fear was that he would die before seeing his extended family again. In May 2007, he went to a phone booth and tried to call his estranged sister. He could not reach her. While still in the phone booth, he tried to overdose on Valium. The battalion, seeing that he was in no shape to be in Iraq, sent him home a few weeks later.[18]

Sending soldiers home was always the last option. After all, if other soldiers saw you could go home by acting crazy, many might follow suit. So guys were usually moved to easier or less lethal details. They were put on guard duty for a while, or sat in the radio room monitoring missions. Many eventually returned to duty. The army has since decided that soldiers often recover better when with their units, but in 2007, if a soldier was suicidal he was sent home.

———

In the spring of 2007, Eastridge was moved from gunner to driver in his Humvee, perhaps because his command decided he was dangerously trigger-happy. Even so, Eastridge continued to find ways to lash out. One morning, he was leading a search of a house in Al Dora with a handful of other soldiers when he found bullets for a palm-sized .25 caliber pistol. The battalion let every family in Al Dora own one AK–47 for security, but handguns were strictly forbidden. They were too easy to conceal. When Eastridge saw the handgun bullets, he asked his interpreter, or "terp," to ask the homeowner where the pistol was.

The homeowner, a middle-aged man with a mustache, shook his head and raised his hands. He said he sold it long ago. Eastridge didn't buy it. He knew the man was lying. He had the evidence in his hand. So he told the other soldiers to start looking for a pistol. They sifted through rooms, emptying drawers on the floor and dumping out cabinets. In a bedroom, Bruce Bastien found more ammunition—this time to different kind of pistol, a 9 mm.

"OK, ask him where this fucking pistol is? Did he sell this one, too?" Eastridge said to the terp.

The man said yes, he sold both.

Eastridge was furious. He viewed all Iraqis as sniveling, cowardly liars. If they were not actively fighting the Americans, they were at least supporting those who were. Everything was crooked and corrupt. The women and children were in league with the bomb planters. The cops and army were thieves and terrorists just like everyone else. He knew the man sitting on the couch in front of him was lying and he was going to teach him a lesson.

"Look, this guy has another pistol," he told the other soldiers. "Find it for me so I can shove it up his ass."

The others rifled through closets and under beds, turning up two AK–47s and more bullets. Again, Eastridge shoved the evidence in the man's face and asked where the guns were. Again the man stuttered and said he had no idea.

Eastridge snapped. He started breaking everything he could reach. He pulled out a long, sharp combat knife and sliced up the couch, saying, "There's pistols here, I know it!"

He ordered the other soldiers to ransack the place. He took a hatchet he always carried and chopped a hole in the refrigerator. He bashed furniture and knocked holes in the walls. Eventually the soldiers found the two pistols. In retribution, Eastridge told the others to go on a rampage.

"We wrecked everything in the motherfucker," he said later. "If something could go inside it, I broke it and just used the excuse I was searching. We weren't supposed to do stuff like that, but we did it all the time. If we thought [an Iraqi] was out of line, we made them pay for it. You make me mad, I'll wreck your whole house, tear it to pieces, and make you pay for it. I'll chop your fucking refrigerator up with this ax right here, I don't care, you're a terrorist. Maybe I can't prove you are a terrorist, but I know you are a terrorist. And if you don't like it, fine, I'll just hand you over to the Iraqi police and they will kill you."

The homeowner filed a complaint against Eastridge's platoon, and the battalion investigated. The sergeant in charge of the squad was knocked down in rank and Eastridge was reprimanded, but nothing more serious came of it. As was his habit, Eastridge turned in half of the guns he found in the house and kept the other half, including the palm-sized .25 pistol.

Eastridge was increasingly turning dark—he would openly argue with his lieutenant, swearing at him and calling him a hajji lover and a coward in front of the men. He had once been a capable and well-liked member of the team, but by the middle of the tour, soldiers said, even his own lieutenant started to fear him.

A few months later, the platoon was on patrol on the northern edge of Al Dora when someone shot at them from the vicinity of a farmhouse set off in a field. The whole platoon instinctively unloaded on the house, peppering it with machine-gun fire. Eastridge grabbed a grenade launcher from a sergeant and fired every grenade he had—about two dozen—into the house, battering the walls with one explosion after another. When the smoke cleared, the platoon rushed in to search the house and found a farmer and his two dogs cowering in a back room.

They pulled the man into the courtyard, and, through the terp, Eastridge asked where the shooter was.

"No, no. No bad guys here," the man said.

"That's bullshit!," Eastridge said, kicking the dirt near his feet. "Look, there are AK–47 shells right here."

The man said he did not know where the shells came from.

Eastridge started to feel a familiar rage envelop him. He lifted his rifle and shot one of the man's dogs.

"Where is the shooter?!" Eastridge fumed.

The man raised his hands and insisted there was no shooter.

Eastridge shot his other dog.

"Where is the shooter?" he yelled again.

At that moment his lieutenant stepped in and said, "You need to go cool down and sit in the truck, Eastridge."[19]

"Yeah, I'll go sit in the fucking truck," Eastridge snorted. He stormed out of the yard, but on the way, he passed the pen where the farmer kept a small herd of about a twenty goats. He mowed them all down with his gun. Then he told another soldier to shoot the farmer's two cows. He spotted the man's horse. He raised his rifle and killed it.

———

Eastridge's actions were contrary to almost everything the Warriors were trying to achieve in Al Dora.

A new military counterinsurgency strategy in Baghdad introduced by General David H. Petraeus in early 2007 stressed that brute force was only making the situation worse and military units had to position themselves as allies of the locals, not occupiers.

"This balance is not easy," Patraeus wrote in the foreword to a new military counterinsurgency manual. "It requires leaders at all levels to adjust their approach constantly. They must ensure that their Soldiers and Marines are ready to be greeted with either a handshake or a hand grenade . . . be nation builders as well as warriors."[20]

In light of Patraeus's directive for the military to employ more than just firepower, commanders in the Warriors shaped their mission to include much more than hunting the bad guys. The Warriors' commanders believed Al Dora was infected by a relatively small number of ideologically driven, hard-core Al Qaeda terrorists. The terrorists supplied guns and bomb-making materials to a much larger group of local Sunnis who were primarily interested in protecting their neighborhood from the Shia. The terrorists also played an important role in the local economy, paying young men $50 to $200 to plant IEDs and act as spotters, which, in a place like Al Dora with almost total unemployment, was some of the only work locals could find.

The locals "were linked to Al Qaeda because there was, in their minds, no alternative," Captain Jim Keirsey, the commander of the Warrior's Baker Company, wrote in a summary of the battalion's strategy published in *Army* magazine. "Al Qaeda scared them, but they fought alongside them for the money and to reach the common end of protecting Sunnis."[21]

The command knew the only way to catch Al Qaeda was to get the locals to snitch. The only way to get them to snitch was to first win their trust. The only way to win their trust was to provide the security, electricity, clean water, and jobs the locals so desperately needed. The battalion started to gain their trust by first building twelve-foot concrete walls around each section of Al Dora, leaving only two entrances that were guarded twenty-four hours a day. This allowed the army to protect locals from Shia death squads and seach everyone for guns and explosives. The soldiers jokingly called them "gated communities."

The second step was to replace the sectarian mobs of the Iraqi police with the more reliable Iraqi army units from outside Baghdad. At the same time, the battalion started handing out small grants of a few hundred to a thousand dollars to help locals reopen businesses. Then American troops started the hard work of restoring basic services like cooking-fuel deliveries. Finally, the battalion created small neighborhood watch groups employing young Sunni men to watch for Al Qaeda instead of working for them.

"That is how we won trust," said Lieutenant Colonel Stephen Michael. "It was working with the neighborhood counsels, school principals, getting books, getting kerosene and fuel. But it took a long time."

Brute force and contempt for the Iraqis had no place in the strategy. Company commanders knew that if the locals liked the soldiers, they would tell them where IEDs were hidden, so a good relationship was vital. Captain Keirsey warned his troops not to smoke on patrol, ogle women, swear, or leave helmets on inside, cautioning the men, "Simple actions from your patrols will either make or break your relationship."[22]

But the army is a human organization full of human error, misjudgments, pride, anger, revenge, fatigue, frustration, and innumerable other factors that can shatter the best intentions like a well-placed IED.

The strategy to revive civilization in the mean streets of Al Dora relied on a crucial first step called "clear and hold." The Warriors had to clear out the defensive network of massive IEDs and hold the neighborhood so Al Qaeda could not plant more. It was a deadly business. To achieve it, soldiers often felt they needed to call on the very brute force they were admonished to control. They were kept out on patrols for days on end so terrorists could not retake cleared ground. They went out at all hours with little time for sleep. Many survived multiple IED blasts and the concussions and other unseen brain injuries that accompany them. Almost everyone saw close friends killed. They were worn down and burnt out. Trying to restore order in Al Dora exacted a heavy toll on the Warriors, measured in dozens of lost comrades and more than two hundred purple hearts. Some men who sought tirelessly to bring peace to this seething corner of Iraq eventually lost their own peace of mind. The soldiers later arrested for murder in the United States and some of the friends who fought alongside them generally agree that the violence that spilled out back home started in the heart of darkness that was Al Dora.

———

On March 13, 2007, Eastridge's platoon went out to act on a tip from one of their local sources about the address of a secret Al Qaeda bomb maker. The plan was to cordon off the neighborhood and search every house on the block. That would give the platoon a chance to scope out the bomb maker's house for a subsequent raid without arousing suspicions. They parked their Humvees in the middle of the street and spread out for a block party. Jose Barco crouched in the turret of the lead Humvee, watching other soldiers block off the street. Bruce Bastien sat in the backseat of the Humvee at Barco's feet—a medic safely stowed in case of emergency. Just a few feet behind them another truck sat idling. As Barco swiveled in his turret, he watched the driver of the second Humvee, a twenty-two-year-old sergeant named Robert Carr, scan the rooflines. Above Carr, another gunner turned in a circular sweep.

The rest of the platoon went door to door, doing the slow work of getting to know the neighbors. Minutes stretched into hours. The soldiers in the trucks surveyed the streets, always vigilant, always watching, always prepared to fire—never aware that just below Carr's feet, 150 pounds of explosives sat poised to blow.

The IED had somehow been hidden under flawless asphalt, leaving no clue of its presence. The triggerman was watching. No one knew from where, but he waited to pull the trigger, perhaps wanting to take out as many soldiers as he could. Before long, an opportunity presented itself. The first sergeant, James Naughton, stepped out of a nearby house with two other soldiers and started walking toward the trucks. Barco watched them pass his truck out of the corner of his eye as he continued to scan the street, then *boom*.

The triggerman had pulled the trigger.

The deafening explosion shot an instant shock wave down the street, whipping up every ounce of dust and grit into a fine cloud that stretched for blocks. A concentrated blast shot up through the earth, through the asphalt, into Robert Carr's Humvee, splintering the engine, the axel, the chassis, and the inch-thick armored passenger cocoon. The shattered metal of the Humvee became jagged spearheads shooting out in a deadly burst. First Sergeant Naughton and his soldiers were thrown to the ground. Barco was hit with such force that he thought it was his Humvee that had exploded. A cloak of black oily smoke swallowed him. He could not see or hear. As he choked on the burning air, he did not know whether he was alive or dead.

Eastridge heard the blast and ran out of a house he was searching, rifle up for another attack. He saw the first sergeant stumble to his feet in a daze, so covered with soot and singed oil that he was raven black from head to toe. The smoke cleared just enough to show a burning Humvee. The whole front of it was gone. The gunner had been blown out.

Bruce Bastien jumped out of the lead Humvee just feet from the blast and ran to help pull Robert Carr from the fire. Carr didn't look good. His legs had been shoved above the steering wheel by the blast and hung limp at odd angles possible only when bones have completely crumpled. A shard of the Humvee had punched up through his chest, exiting through a gaping gash in his neck. Another shard had ripped off half of his arm. The bones jutted out past singed flesh. He was burned and black and bleeding from a dozen places. But he was breathing. The soldiers dragged him out and Bastien jumped on top of the bleeding sergeant to start CPR. The platoon piled medic and patient into the back of Barco's Humvee, shoved the first sergeant, who was covered with shrapnel wounds, into the passenger seat, and the truck took off.[23]

As the Humvee sped through the IED-laced streets, Bastien shoved a tube down Carr's throat and started breathing for him.

"Barco!" Bastien said between breaths, "I need you to get down here!"[24]

The dazed gunner swung down from his sling in the turret.

Carr's pulse was fading away. Bastien yelled that Barco needed to do chest compressions while Bastien alternately pushed breaths through the tube. After every few breaths, Bastien grasped Carr's one remaining wrist, searching for a pulse. He tried desperately to save Carr. He had to. Carr was one of the favorites of the platoon, always joking around and sharing anything he had. He had been with them since Korea. He was getting ready to go home to Ohio in a few weeks to see his wife for their first wedding anniversary. Bastien pressed his fingers on Carr's wrist and held his breath. The pulse was thready, but it was there.

He told Barco to keep pumping. Pump and breathe. Pump and breathe. The heart was still beating. But every time Barco pumped, he could feel the sickening crepitus of broken ribs grating under his palms. Carr's lungs were full of blood. Every time Bastien would blow in, a fountain of blood and chunks of lung would spurt out into his mouth and all over his face.

Bastien never quit, though. The whole way to the hospital he kept checking the pulse, breathing for the sergeant, and bracing for the exhale of gore that spit up at him. Even when Carr's pulse faded away, Bastien kept going, trying everything he could to save the young sergeant.

"He never gave up, all the way to the hospital," Barco said later.

Eastridge saw Bastien stumble back into the barracks after Carr was pronounced dead. The medic's face and front of his uniform were so covered in blood that, Eastridge recalled, "He looked like he had eaten somebody."

"He seemed to take it in stride," Eastridge said later. "It did not seem to affect him."

But like almost everything else Bastien did, his composure seemed to be just another tough-guy act. The bloody event shook him to his core. A few weeks later, Bastien asked Eastridge for a favor. He had heard the stories of how Barco had shot their friend Josh Butler so he could get out of duty back at Fort Carson. Now Bastien wanted Eastridge to shoot him so he could go back to the United States. A week later, Eastridge tucked the palm-sized .25 pistol he had stolen during a search in his pocket when the platoon went out on a night mission. He and Bastien went up on a rooftop alone to watch the street for insurgents. They decided the time was right. Eastridge said he would shoot Bastien in the biceps, then shoot a few more rounds in the air. Bastien would then tell the platoon he had been nearly fatally shot by a sniper.

Eastridge pulled out his pistol and Bastien held out his arm. First he pointed the little gun at Bastien's forearm then traced the barrel along the arm to the biceps. He took a deep breath. But he did not pull the trigger. He slowly moved the barrel up to Bastien's shoulder.

Bastien glared at Eastridge, not sure what he was doing.

Eastridge wordlessly traced the little gun to Bastien's chest and held it there for a second, then brought it up to his face. Eastridge had a funny look in his eye that Bastien did not like. He grabbed Eastridge's wrist and guided it back down to his biceps. Eastridge pulled the trigger. At the same moment Bastien flinched and the round missed his arm, punching a hole in his uniform right through the Warriors patch.[25]

"Bastien got scared after that and never tried it again," said Robert Forsythe, who talked to Bastien about the shooting before they went to bed that night. "I don't know if he was scared of the pain from the shot, or of Eastridge killing him."

Instead, Bastien searched for another way to go home. He told other medics he was thinking about going AWOL. In May, he was secretly smoking a blunt with Eastridge and the platoon's old medic, Ryan Krebbs, in an out-of-the-way corner of the FOB. Bastien said he had two weeks of leave coming up and he wasn't going to come back from it. He told Krebbs if he was arrested in the States they could not send him back.

"I rolled my eyes and said 'whatever,'" Krebbs said later. "But then a few weeks later we heard Bastien had gotten arrested on leave for beating his wife."

Bastien got out of jail on bail and immediately went to the fourth floor at Evans Army Hospital, saying he had PTSD and was out of control. The army kept him at Fort Carson to receive treatment. Bastien's past made many Warriors suspicious of the diagnosis. They viewed it as just another one of his convenient lies. But there is evidence to suggest that being a first responder in Al Dora, with all the blood, violence, helplessness, and guilt associated with trying to save soldiers' lives, was enough to make medics crack.

Two other medics who worked with the platoon, Ryan Krebbs and Robert Forsythe, also started to lose it in Al Dora. Krebbs started abusing prescription drugs, alcohol, and marijuana and stopped loading his weapon on missions, hoping, just slightly, that he would be killed. "I didn't want to shoot at anyone else," Krebbs said later. "I didn't believe in what I was doing, and I wasn't going to kill someone for something that I didn't believe in, so, to me, it just seemed pointless to load a weapon, and at the time I thought so strongly against [killing that] I thought that I would rather die than take another man's life for something that I don't believe in."[26]

Forsythe went the opposite direction, focusing the anger and shame he felt for the casualties not at himself, but at the Iraqis. He took pleasure in beating detainees. He would beat them while his lieutenant interrogated them. He shot unarmed Iraqis in the street that he suspected of being watchers. At one point, after a firefight, he was called to give aid to an insurgent who had been shot several times. He knelt down by the bleeding Iraqi, gave the other soldiers standing around him a cold, solemn look, and said, "Get out of here. I got this." The others looked at him quizzically but did not leave, so he pulled out an old Iraqi bayonet he had found on a mission, held up the sharp tip, and said, "I got this."

When they left, he thrust the blade into the wounded man, killing him.[27]

"I hated the hajjis. They are vile, disgusting people," he said, recalling his urge for vengeance. He was later court-martialed for the stabbing and other alleged crimes, including stealing from Iraqis, but other soldiers testified that none of it happened, and he was cleared of all charges. After the tour, Forsythe was arrested twice for drunk driving and reckless endangerment, and eventually diagnosed by the Veterans Administration with PTSD.

Looking back, he said, one statistic shows just how caustic and damaging the tour was for the battalion's medics. In the medical platoon of thirty men, he said, twenty were married when they left for Iraq. Four were still married a year after they returned. Forsythe was not one of them.

He said it has taken years to begin to recover. "I am looking forward to a peaceful life now," he said via email from Lebanon, where he moved in the spring of 2010. "I'm on medication, and go to meetings when I'm back in the States. I still drink a lot, and will forever, but I'm not as violent as I was during that first two years back from the war."

The crumbling of so many personal lives was juxtaposed to dramatic strategic success in Al Dora. In the spring of 2007, as part of U.S. military's surge to take back Baghdad, the city and surrounding areas were flooded with 30,000 additional U.S. troops. The reinforcements allowed the Warriors to focus on the worst corners of Al Dora. Commanders increased the troops' workload, keeping them out on the street for long hours every day in order to hold the tenuous peace. Concrete walls went up to hamper terrorists' movements and supply lines. Neighborhood watch teams employed hundreds of young men. After several months of near-daily battles, the surge worked. Bomb blasts in Al Dora dropped from daily to rare. Murders in Baghdad plummeted from almost forty per day in January 2007 to fewer than seven per day by December.[28] Five hundred shops reopened in the Dora market and a handful of the neighborhood's Christians returned to rebuild their church. But in the grim process of peacemaking a number of soldiers lost their minds.

CHAPTER 9

"THROW ME A LIFE WORTH LIVING"

As the grind of Al Dora wore on into the summer of 2007, one by one Louis Bressler, Kenneth Eastridge, and John Needham started to break down. The soldiers grew unpredictable and increasingly prone to rage. Many stopped caring about anything. They eventually became too dangerous to handle firearms or be trusted with the civilian population. They became too dangerous to keep in Iraq. So the battalion did something that in hindsight seems even more risky: they sent the soldiers back to Colorado Springs.

Louis Bressler was the first to break. The relentless threat of death every day started to get to him after a few months, but he was able to keep it together until May 30, 2007. That night, at around midnight, his platoon went on a mission to set up a sniper outpost in a house overlooking a stretch of road infamous for IEDs. The idea was to catch the bomb planters red-handed, then shoot them. Bressler's squad set up a security perimeter on the street while a second squad crept into the courtyard of a nearby house to place the snipers. Without warning, the rattle of heavy machine guns shattered the night. One of the four soldiers in the courtyard, a twenty-year-old private from Long Island named Matthew Baylis, was shot square in the chest. He dropped to the ground. A sergeant taking cover from the hail of bullets in the shelter of a low curb a few feet away crawled to the wounded private, threw him over his shoulder, and started running for cover, but both were knocked to the ground by another bullet that went through Baylis's neck.[1]

Bressler had grown especially close to Baylis in the previous months. He had taken the younger soldier under his wing, and thought of him as a brother.[2] When the shooting started, Bressler rushed in with the others and fought his way toward Baylis. By the time they reached him, he was unconscious. Bressler helped load him into a Humvee and rushed him to the hospital. As he drove, he kept saying, "Hold on, you're gonna make it!"[3]

Baylis died a few hours later, and Bressler took it hard. He believed his friend had died for no reason. He felt guilty that it was the young private who had died, and not him. He started having the same dream over and over. A green tent stood alone in a featureless desert. Bressler would walk across the sand into the tent and find Baylis standing there. "You're dead," Bressler would say.

Baylis would ask him why.

Bressler's response was always the same. "I don't know."[4]

Bressler started acting erratically. He would make disjointed comments only tangentially connected to what others were saying. He started getting counseling, sleeping pills, and antidepressants from the FOB psychiatrist, but soldiers said he still seemed completely out of it. "He always looked like he had tears in his eyes," said Ryan Krebbs. "And he just was not coherent."[5]

The wars in Iraq and Afghanistan mark the first time soldiers have been given prescription drugs in the war zone for depression and anxiety, and by most accounts, the use of sleeping pills and antidepressants was widespread in the battalion. "They would offer that stuff to everyone every five seconds, it seemed like," said Paris Taylor. The drugs allowed soldiers to ignore or at least tolerate their combat stress symptoms. But that only let them do more missions, exposing them to more trauma. Since the use of these drugs in combat is new, it is too soon to know the long-term effects, but by making soldiers feel better they may ultimately have been making them worse.

Bressler continued to go out on missions, but he could not focus. He often could not remember orders or perform simple tasks. He had always loved being a soldier in Iraq. He had rarely complained, but now he was unable to do his job. In mid-June, he got in a shouting match with a sergeant who was criticizing his low performance. Bressler flew into a rage and punched the sergeant in the face, then ran to a nearby weight room and started throwing the equipment around. Other soldiers rushed in and tackled him. Bressler fought back as they zip-tied him and shut him in a room to cool off.[6] The battalion was unsure of what to do with Bressler. He had been a dependable, hardworking soldier, and no one wanted to formally punish him for assaulting a superior, but he obviously could not stay in Iraq. Commanders decided to send him back to Fort Carson, hoping he would get the care he needed.

———————

By the time Bressler was sent home, his buddy Kenneth Eastridge was already pretty far gone. In the spring of 2007, the constant fear of IEDs started haunting him, so he went to the company doctor, complaining of stress and depression. The doctor gave him antidepressants and sleeping pills. Almost half of the Warriors were referred to mental health at some point during the tour.[7] But with limited time and staff, health providers could not offer true treatment; they could often only offer pills. Eastridge found he could not take the sleeping pills and still do his job. He felt like the antidepressants were not working. When he told the doctor this, the doctor doubled the dose.

"They tried all kinds of stuff and nothing worked," Eastridge said. Eventually an Iraqi interpreter introduced him to Valium, which is available over the counter in Iraq. First Eastridge was taking just a little before missions to ease his nerves, then he was taking a little all the time. Then he was taking a lot. Often he would go out on missions completely giddy and strung out.

Around the same time, Eastridge had someone from home send him a package of hollow-point ammunition for his rifle. Hollow points are banned by international treaties, but soldiers valued them because they expanded on impact, causing more damage, while army-issued ammunition shot right through an Iraqi. Over time, more and more soldiers were secretly using them.

"Once I realized I could get bullets through the mail, I started ordering all kinds of stuff," Eastridge said. He had boxes of top-shelf liquor and marijuana sent from home; he drank and smoked his fill and sold the rest at outrageous prices.[8]

"He pretty much became the company drug dealer," one soldier said.

As he grew more stressed-out and medicated, Eastridge seemed to stop caring about the rules of engagement. He and others in his Humvee started to shoot Iraqis along the road with the stolen AK–47s, two soldiers said, claiming the fire came from Iraqis.[9] If anyone noticed, they claimed self-defense. In a place like Al Dora, murder was easy to hide. No one, not even the soldiers themselves, may know how many people they murdered.

Eastridge later suggested the murders and trumped-up evidence were the dark side of unit cohesion—the modern practice of training and deploying the same group of soldiers together as a team. "We learned habits in the first tour and perfected them in the second tour," he said. "Maybe if you mixed guys up, they wouldn't feel comfortable doing some of those things."

He started to notice that he was slowly losing his mind. He could not sleep. Behind his calm, dark-humored exterior, he felt like he was always on edge. He felt like he did not know himself anymore. The only way he could feel in control on missions, he said, was by acting aggressive. "I could make myself feel better by taking the initiative, going on the offensive, if you will. I'm smashing through some dude's house, I'm getting to the rooftop, just getting aggressive to put them on the defensive."

By the summer of 2007, Eastridge's running tally of confirmed kills hovered at seventy.[10] He shot everything, even dogs and cats. His command put him on radio duty and gate duty at the FOB to keep him from causing too much harm, but with the constant casualties from snipers and IEDs in Al Dora, troop numbers were dwindling. Humvees designed for five people were often rolling with three. Noncombatant soldiers were shifted into combat positions. At one point the battalion even had a few women from a supply company manning gun turrets on their Humvees.[11] And so Eastridge kept being sent out on combat missions until the day it became clear that his participation would have to stop.

That day in June 2007, right around the time Bressler was sent home, Eastridge's platoon pointed their convoy into the heart of Al Dora to place a sniper team in the bullet-riddled bell tower of a burned-out church. It was a rare nice morning in Baghdad, sunny but not too hot, with a breeze that had chased away the normally fetid smell of standing sewage and burning garbage. In the sun-bleached street, women in headscarves chatted in a doorway, and a gang of boys chased a soccer ball up and down the broken pavement. Several families were outside barbecuing. On the corner, someone was selling grilled chicken. The crowd milling in the street was a sign that the chance of an attack was low.

Eastridge was the gunner in his lieutenant's truck. As usual, he and his lieutenant were quarreling. The officer was telling Eastridge he could not leave the truck.

"I was telling him he was a coward and that I would fuck him up one day," Eastridge said, recalling that morning. "When we parked the trucks, I told him, 'As soon as you walk around the corner, I'm going to kill all these people.'"

The lieutenant gave Eastridge a "yeah, whatever" kind of look as he got out of the truck and left with the rest of the platoon to go into the church. Eastridge told the truck driver to "put some killing music on the iPod." The angry guitar riffs of a heavy metal band called Drowning Pool rumbled through the speakers. The song was called "Let the Bodies Hit the Floor." As the guitars started to thrum, Eastridge scanned the street with the barrel of his heavy machine gun. His hands instinctively gripped the triggers.

He watched as a boy crossed the alley to bring a tray of tea to a group of men in long cotton shirts sitting in the shade of an ancient palm tree. The men sipped their tea.

Then Eastridge started shooting. He pumped a long, loud burst into the palm tree just above the heads of the men drinking tea. Eastridge said later he was not sure why he shot. After being in Iraq for two tours, he had learned that asking why didn't matter much.

The shots echoed up the street followed immediately by a ripple of panic. People scurried for cover, ducking into doorways or down alleys. The soccer boys broke into a run. The women who had been chatting in the shade ducked inside. A number of people piled into cars and started to speed away.

Eastridge started to panic. He had meant the burst of bullets as a joke—something to piss off his lieutenant. Instead it had unleashed chaos. The Warriors had imposed a vehicle ban in the neighborhood to protect against car bombs and drive-by shootings. Now, suddenly, in the mayhem he had created, fleeing cars swarmed into the streets.

The damaged parts of Eastridge's brain that normally separate friend and foe faltered. The rider could no longer calm the horse. He swung his gun and centered it on the first moving car he saw. It was almost a reflex. In his mind, after spending twenty months in Iraq, every vehicle on the road was potentially packed with explosives. His friends were on foot around the corner. He had to protect them. His gun was built to spray 850 bullets per minute. A three-second burst could waste everyone in a car. Eastridge peppered the street off and on for twenty minutes, shooting almost 1,700 rounds. Yells kept crackling over the radio to cease fire. He screamed, "Negative! Negative!"

"It was crazy. Insane. I had completely lost it," he said later.

Asked how many people he thought he killed that day, he said, "I don't know. Not that many, maybe a dozen."[12]

After that, Eastridge was confined to the FOB. He guarded the gate and did other light duty while continuing to sell drugs. He was high almost all the time. While on gate duty, he fell in love with a woman from a supply company attached to the battalion. In late August 2007 he was caught with her in his bed by Chosen Company's first sergeant. For the Warriors, it was the last straw.

The first sergeant had other soldiers drag Eastridge into his office, where he was searched. They found 463 Valium pills in the bedraggled soldier's pocket. The first sergeant had known Eastridge since Korea. He looked at what a mess the soldier had become and just shook his head. He knew Iraq had been hard on his men, but he also knew that most of them were not screwing up,

selling drugs, shooting people, or breaking the rules against sex with other soldiers. He told Eastridge he had given him too many chances to clean up and
Eastridge had blown them all. He said he was throwing his army career away
on a tramp.[13] Eastridge lunged at the sergeant, and two other soldiers in the
room had to hold him back. He kept struggling and thrashing, his whole body
trembling. He shrieked that he would kill the first sergeant, suck out his blood,
and spit it at his children.[14]

Eastridge was court-martialed on nine counts, including drug possession,
disobeying orders, and assaulting an officer. He was never charged with killing
civilians. As part of the court-martial, he was assessed by a doctor and found
to have chronic PTSD, major depression, antisocial personality disorder, and
homicidal thoughts, but he was not given any treatment. The army had spent
years training him to be lethal and Iraq had spent just as much time turning him
into a sociopath, but no one spent a minute trying to rehabilitate him. Instead,
Eastridge was sent to do hard labor at a detention camp in Kuwait for a month
as punishment, then sent back to Fort Carson to be kicked out of the army and
let loose into the civilian community of Colorado Springs.

———

John Needham had none of the antisocial leanings of Kenneth Eastridge, but
a month later he had a similar exit from Iraq.

Early in the tour, the California surfer landed in a platoon in Baker Company that became famous for being the best IED hunters in Baghdad. They
called themselves the Dead Rabbits. In the "clear and hold" counterinsurgency strategy for winning over Al Dora, defusing the IED threat was the crucial first step. Without it, there could be no regular military patrols, which
meant there could be no delivery of propane, water, and electricity, which
meant the troops would never win the trust of the people and Al Qaeda would
keep planting IEDs.

To break the gridlock, the captain of Baker Company, Jim Keirsey, made
finding the hidden bombs his top priority. Through intelligence gathered by his
platoons and tips left through an anonymous hotline, his company began to plot
the locations of known IEDs in their small section of Al Dora as red Xs on a
map of the neighborhood. By the time they finished, almost every intersection
had an X—forty IEDs in all. And those were just the ones they knew about.

Keirsey called together his platoon leaders one night in mid-May 2007 to
tell them the plan. He unrolled the map laden with Xs in front of them.

"Look, guys, no one else will take care of this problem for us," Keirsey
said. "The only thing for us to do is go in there and dig them up."

"What EOD team do we have?" one of his platoon sergeants, Jeffrey Althouse, asked, referring to the army's specialized explosive ordnance disposal teams—the bomb squad.

Keirsey shook his head. None, he said. EOD was afraid to enter the neighborhood. They would not hunt down bombs. They would only come in with an escort and explode IEDs once they were uncovered. That meant Baker was going to have to find the IEDs and dig them up themselves.

"That's crazy," Althouse said. He was opposed. Digging up Al Dora's massive bombs was suicide. The EOD guys had bomb-diffusing robots and specialized blast suits. The only protection the guys in Baker Company had were flack vests and combat boots.

The captain agreed, but said, "You have a better idea?"[15]

Baker Company was going to have to suck it up. Keirsey's plan was to go in at night when triggermen could not see them scouring the dark intersections. They would work all night, every night, until the neighborhood was cleared. The captain picked his best platoon for the job: the Dead Rabbits.

The next night the Dead Rabbits crept into the neighborhood on foot. One of the sergeants who had grown up hunting coyotes outside a small town in Texas had devised a method for finding bombs. He would search for a wire—usually peeking out of the asphalt and sneaking under trash and dirt to a nearby utility pole, where it would snake up and disappear into a tangle of other power lines and telephone wires. Clip the wire and the IED was disabled. Then the Rabbits followed the wire, carefully chiseling it out of the asphalt until they reached the bomb. (Later they realized they could be even more effective if they cut the wire, hid, and then killed the bomb-planter when he came to investigate.)

That night at the first intersection, after the wire was cut, Needham and the other soldiers dug delicately through the dirt with screwdrivers and tire irons, holding their breath.[16] The IEDs in Al Dora were designed to obliterate five-ton armored Humvees. If they went off on a bunch of infantry grunts scratching in the dirt on their knees, nothing would be left but a fleeting red mist. Everyone was on edge as they chiseled and scraped. Eventually, their screwdrivers hit metal. They carefully brushed away the dirt to uncover a long, heavy 155 round. Their hearts pounded with such force that they seemed to echo in the dark street. The platoon had clipped the wire to disable the bomb, but the terrorists were crafty. It could have been a decoy wire. Just as the massive round was almost uncovered, they found another wire. They followed it through the dirt to another 155 round, and another. And the wire kept going. Beneath the artillery shells sat an antitank mine like the one that had almost killed Eastridge during the first tour. Beneath the mine was an EFP. The soldiers' eyes widened: they could not believe how big the bomb was.[17]

The Dead Rabbits called in EOD and roared on to the next intersection. And the next. And the next, repeating the same harrowing procedure all night. The controlled booms of the IEDs being neutralized roared out seemingly every hour. The Dead Rabbits went back night after night. At the end of three days they had destroyed eighteen deep-buried IEDs.

"That shit was fucking crazy," said Ryan Krebbs, who had been assigned to the platoon after one of the Dead Rabbits' original medics was killed. "EOD would put C4 on the bomb and blow it in place. Because, I mean, there's no way to move those things." Sometimes the blast would shatter all the windows on a block and the medics would have to go door to door, bandaging the neighbors cut by flying glass.

Needham could handle the stress of digging up massive IEDs by hand. Seven months into the tour, he had already seen the worst Baghdad had to offer and shown himself to be resilient. For the first four months he had been split off from the Warriors and attached to a neighboring infantry unit, the 1st Squadron, 4th Cavalry. There his platoon sergeant said Needham proved to be an "exemplary soldier"—smart, kind, and brave.[18] He was put in for a commendation medal. But Al Dora wore a little bit of him away every day. One afternoon a fellow private was shot in the head by a sniper so close to Needham that the other soldier's brains splattered on Needham's uniform. Another day he was hit by an IED.

"He was not giddy to be there," his father, Michael Needham, said. "But he was secure in what he was doing, serving the country in an honorable way."

When the tall, sandy-haired surfer moved back to the Warriors in March 2007, his easygoing competence and charisma instantly won him a spot as the lieutenant's right-hand man. But the relentless tempo of attacks started to grind Needham down. In April, an IED ripped into his Humvee, knocking him out and killing the interpreter in the backseat. On June 7, after stopping a suspicious vehicle, Needham ordered two Iraqi men out of a car only to see one of them holding a grenade with the pin pulled. Needham shot the man three times in the chest and once in the face, then turned to run. A few steps later the blast of the grenade knocked him to the ground, peppering his legs with shrapnel. He was recommended for a commendation medal for the act of valor. A week later, Needham and his lieutenant, Scott Flanigan, were hiding in a house, waiting for a triggerman to inspect an IED they had disabled, when suddenly they were hit by machine-gun fire from several directions. Needham pulled Flanigan to the floor and returned fire. He held them off with his rifle, burning through sixteen thirty-round magazines before backup could arrive. He was later nominated for a Bronze Star with valor for his actions.

The attacks seemed to be endless. On June 18, a mortar shell disguised as a piece of trash blew up on Needham's Humvee, giving him another concussion.[19] On June 28, Needham's platoon responded to a massive attack on another Warrior platoon in their corner of Baghdad. The local terrorists, realizing that Baker Company had learned to detect and defeat their bombs, had dug under the road from a nearby courtyard and packed the tunnel with explosives, leaving no wires to detect. When a Warriors Humvee rolled over the spot, the blast was so powerful that it tossed the vehicle thirty feet in the air and destroyed several surrounding buildings. The flaming truck crashed to the ground a block away, crushing and killing all five soldiers in the burning wreckage.[20] When Needham and dozens of other soldiers rushed to the rescue, more than a dozen insurgents ambushed them with heavy machine guns, armor-piercing grenades and RPGs. The firefight lasted for hours, seriously wounding another thirteen soldiers.[21] At the end, there were so many dead and wounded that soldiers piled many of the bodies in the trunks of their Humvees.

In July and August, Needham was hit by two more IEDs. One blast made him hit the roof of his Humvee so hard that he fractured two vertebrae. Another afternoon, the gunner in a Humvee in his convoy was taken out by an RPG. Needham jumped out of a Humvee, took his place, and returned fire, only to be almost knocked out when another grenade tossed over a wall hit the truck.

Needham went to the doctor for his wounds but always went back out on missions. His platoon prided itself on being the toughest, best unit in the battalion and its philosophy was just to suck it up and keep going. Twice, though, he quietly went to the battalion doctor and said he was depressed, couldn't sleep, and was "starting to lose it."[22] As with Eastridge and Bressler, the doctor gave him a handful of antidepressants and Ambien and told him to come back in a few weeks.

John later told his father that his platoon would not give him the time to get counseling and other care for his combat stress, and evidence suggests this is true. His platoon sergeant and squad leader were both on record saying PTSD was a made-up excuse for soldiers that could not hack it. They had told National Public Radio in 2006 that they sometimes did not let soldiers seek mental health care if it meant missing training. Both sergeants told NPR that PTSD was just a cop-out soldiers used when they got scared or did not want to work. But even if he was allowed to see a doctor regularly, it is questionable what good it would have done. Both Eastridge and Bressler were able to get regular mental health appointments, and they all ended up in the same place.

Something besides the relentless attacks started gnawing at Needham. In a quest to win in Al Dora, he said some of the Dead Rabbits turned ugly. Like Eastridge, the Dead Rabbits started loading their weapons with illegal hollow-point bullets sent from home, he said. Some of the sergeants would go out into the neighborhood at night with a homemade zip gun, hunting dogs.[23] One of the sergeants made a poster where he could chalk up every kill. It boasted over eighty dogs. Soldiers sometimes shot unarmed locals, including teenagers, and then refused to give them medical care, he said, letting them die on the street. One sergeant shot an unarmed man in the head during an interrogation, Needham said, then mutilated the body, pulled out the brains, lashed the limp, bloody carcass to the hood of his Humvee, and drove around the neighborhood blaring warnings to insurgents in Arabic that they would be next.

The army's Criminal Investigation Division later interviewed several soldiers from the Dead Rabbits after Needham made his accusations publicly and said it was "unable to substantiate any of his allegations,"[24] but Needham took a handful of graphic photos of the dead bodies. It is impossible to know the context in which they were taken, but one clearly shows an Iraqi body on the hood of a Humvee and a soldier pulling out the brains.

Experts in the field of combat stress have noted that PTSD rates are particularly high among soldiers who report witnessing or participating in atrocities. Something about violating the inate morale code against cruelty seems to be especially toxic to the human mind. Whatever was going on in the platoon, it was enough to make the once mellow surfer crack.

Needham said he refused to participate and was ostracized by the Dead Rabbits. In September 2007, he posted a note on his MySpace page saying he was falling apart. "These walls are caving in my despair wraps me in its web, I feel I'm sinking in, throw me a lifesaver throw me a life worth living. I'm a part of death I am death this is hard to admit but this shit's getting old."[25]

A few nights later, on September 18, Needham and a fellow soldier, Christopher Smith, got a bottle of contraband whiskey from their medic, Ryan Krebbs, and tried to drink away their sorrows. They were talking about how much they hated the ugly situation they were trapped in when Needham took out his loaded pistol. He walked out of his room into the hall of the barracks, thinking to himself that if anyone challenged him, he was going to kill them. He walked up and down the hall. No one came out.[26]

What happened next is unclear. Soldiers say Needham shot off his gun in anger in the hall of the barracks. Needham told his father he put a pistol to his head and his roommate knocked it away just as he pulled the trigger. Either way, a gun went off in the barracks. Soldiers ran out of their rooms and pinned

Needham down. He was detained by his commanders for illegally discharging a firearm, kept in his room for twenty-two days, and not allowed to leave or make any contact with the outside world. A friend tipped off Needham's family to what was going on via email. His father, a former army officer, called the battalion commander, Lieutenant Colonel Michael, furious that his son was being mistreated. He said his son needed to see a psychiatrist. The officer countered that John had broken several rules and needed to be punished. The two got in an argument over the phone. Each says the other started hurling profanities and hung up in anger. Needham's father called authorities at Fort Carson, demanding that his son get medical attention. Fort Carson contacted the Warriors, and Needham was let out of his room to see a doctor.

Like Bressler and Eastridge, Needham had been a good soldier but eventually turned against his own battalion. He had survived almost a dozen IEDs and constant firefights. He had seen friends die and said he watched people be murdered by the very troops who were supposed to be protecting them. He was suicidal and homicidal and could not be trusted around weapons anymore. The doctor diagnosed him with injuries to his spine and brain from IED blasts and with PSTD, and said he was too dangerous to be in Iraq. So, like the others, they sent him back to the United States.

———

Not everyone who was suffering from combat stress was sent home.

The scout platoon set up dozens of sniper nests overlooking Al Dora. For weeks they manned a post ten stories up on a power plant overlooking the neighborhood with little contact with the rest of the battalion. Jomar Vives would pull security for days on end.

Vives seemed to handle the stresses of Al Dora well enough, but he could not handle what was going on at home. He started to suspect his wife was cheating on him, using drugs, and neglecting their child. He would obsess over it and talk constantly to his sergeants and fellow grunts about how much it tortured him.

"I was going through the same thing and we talked about it often," said Paris Taylor, who was a private in the platoon at the time. "It really got to him, but he was able to focus his rage into his job." As a SAW gunner, Vives never hesitated to shoot.

In late September, Vives went home on leave and caught his wife cheating on him and allegedly neglecting his son. The army allowed him to stay at Fort Carson while he sorted out his family problems.[27] Like the others, he was now at home.

Most of the battalion made it through the whole tour, but that did not mean they all made it through unscathed. Jose Barco seemed as healthy at the end of the tour as he did at the beginning. He smiled and joked almost the whole time and never hid from a firefight. He was in five IED blasts and had several concussions, but felt almost invincible. His favorite photo from the tour showed him grinning next to the blast shield around his gun turret, which had been shattered by a sniper moments before, just missing his head.

"We had to joke about that kind of stuff all the time," said a former sergeant and friend of Barco, John Duval. "There was no other way to make it. You just accepted your fate. Getting scared or worrying about it was not going to save you. If you got killed, so what? You were dead."

But the constant high level of alertness, the aggression, and the deeply entrenched fatalism soldiers used to remain normal and functional in Al Dora almost guaranteed they would not be normal in Colorado Springs. They hungered for a respite from the danger of Al Dora and yet feared the moment when it would be gone. In Iraq they were lords of the neighborhood. At home they were nothing. Their hard-won skills had little use. By 2007, the American public showed little appreciation for or interest in the troops fighting their wars. As the date of return to the United States drew near, soldiers increasingly talked about what they would do when they got home. Barco joked that he would never be able to survive civilian life, he would just end up in prison.

One day, the subject of life after the army came up between Barco and Robert Forsythe. They had forged a strong bond during the tour, in part because both were willing to shoot unarmed watchers. Barco told the medic he couldn't really imagine ever getting a normal job. Plus, his job skills did not really translate to the civilian world. Forsythe agreed. He had no interest in a nine-to-five job. After discussing it a bit more, they decided to try a new profession somewhere along the United States–Mexico border—something that employed their infantry skills. "We planned on killing drug dealers as they crossed the border," Forsythe said, recalling their idea, "and stealing their money, drugs, and weapons."

The Warriors returned to Fort Carson in December 2007 after fifteen months in Iraq. A few months later they were reflagged again through another reshuffling of army units, changing from the 2nd Brigade Combat Team to the 4th Brigade Combat Team. They gave themselves a new nickname. This time they called themselves the "Lethal Warriors."

CHAPTER 10

ESCALATION
OF FORCE

Kenneth Eastridge pulled Louis Bressler into the back bedroom of Bressler's apartment on the east side of Colorado Springs and closed the door. It was October 26, 2007, just over a month before Kevin Shields was murdered. Both soldiers were dressed head to toe in black. Eastridge had a knife in his pocket and a silver .38 revolver in his waistband. He looked at Bressler and said, "What are you doing inviting him?"

In the next room, Bruce Bastien slouched on the couch watching TV wearing white sweatpants and a bright yellow shirt. The vast majority of the Warriors were still in Iraq, but Bastien, Bressler, and Eastridge had all been sent home early. Eastridge was planning a robbery that night, and the arrival of the medic from his platoon had thrown a wrench into the plans. Not only was Bastien inept and untrustworthy, Eastridge told Bressler, but he was dressed like a canary. Eastridge looked at Bressler and quietly, through a clenched jaw, said, "He's not coming."

"Don't worry," Bressler said calmly as he tucked a black .45 semiautomatic pistol into his belt. "I know him. We've been hanging out. We've done shit together. He's cool."

"He was in *my* platoon in Iraq. I know he's *not* cool," Eastridge shot back.

"No, we've been hanging out, we've *done* shit together," Bressler said. "Way more serious shit than this. Trust me, he is cool."

"Look, I don't even want to get you involved in this. I can't share the money, I need it all," Eastridge said.

"Don't even trip. We'll do it. You can keep the money," Bressler said. "I don't care, I'm fucking down."

"Well, if you don't want the money, then what is the point?" Eastridge said.

"Just to do it," Bressler said. "Look, it's my guns, my car. If you are going to use my shit, you have to let us come."[1]

Eastridge could see he was not going to win. Fine, he said, but if Bastien was going to come, it wasn't going to be in white sweatpants and a yellow shirt. Eastridge dug out dark clothes and threw the heap in the medic's lap. As they walked to the car, Eastridge also tossed Bastien a four-inch black folding combat knife.

For more than a week, Eastridge had been devising a string of armed robberies he hoped would help him get back on his feet. Since coming back from Iraq, he had been on the run from the law and the army. He had no money. He had no job skills. He wanted to scrape enough cash together to get a small apartment where he could live with his girlfriend until he figured out what to do next. So he mapped out a series of heists as if he were planning raids in Baghdad.

One idea was to steal a car, crash it through the front of a Sportsman's Warehouse in the middle of the night, and grab armloads of shotguns, pistols, rifles, and cash. He had driven Humvees through walls in Al Dora. He knew how easy it was. The whole thing would take just minutes. They could easily sell the guns to other Lethal Warriors.

Another idea was to knock off a bank, infantry style, bursting through the door and moving to the corners like they were clearing an insurgent stronghold. Stick a rifle in the teller's face, bag the money, toss out the booby-trapped dye packs disguised as stacks of bills, and get out. But the idea Eastridge decided to try first was the simplest, safest, and most likely to land a large, instantaneous payoff. They would stake out one of the Tejon Street bars where soldiers burned thousands of dollars a night on drinks. When the manager left with the receipts after closing, they would grab the money. Compared to what they did in Iraq, it would be easy.

After staking out a few places, Eastridge decided to hit Eden, a club in a renovated stone church two blocks off Tejon Street.

On the night of October 26, the three soldiers, now all wearing black, piled into a new Suzuki Forenza Bressler had bought after getting back from Iraq. They drove downtown, cruised up Tejon Street, past the crowds and ever-present police cars outside Rum Bay, then turned onto a cross street called Pikes Peak Avenue and pulled into a dark parking lot behind Eden.

―――――――

Bressler had not been kidding with Eastridge when he said he had done more serious stuff than an armed robbery with Bastien. The two had been on a drug- and alcohol-fueled spree of violence for months. It included shootings and mur- ders so senseless that not even the two soldiers involved understood them. It started just a few weeks after the Warriors sent Bressler home from Baghdad in June.

When Bressler's wife, Tira, picked him up at the airport he had a textbook case of complex PTSD. He was twitchy and unable to concentrate. He swung wildly between rage and apathy. He couldn't be around crowds, so he holed up most of the time in their little apartment. On returning to Fort Carson, he was assigned to the Lethal Warrior's Rear Detachment. The Rear Detachment, or Rear D, was the fraction of the battalion that stayed at home during deploy- ments to handle all of the supplies, travel, communication, and other logistics for the rest of the battalion. The Rear D also increasingly functioned as a sort of purgatory for soldiers too injured for Iraq, but not injured enough for the hospital—some of the injuries physical, some of them, like Bressler's, mental.

The Rear D is often staffed by soldiers who, for one reason or another, could not go to Iraq. Oftentimes they were in the Rear D because they were going through issues of their own. In 2007, the staff was not trained to deal with wounded soldiers, especially serious combat stress cases like Bressler. And so Bressler was treated with what can only be described as neglect.

When Bressler arrived in the Rear D, he was required to go to the fourth floor of Evans Army Hospital. The wave of PTSD cases that had crashed into Evans in 2005 and 2006 was topped by an even bigger wave in 2007. PTSD takes time and repeated sessions with counselors and psychiatrists to treat. With the medical retirement process bogged down, patients piled up. Three years of cases had left the hospital with about 1,200 patients and only about 35 staff to treat them.

Desperate to stabilize potentially dangerous soldiers, the staff's first tactic was almost always to medicate. When Bressler arrived for a brief appointment with a psychiatrist, he was prescribed a barrage of strong sleep medication, antidepressants, antipsychotics, and antiseizure drugs that had become the standard cocktail for soldiers with PTSD. From there he was sent back to the Rear D, where he was expected to report every day so commanders could make sure he was going to his psychiatrist appointments as he crept through the slow process of medical retirement. Like soldiers stuck in the shit bag brigade after the previous tour, he had nothing to do but menial tasks designed to punish malingerers and discipline problems. Because of his condition, he was not allowed to use a gun, so he could not help train replacement troops. He yearned to be back in Iraq with his buddies; instead, he was stuck in a pointless netherworld. He felt betrayed by the two things he thought he could count on most, his platoon and his own mind. Often, he would just not show up to work.

In the Rear D, Bressler ran into Bruce Bastien. After beating up his wife, Jackie, while on leave, Bastien had told commanders he had PTSD and had persuaded his wife not to cooperate with prosecutors so his case would be dismissed. In Baghdad, Bressler and Bastien often hung out after missions because of their mutual friendship with Kenny Eastridge, but they were never very close. Now Bressler needed someone. His wife, Tira, was working nights as a nurse at a hospital. Often he would only see her a few hours a day. He missed the Lethal Warriors desperately. He missed life as a real soldier. He missed talking to people who had experienced what he had experienced. One day at the Rear D, he asked Bastien if he wanted to get a drink.[2]

They soon grew inseparable, spending hours each day at each other's apartments, smoking weed and plowing through Jack and Cokes while playing war games like Halo or Call of Duty.[3]

Bressler was still having nightmares and flashbacks about Iraq, even with the strong drugs. He would often wake up his wife with his thrashing. At first, he tried to talk to his psychiatrist about the war—about killing and seeing peopled killed—but the psychiatrist at Evans had never seen combat, so Bressler felt like he was wasting his time. "It was like I was speaking in a foreign language," he said years later. "He didn't understand what the hell I was saying."[4]

Instead Bressler numbed his bewildering storm of feelings with pot and booze and the pills the army gave him. He did not like the way the pills made him feel, but he did not like how he felt without them, either. Sometimes he would stop taking them, then he would go back on them, then stop taking them again.[5] Many of the drugs he was taking came with the warning that sudden changes in dose could lead to violent mood swings, but he did not know the risks. He was paranoid, and though the army forbade him to carry a gun because of his mental state, he found a .38 revolver and a .45 pistol he had bought his wife for protection while he was in Iraq in a kitchen cabinet and started carrying one or the other everywhere.[6]

On Friday night, July 27, Bastien and his wife invited Bressler and his wife over to drink. They kicked off the night by funneling cans of Coors Light through a beer bong on the apartment stairs while Bastien's one-year-old daughter slept in the back room. By 3:00 A.M. all of them were plastered. Bastien's wife went out to get cigarettes and rushed back into the house a few minutes later in a panic, saying some guys had tried to chase her. Bastien was furious. He turned to Bressler and said, "Let's go find them."[7] They ran down the stairs and hopped into a new Audi A4 that Bastien's parents had just helped him buy.

A few blocks away, a twenty-five-year-old soldier named Mathew Orrenmaa was walking down the sidewalk. He had not said anything to Bastien's wife, or even seen her. He did not know Bastien or Bressler. He did not even live in the area. He had been out all night at a party with friends from his unit and had run out of gas on his way home. He was walking to a nearby Shell station when Bastien's Audi sped out onto the main road, took a sharp turn, and pulled up right next to him. Bressler leaned out the passenger side window. "Hey, man," he said. "You trying to fuck with some girl?"[8]

Before Orrenmaa could even figure out what the guy in the car was talking about, he saw Bressler pull out a black .45 pistol and fire three shots. One of them sliced through Orrenmaa's deltoid, just missing his ribs and lung. Orrenmaa reflexively ducked and sprinted around the corner into a suburban neighborhood. He hopped a six-foot wooden fence into a backyard and then another. He could hear the whiny tailpipes of the Audi troll past the dark houses, as if Bastien and Bressler were looking for him.

Bressler and Bastien's actions can, in part, be explained by the fact that the parts of their brains that assess threats were so fried by combat. What normal people might have seen as a slight cause for alarm pushed them into violent overdrive. Their learned reaction was to respond with lethal force. In Baghdad, it was a normal way of dealing with a threat.

They never found Orrenmaa, and he later called 911 from a house in the neighborhood, but he could not identify the car or the men so the police did not have much to go on.

That was the first time Bastien had ever seen Bressler snap. It is unclear whether the medic was mortified or impressed. Bastien never said anything, even to his wife. The two soldiers drove back to the party as if nothing had happened.

The next weekend they did almost the exact same thing. On Friday, August 3, Bastien invited a handful of soldiers from the Rear D over to get drunk with him and his wife. At around two in the morning, Bastien and Bressler went to get cigarettes at a nearby gas station. At a stoplight blocks from his apartment, they spotted a twenty-three-year-old private named Robert James. They had never met him, they did not even know he was a soldier, but they offered him a ride.

James was a little guy with a round face and a black buzz cut. Like Bressler, James loved sports growing up but had struggled with school. Like Bressler, he had dropped out and struggled with dead-end jobs before settling on the army. And like Bressler, that night he was totally wasted. He had spent hours drinking at a pool hall with a soldier from his unit, and had gotten so obnoxiously drunk that he was thrown out of the bar. When his friend drove him to the gates of Fort Carson and told him to walk back to the barracks, he inadvertently walked in the opposite direction, back toward town.

After picking up James, Bastien suggested they should all smoke a blunt, so the three went to a nearby 7-Eleven to get a few cheap cigars to stuff with pot. Bressler and Bastien went into the convenience store while James waited in the backseat. While inside, Bressler said, "Hey, you want to rob this guy?" Bastien was caught by surprise. There was no reason to rob James. But the follower in him didn't want to seem uncool. "Yeah, whatever," he said.[9]

In the car, they rolled up a blunt and drove through the winding, quiet streets of a nearby wealthy neighborhood called the Broadmoor. Bastien often cruised the Broadmoor while smoking blunts because the mansions and mature trees reminded him of the tony neighborhoods where he grew up in Connecticut. They were blasting music and passing the blunt, talking about nothing in particular when Bressler turned and asked James how much money he had.

"Not much, like a couple bucks," James said.

"No, how much do you have?" Bressler said with a cold glint in his eye. He showed James the silver .38 revolver he nearly always carried.

James started shifting uncomfortably in his seat.

Bastien pulled into the dark parking lot of a bank thinking they were going to pistol-whip the guy, take his money, and leave him there.

"Look, leave me alone. Leave me alone," James said as Bastien pulled to a stop. James had his wallet out and was throwing a few small bills into the front seat.

"Get the fuck out of the car," Bressler said as he opened his own door and came around the front of the Audi. He pulled James out of the back seat.

"Look, just leave me here. Take the money," James pleaded.[10]

Bressler stood a few feet in front of him with a gun to his face. James raised his hands and begged for his life.

Bastien was fishing between the front seats for the bills James had thrown when he heard a loud *pop!* He looked behind him and saw James drop to his knees with a bullet hole through his forehead. As he fell back on the pavement, Bressler popped two quick shots at James's head. It was a move, known as the "double tap," that soldiers routinely used in Iraq to make sure their targets were dead. Anthony Marquez had used a similar technique when he killed a drug dealer the year before. The bullets hit just under James's jaw and shot up through his tongue, lodging in his brain and spine.[11] He died instantly. Without a word, Bressler got back in the car.

Bastien peeled out of the parking lot and looked back at the body in a growing pool of dark blood below the yellow streetlights. No one knows why Bressler shot Robert James, whether it was the moral injuries of Al Dora, his perceived betrayal by his unit, a PTSD flashback, the prescriptions, the booze, or a mix of them all. All anyone that knew him could be sure of was that he came home from Iraq different.

Bastien's thoughts were racing as they pulled away. It was a bank parking lot. A bank! It was sure to have cameras. They had parked near a streetlight. He was done for. It was just a matter of time until the cops came to his door. He had not known what was coming. He thought Louie was just going to kick the guy's ass, maybe put a gun in his face and watch him squirm. But Louie was not the same Louie anymore. He was not even the crazy Louie from Iraq. He was full-on nuts. He was on all kinds of medications and it was becoming obvious that when he got drunk he would snap. Bastien did not know what to do, so he just said, "Let's just go home."[12]

They drove back to the party with cigarettes as if nothing had happened. It was late, and most of the soldiers had left. One was passed out on the couch. Bressler went home. Bastien, still upset over the murder, picked a fight with his wife. Jackie wanted to take a bath; he said she was too drunk and would drown. He slapped her, calling her a bitch and a whore. She ran to get a phone to call the cops. He dragged her into the bedroom and told her to shut up. She came out again, screaming. The soldier who had passed out on the couch woke up and called 911. When the police arrived, they found scabbed-over burns on Jackie. She had tried to go out with her friends a week before and he had held her down, pushing his cigarette into her chest again and again as he told her she wasn't going anywhere.[13]

Bastien was taken to jail, but didn't think much of it. He would get his wife to refuse to testify, just like the time before and the time before that. The case would be dismissed. The next afternoon, when Bastien bailed himself out of jail, he called Bressler to pick him up. They used the money they had taken from Robert James—about thirty dollars—to buy a small bag of weed.

Neither of them ever mentioned the murder to anyone. That is why, months later, Bressler could assure Eastridge that the medic was cool. But Bastien and Bressler's relationship went deeper than a shared vow of silence. Bressler felt he owed the medic his life.

Four days after the murder, Bressler took his wife out to a fondue restaurant around the corner from Rum Bay to celebrate their first wedding anniversary. They had cheese and chocolate dips, and had the waitress take several photos of them smiling arm and arm. In the photos, Bressler's eyes looked vacant and deranged. The lids drooped unevenly. The smile was crooked and forced. It was a different face from their wedding a year before. Late that night, the couple went to a topless bar just a few blocks from their apartment called PT's Show-club. By the time they left, Bressler was too drunk to drive. His wife tried to take the keys, but he grabbed her by the hair and slammed her head against the car door. He screamed and talked gibberish as if he was out of his mind. Back at the apartment, he became enraged because he had left his ID and credit card at the strip club. Tira ran to the bathroom and tried to lock herself in, but Bressler pushed open the door. He had her silver revolver in his hand and growled, "Kill me! If you don't kill me right now, I'm going to kill you!"[14]

He kept shoving the gun toward her, saying, "Here, do it! Do it!" Tira grabbed the gun and shook the shells into her hand. She shoved her husband out of the bathroom and locked the door.

The next morning, Tira could not wake her husband up. That night, Bressler had uncapped a bottle of antidepressants called Remeron and another of antiseizure pills called Depakote and swallowed them all with a chaser of Jack Daniels. Tira found him almost dead in his own vomit on a mattress on the floor the next morning. She immediately called Bastien, since he was a medic, and said, "What should I do?"

"Call 911!" Bastien said and rushed over.[15]

Just over a month before, the Food and Drug Administration started requiring the maker of Remeron to add a stern "black box label" to the drug, warning that it increased the likelihood of suicidal behavior. Just over a year later, the FDA required the maker of Depakote to add a similar warning. One of the problems with prescribing so many drugs to troubled soldiers is the murkiness its adds when things go wrong. How much of Bressler's actions were due to his combat stress injuries and how much were due to his regimen of prescriptions? It is impossible to know. Even so, the habit of medicating soldiers continues to grow. By 2009, 106,000 soldiers were on prescription drugs, many of them for behavioral health issues.[16]

Bressler was in a coma for a week, then doctors moved him to a locked suicide ward in Cedar Springs, the local civilian psychiatric hospital. Bressler and Bastien's crime spree could have ended there. Bressler's commanders in the Rear D at Fort Carson could have acknowledged that the soldier was deeply disturbed and needed help. They could have visited him to offer words of encouragement and followed up to make sure he was on an effective treatment plan, but to much of the battalion Bressler was just a shit bag who had tried to punch a superior. The fact that he was now trying to commit suicide just proved how worthless and unfit for the infantry he was.

The old lines from Shakespeare, "For he to-day that sheds his blood with me, Shall be my brother; be he ne'er so vile," that the battalion had introduced soldiers like Bressler to in Korea—the vow the Band of Brothers made to stand by each other no matter what—was now gone, just like the Band of Brothers name.

No one from the battalion came to see Bressler at Cedar Springs. The hospital at Fort Carson was in such disarray that no doctors there ever checked on him.[17] Bressler hated the nurses at Cedar Springs. He hated the fact that he was trapped there. He felt abandoned by the soldiers he identified with most. Everything had been taken from him. Finally, after three days, a soldier from the Lethal Warriors came in and told the nurses he was Bressler's sergeant and had orders to take Bressler back to the hospital at Fort Carson. He signed some papers and they brought Bressler out. As Bressler shuffled into the waiting room, he saw Bastien standing there in uniform, giving him a knowing look. He was there to spring his friend.

Bressler was sneaking out of the hospital at about the same time Eastridge was getting in trouble in Iraq. After getting a court-martial in Baghdad in August, Eastridge was sent to Camp Arifjan, Kuwait, to perform thirty days of hard labor. So was the woman who was caught naked in his room, Krystal Holloway. They spent weeks on work details, often filling sandbags for hours in the sun. When their sentence was up, they were sent together back to Colorado Springs to be dishonorably discharged from the army. On the multiflight trip, they had six army escorts who were ordered to not let them out of their sight.

Before the flight, Eastridge had spent days planning an escape. He had some money saved up from selling guns and drugs. The only thing waiting for him in the United States was the old felony charge he had skipped town on. He had nothing to lose. So he was going to make a break for it. "If the plane lands anywhere in mainland Europe, we'll bounce," he told Holloway. "We can live on our savings, then if we get desperate, turn ourselves in at an embassy somewhere."

Eastridge turned the charm on with his six escorts so they would let down their guard. He waited for a chance to escape, but their plane from Kuwait stopped in Ireland, cutting off any chance, he thought, of fleeing to the mainland. Eastridge abandoned the plan. It was not until his plane touched down in Colorado Springs that he saw another opportunity.

At the baggage claim of the Colorado Springs Airport, two big army duffels belonging to Eastridge and his girlfriend came out first. Eastridge and Holloway waded through the crowd to claim them, then came back to their escorts.

One by one, the escorts' bags came out and the escorts stepped into the crowd. Suddenly Eastridge and his girlfriend were standing alone.

He grabbed her by the hand and ran to a waiting cab, jumped in, and said, "Just drive!"

Eastridge was still wanted by the police in Colorado Springs for pointing a pistol at his old girlfriend. Now he was wanted by the army, too. But he didn't care. Iraq had taught him to live one day at a time. He and his girlfriend holed up in a hotel, spending all their savings on booze and restaurants and room service. When Eastridge needed a ride anywhere, he called the only guys he knew in town who were not in Iraq, Bressler and Bastien. Soon they were hanging out all the time. When the money ran out about four weeks later, Eastridge's girlfriend went home to Arizona and Eastridge moved in with Bressler.

———

That October, not more than a week after his money ran out, Eastridge, Bressler, and Bastien dressed all in black and headed out to stake out the nightclub. The cops had never tied Bastien and Bressler to the James murder or to the Orrenmaa shooting. It must have given the soldiers a sense of invincibility, because they were eager to pull more crimes. They had been pestering Eastridge about it for weeks. Every time they seemed to be at a loss for something to do, they would ask him, "Hey, you want to go murder someone?"[18]

Eastridge always thought they were kidding. He did not want to hurt anyone. He just wanted money.

Everything seemed to go perfectly that night. Not long after the bar closed at 2:00 A.M. a lone woman came out the back door with a money bag so stuffed with cash that she could not fit it in her purse and had it clumsily jammed in her jacket. The three watched her walk down the alley and get into a Range Rover. Bressler quietly pulled out a few cars behind and tailed the Range Rover north several miles to a cluster of two-story apartments. On the way, Eastridge went over the plan: Bressler would stay in the car; Eastridge and Bastien would sneak up on her infantry-style, low and silent, using hand signals to communicate. No shooting, Eastridge said. They would just grab the money and take off.

The Range Rover pulled into a spot next to the apartments and Bressler parked a dozen spaces away. Eastridge and Bastien slipped out. Eastridge crept behind the rows of cars, staying low. He was a car away from the Range Rover—so close that he could see the club manager get out with her big bag of money—when suddenly Bastien came running up in plain sight, yelling for her to get down. The club manager jumped back in her SUV and slammed it into reverse. Eastridge had to jump out of the way of the screeching tires. He watched the SUV with the money bag peel out into the night.

"I fucking hate you!" Eastridge said as the three drove away empty-handed. He was turned around in the passenger seat, pointing Bressler's silver revolver at Bastien and lambasting him for ruining the heist. Bastien tried to make excuses. He said he wasn't to blame. He swore he would make it up to Eastridge.

"Stop fucking talking," Eastridge said. "Don't ever talk to me again." He turned to Bressler and said, "This is all your fault. I told you he was a piece of shit."

Bressler stared silently ahead as he steered toward his apartment through a deteriorating neighborhood of cheap ranch houses just east of the center of Colorado Springs. Bastien was still trying to shovel excuses at Eastridge from the backseat to make things right. Eastridge was still berating him. Up ahead Bastien saw a young black woman walking on the side of the road in the dark.

Bastien said he would rob her to make up for his mistake.[19]

"Dude, it's five in the fucking morning in the poorest neighborhood in the city," Eastridge said. "This girl's got nothing. She's broke, I guarantee you."

Pull over anyway, Bastien said. Whatever she had, he would give it to Eastridge.

"I don't want it. She ain't got nothing," Eastridge said. "Shut the fuck up. Stop talking. We're going to drop you off at your hou—"

Eastridge was interrupted by the sound of the woman hitting the hood of the Suzuki. Bressler had swerved onto the shoulder and clipped her. She flew up onto the hood and slammed into the windshield.

The woman's name was Erica Ham. She was nineteen and had just graduated from high school. At home she had a five-month-old son. She was dressed in dark blue scrubs and was on her way to the bus stop at dawn to catch a ride to work at a local retirement home. When the car hit her, she thought it was an accident. It did not even occur to her that someone would run her down on purpose.[20]

The loud thump of her hitting the hood forced Eastridge to turn from yelling at Bastien. He was shocked to see a face pressed against the windshield, and yelled, "Stop the car! Stop the car!"

Bressler slammed on the brakes and the girl hit the pavement. Bastien jumped out of the backseat and tried to grab her backpack. At first Ham thought Bastien had gotten out to help her. Then he started punching her in the head.

"I ain't got no money. What do you want?" Ham stammered as Bastien tugged at the bag.

One of the things Iraq does, Eastridge said years later, is warp a soldier's sense of what he called "escalation of force." "Before Iraq, if someone had talked shit to me, I might have ignored them or insulted them back," he explained. "If someone had pushed me, I might have pushed them back. In Iraq, that is dangerous. If someone is acting aggressive in any way, you just kill them and end it. If you don't, you are taking a risk. And that is how some guys are when they come back, too."

When Ham started pushing Bastien away, he pulled out the knife Eastridge had given him earlier that night and slashed Ham across the forehead, opening the skin to the bone. Then he stabbed her in her left eye, then in the left arm, then three times in the ribs, and left her for dead. Air whimpered out of the hole Bastien cut in her lung as she gazed at him in shock. Bastien ripped the bag away and took a step back toward the car. Ham started to get up and Eastridge jumped out with his pistol and yelled, "Get the fuck on the ground!"

They climbed in the car and sped off.

"Check it out. I stabbed that bitch," Bastien said as they pulled away.[21] In the bag they found a few dirty baby clothes, a can of spaghetti, and a Bible Ham liked to read at work.

Ham stumbled to her feet with blood streaming down her face. She tried to flag down a passing car, but the driver steered past. She pulled out her phone and called 911, giving woozy directions before collapsing and passing out with the phone still to her ear. She was in the hospital for a month. After getting out, she returned to work but was fired from her job because she missed too many days from constant lung infections. She became so terrified of Colorado Springs that she moved to another state. She had never thought much about the war. She did not know what PTSD was. That night changed her forever, she said. "I'm so angry now, and scared. I'm reminded of them every day when I look at my scars."

Erica Ham paid a heavy price for the army's shortchanging of the hardest-hit troops. And in some ways, everyone does. The combat stress wounds and moral injuries that go unaddressed in returning troops do not simply disappear. They seep into society. They become alcoholism and domestic violence, divorce, unemployment, drug abuse, and bad parenting that can echo for generations. Only in the rarest occasions do they lash out like they did at Erica Ham, but when they do, it is a warning sign of a much broader problem. Each damaged veteran who returns is a stone tossed into the pool of the nation's well being. The ripples spread to every bank. Though most Americans' lives changed little during the Iraq War, and the sacrifices made by troops and their families are easy for most to overlook, eventually we all pay the price.

After the stabbing, Eastridge stared silently out the car window at the first gray signs of dawn and thought to himself, "That's the end of it. These guys are totally nuts. I want nothing to do with them." Two days later, he turned himself in to the Colorado Springs police for his eighteen-month-old felony charge. He spent thirty days in jail before his mother and Bressler bailed him out to await trial. During the month Eastridge was behind bars, Bastien got arrested again for domestic violence, and Bressler shot up another house in the neighborhood. For Eastridge, time in a cell was a good thing.

"Locked up I felt safe," he said later. "No one was going to shoot me. No one was going to blow me up. I had constantly been having nightmares about me killing people or me getting killed. And I started to feel more secure. I started to get over some of my PTSD."

When Eastridge got out of jail on November 28, 2007, the army picked him up in the jail lobby, took him to Fort Carson, and gave him an "other than honorable" discharge. He did not receive any kind of medical exam or mental health screening on his way out. He was not given medical retirement.

After two tours in the worst places in Iraq and multiple IED blasts, Eastridge was depressed, paranoid, abusing drugs, and haunted by nightmares, and he was a violent, trained killer. Doctors in Baghdad had diagnosed him with PTSD, anxiety, and depression, noting that he had thoughts of homicide. Doctors at Fort Carson had diagnosed him with a traumatic brain injury. Commanders in Baghdad had flagged him as too dangerous to keep in Iraq, but his unit at Fort Carson tossed him out on the streets of Colorado Springs with no supervision. He had more kills than most serial murderers, but once he was out of the army, he was no longer Fort Carson's problem. He was on his own.

"I had no job training," Eastridge said later. "All I knew how to do is kill people."

Almost immediately after his release, he started planning to rob club owners again.

On the night of November 30, 2007, Eastridge and Bressler went to pick up Bastien at his apartment, ostensibly to celebrate Eastridge's newfound freedom. When they arrived, they told the medic it was actually a "work night" and they were going out to case the bars on Tejon Street for another stickup.[22]

A few hours later, they sat drinking beers at a martini bar on Tejon called the Rendezvous Lounge when Specialist Kevin Shields walked in. Shields, too, had been sitting for months in the Rear D after a suicide attempt. He was just a few days from being medically retired and had a job lined up with Hewlett-Packard. That night was his twenty-fourth birthday—the first birthday he had spent in the United States since turning twenty-one—and he wanted to go out to celebrate. His wife, Svetlana, was nine weeks pregnant, so she told him to go out without her.

When he walked into the bar, Bressler said, "Check it out, there's Shields."

Bastien knew Shields was celebrating because he had ordered pizzas for everyone at work that day. "Yo, it's his birthday," Bastien said. "Let's buy him a shot."[23]

They did not really like Shields. They thought he was a pussy for getting out of combat duty and trying to commit suicide in Iraq.[24] But the bonds of the Warriors ran deep. Despite their many differences, the four men had more in common with each other than anyone else in the city.[25] They yelled to Shields over the music and waved him to an adjoining seat, then they ordered a round of Patron tequila.

They sat around drinking beers for a few hours. "We were just bullshitting about Iraq and shit, that's all we ever do really," Bastien later told the police. "Just stories . . . like 'Hey remember that time we blew that guy up?' That's all there is to talk about really."[26]

Around midnight, they wandered two blocks down to Rum Bay, where they bought uncounted shots from a short-skirted waitress who kept coming around with a tray. They played pool and drank until the lights turned on and the music turned off at last call at 2:00 A.M. When the crowd flowed out of the bar, the four almost got in fights with two other groups as they made their drunken way back to Bastien's Audi, a few blocks away. In the car, Bastien lit up a blunt. They drove around and passed the pot-stuffed cigar from soldier to soldier, not really going anywhere.

The four drove Bastien's Audi west from downtown toward the mountains on Colorado Avenue. They turned off onto a century-old street packed with crooked bungalows and bare trees lacing the sky, and drove slowly, passing a blunt from hand to hand. Then, without warning, Bressler started throwing up. He had downed one too many shots, and the stinking, watery vomit streamed down the inside of the door.

"He's puking in your car! He's puking in your car!" Shields chanted with a drunken laugh.[27]

Bastien pulled over and yelled for Bressler to open the door. While Bressler finished heaving, they all got out to take a piss on the frozen sidewalk. Shields said something snide to Bressler—no one can remember what—and Bressler took a swing at him. Shields, who was relatively sober, easily dodged the punch and when Bressler rushed him, Shields used one of his old high school wrestling moves to throw Bressler over the hood of the car.

Bastien and Eastridge pushed the two soldiers apart. Bressler was furious. His battle-scarred amygdala had kicked his body into full-threat mode, and his drug- and alcohol-addled brain could not calm it down. Eastridge sat Bressler down on the grass and told him he needed to chill out. He held him there for a few minutes. Shields asked Bastien what the fuck the problem was with his friend. Bastien just said Bressler sometimes got a little crazy when he was drunk, that's all.

After a few minutes, they all got back in the Audi and Shields told Bastien to take him back to his car. Bastien tried to find his way back downtown through the maze of bungalows, but he was too stoned and drunk. They circled past the same streets over and over. At one point Bressler lunged at Shields from the backseat and tried to choke him. Eastridge had to peel his friend's hands away. After a while, Bressler said he needed to throw up again. Bastien pulled over and Bressler got out. He leaned his forehead on a utility pole, waiting to vomit.

Shields got out and lit a cigarette a few steps away. Without Shields noticing, Bressler had signaled Eastridge to get him his gun before he climbed out of the car. Eastridge got Bastien to pass him the silver revolver, which was always stashed under the driver's seat. When Bressler leaned against the pole gagging, he had the gun in his jacket.

Eastridge figured Bressler was going to pistol-whip Shields, make him cry, and leave him there. He was not a huge fan of Shields. After all, Shields had bitched out in Al Dora and gotten a cushy assignment training Iraqi recruits in the Green Zone, but he saw no reason to kill him. Eastridge and Bastien watched from the Audi. Bressler stood up from pretending to vomit against the pole and turned around. He pointed his silver revolver at Shields. Shields took a step back, his cigarette hanging from his mouth. Then, just as he had done to Robert James, Bressler shot Shields in the face. Then he shot twice more. Just like his training.

Shields dropped instantly. Bressler stood over him and shot him again.

Bressler fished Shields's phone out of his jacket to make it look like a robbery and got back in the car. Bastien sped away. A few blocks later Bressler flung the phone and the spent shells out the window.

"What the fuck? What the fuck?" Eastridge kept saying as Bastien tore through the neighborhood, trying to find a main road.

Bressler was mumbling incoherently in the front seat.

"Did you kill him?" Eastridge said.

"Yeah," Bressler said.

"You just fucked all of us," Eastridge yelled. He was almost crying. While he did not see Iraqis as human or worth grieving over, a fellow Warrior was a different story. "It was his fucking birthday. The guy has fucking kids, and you killed him for no reason. No reason!"

Bressler turned and pointed his gun at Eastridge and said, "Don't fucking lecture me!"

Eastridge raised his hands defensively. There was nothing more to say. There was nothing to do. On the way home, they made a plan to burn their clothes and dump the gun. Maybe they would get away with this attack like they had gotten away with all the others.

They drove across town to Bressler's apartment and went to sleep. Bressler's wife, Tira, woke up a few hours later to her husband's thrashing and kicking in bed. She wordlessly got up and spread out her blanket and pillow on the floor, not thinking much of it—just another one of Louie's Iraq nightmares.[28]

———

Two days later, on December 5, 2007, the police asked Bruce Bastien to come down to the station to answer a few questions. After the newspaper delivery-man found Shields's body, the cops traced Shields through his military ID to Fort Carson, then to the Rear D of the Warriors. When sergeants asked every soldier in the Rear D if they had seen Shields recently, Bastien shrugged inno-cently and said, "Yeah, I ran into him Friday night, why?"

At the police station a veteran homicide detective named Derek Graham sat him down in an interrogation room and questioned him for hours. Who was Shields? Why would anyone want to kill him? What was his relationship with his wife like? And what was he doing Friday night?

Graham had a soft voice and a kind demeanor, making him seem more like a pediatrician than the senior homicide detective on the squad. The soft ap-proach worked for him. He was so good at getting suspects to talk that local defense attorneys called him Oprah.

Bastien seemed at ease with Graham. He said he had gone out with two friends, Eastridge and Bressler, and they ran into Shields at the bar, had a few drinks, went to another bar, had a few more drinks, then drove around smok-ing a blunt. Bastien told Graham the truth until he reached the point where he and the others had concocted a story to cover the crime. After they left the bars, he said, Shields called a woman who was not his wife and asked them to drop him off at her place. Bastien could not remember where it was, but he seemed to recall it was somewhere on the west side.

Did he not get along with his wife? Graham asked.

"I don't know. He was never talking about her like he loved her, but he wasn't talking about her like he hated her, either. I mean, you know, he was married," Bastien said.

"Anything we missed? Any problems he had with anyone?"

Bastien shrugged. "I know a lot of people in Iraq really don't like him. I've heard people say one of these times he tries to kill himself, if he doesn't do it, someone is going to do it for him. Not really threats but, you know how it is . . . someone comes home early and the other guys get all upset, pissed. It was one of those things."[29]

The detective eventually thanked Bastien for his time and let him go. The next day he interviewed Bressler and Eastridge and they told the same story about the call to a woman late at night. The police had no leads on the woman Shields had called. They had not found Shields's cell phone on his body. If they could find his phone, they could figure out who this woman was. Without a name or phone number, they were afraid the investigation would hit a dead end. Then, four days after Shields was killed, the detective got a call from another officer. Police combing the weeds near the crime scene had found Shields's phone. The detectives called Bastien and asked him to help them clear up a few things.

When the medic showed up at the police station, they had him retell the whole story of the night Shields was killed. He rambled through the story of getting drunk at the bars and finally reached the phone call at the end. The detectives focused in on the phone call. What did Shields say? How long was he talking? Did he know her address? Bastien was so accustomed to lying that he comfortably filled in details, adding flourishes to the lie each time. After he had told and retold his story, one of the detectives, a longtime veteran named Joe Matiatos, stopped him.

"There is just one problem with this. We found his phone," he said. "There is no girl's number. Just your number."[30]

Bastien shifted in his chair as if it had suddenly turned to ice. He knew he was trapped. He decided to betray his buddies to save his own skin.

———

A few hours later, Bastien pulled his wife's red Ford Escape off a dark street into a pool of neon light at a gas station four miles from Louis Bressler's apartment. Bastien had talked to the cops for eight hours, telling them everything that had happened with Shields. Then he called Bressler from the police station saying they should go get high.

It was now 9:00 P.M. Bastien parked the SUV, pulled out his cell phone and called again.

"Louie, it's Doc," he said. "I know this sounds stupid, but I fuckin' ran out of gas near your house and I don't have my wallet. I need you to come get me and pick me up and bring some money."[31]

Bressler said he'd be over in a minute.

A detective was sitting next to Bastien in the passenger seat. After his confession, the police got a warrant for Bressler's arrest, but collaring an unstable Iraq vet with guns in his house and a track record of violence wasn't going to be easy. Arrests of military personnel in the city had increased more than 300 percent since 2003. The cops had learned that many of the troops packed guns. They knew the guy had done two tours in the infantry. He had more urban fighting experience than almost anyone on the police force. He was a trained killer who had gone off the deep end. The police didn't want to risk knocking on his door and sparking a death-by-cop fiasco in which Bressler might try to take officers down before dying in a hail of bullets. So they used Bastien to lure him to a public place where the SWAT team could sweep in and snatch him by surprise.

At the police station, Bastien was willing to help the cops, even excited. His insatiable urge to fit in came out even in the interrogation room. He switched from killer to cop. He began helping to plan his friend's takedown. He showed no remorse for betraying his friend and no guilt for his part in leaving Shields dead on the side of the road; instead, he enthusiastically offered his own ideas for the trap. "I'll step out of the car as a signal, and that way you'll know it is Louie," he told the cops. "You can even put the zips or the cuffs on me or whatever to make it look like you are taking me down, too." In a way, it was just like Al Dora: hide the truth with a few props.

In the darkness of the parked car, Bastien hung up. The detective took the phone and slipped it in his own pocket so Bastien couldn't call back and yell, "It's a trap!" Then he retreated to an unmarked car across the street. A few minutes later, Bressler pulled his red Suzuki into the island of neon light by the gas pumps.

If Bressler was really the cold-blooded killer Bastien had described, he didn't look like it. For two tours in Iraq, the twenty-four-year-old had worn camouflage and body armor every day. His face had been tan and his eyes bright and alert in the desert sun. Now his skin was pale and his eyes looked dull. His eyelids were heavy. He wore jeans and a black hooded sweatshirt. His once muscular arms had started to go flabby. So had his cheeks. Since getting back from Iraq five months before, he had done little except get stoned and play video games. He was weeks from getting out of the army and had no idea what he would do afterward.

He looked around for Bastien.

Suddenly a staccato of explosions rattled his car windows with a deafening flash. Smoke filled the air. It was a roadside bomb, he thought.[32] Bressler braced for the following ambush of AK–47 fire. In his rearview mirror, he saw men with assault rifles piling out of a white van. He was panicked. He had no gun and no backup. Where were the Warriors?

"Oh fuck, the hajjis are finally going to get me," he thought. It took several seconds for his logical brain to pull the reins so he could ask himself the obvious question, What are hajjis doing in Colorado Springs?[33]

It dawned on him that the guys streaming out of the van were cops. The SWAT team had set a trap with Bastien as the bait, then stunned him with the explosions of loud but harmless flash-bang grenades, designed to produce a confusing roar and a burst of light but cause no injuries. By the time Bressler realized what was going on, the barrel of a police assault rifle was staring at him through the thin glass of the driver's window.

SWAT led Bressler away in cuffs. Bastien, too. They put them in the backs of different cars. When the cop driving Bressler pulled away, another officer opened the door for Bastien and unlocked his cuffs. He was released later that night, unaware that the cops were orchestrating a betrayal of their own.

The police charged Louis Bressler with first-degree murder that night for the shooting of Kevin Shields. Two days later, they arrested Bastien and charged him with being an accessory to murder. His parents bailed him out a few hours later. He told them it was a minor felony charge and if he cooperated he probably would not do any jail time.

The cops went after Kenneth Eastridge next. Eastridge had fled the state the day after the cops questioned him. But Bastien told the cops they would find him hiding at a girlfriend's house outside Little Rock, Arkansas. Eastridge surrendered quietly to an Arkansas police officer who knocked on his door. He arrived in Colorado Springs looking dazed, shaken, and underfed, as if he had just been pulled from the rubble of an earthquake days after anyone expected survivors. Like Bressler, his skin was lifeless and pale. His eyes were sunken into his head. His hair was the shaggy matt of a crew cut gone feral for months.

On December 10, the Colorado Springs homicide detectives once again asked Bastien to come down to the station and answer questions. Bastien was in the process of getting ready to flee to Connecticut. He had the U-Haul all packed. His wife and child had already left. Thinking that cooperating would keep him out of jail, Bastien showed up at the station. Detective Graham once again sat down across a small table from him in one of the interrogation rooms.

"We know about what happened with Shields," Graham said, opening a notebook. "We think there might be some other stuff. It's pretty important. There are some other pretty bad things out there maybe Louie did that you can help us out with."

"What kind of things?"

Graham had worked the still-unsolved shooting of Robert James months before. When Shields's body showed up, he immediately noticed several similarities. Both were young soldiers. Both were shot in the face late on a weekend night. Both shooters left no shells, suggesting a revolver. Graham had nothing to lose by testing his theory with Bastien.

"I think you know what kind of things," Graham said. "Some serious stuff."

Whether it was because months of silence had built up a reservoir of words, or because Bastien hoped confessing would somehow save him from prison, he started to talk. And he talked and he talked. Bastien talked for six hours. He told them everything in detail. He ratted on Bressler. He ratted on Eastridge. For good measure, he even gave them the number and address of his pot dealer.

Louie shot up a bunch of houses around Colorado Springs, he said. One night Louie leaned out the car window for no reason and shot a guy walking down the street, Bastien said. "That guy probably didn't die, though 'cause I didn't see nothing about it in the news."[34]

"What else? I know there is more," said Graham, even though he was just pursuing a hunch. He patted his notebook, which had nothing in it. "I have other crimes here I know you are tied to."

Louie had kicked a guy's ass at a downtown bar, Bastien said. And he punched one of Bastien's neighbors.

"What else?" Graham said.

Louie and Kenny were planning a string of armed robberies. They had already tried to pull one, but it went wrong.

"And?" Graham said.

And Louie ran down a girl with his car.

"There is something else, though," Graham said.

Yeah, there was something else, Bastien said. Louie is behind the unsolved murder the cops are working on—the soldier found dead in the bank parking lot.

There it was. Murder solved. Graham was thrilled, but he never let even an eyebrow twitch.

"What else? Come on. I can't help you unless you are being totally honest with me," Graham said. Inside, his mind was reeling. This soldier was tying together months of random crimes in a matter of hours, but the detective did not want to show the slightest hint of astonishment. He pressed Bastien. "There's more you did. I know. I just can't tell you what."

"Can you give me a hint? We were fucked up a lot, like drunk," Bastien said. "I don't remember all the shit we did."

"No, you know. Come on."

"I don't know, they did a lot of shit," Bastien said. "A lot of shit. I can't remember it all. Fighting people, robbing people. And then there was a whole bunch of shit in Iraq."

He explained the AK–47s they used as drop weapons and the killings of unarmed civilians. The only detail he left out in a six-hour confession was that he had stabbed Erica Ham. But Graham already knew that detail from interviewing Eastridge. When Graham confronted Bastien with it, he sheepishly said, "Oh, yeah."

"Why didn't you tell the police when all this was happening?" Graham asked Bastien.

"I don't know," Bastien stammered. "Like, ever since Louie came back from Iraq, he was crazy. He wasn't really like that before. And I was like, this guy obviously has no problem shooting people, so I was scared."

When Bastien had exhausted all his stories, the detective left the room for several minutes to confer with a small crowd of district attorneys, military investigators, and cops watching the interview from a control room down the hall. Then he came back in.

"We are going to arrest you," Graham said.

"What's the charge?" Bastien asked.

"Murder. First degree. Maybe more, for the girl."

Bastien paused, then asked, "What are my chances of getting away with this?"

———

In July 2008, Bruce Bastien pled guilty to accessory to the murder of Kevin Shields, conspiracy to commit murder in the Robert James killing, and conspiracy to commit aggravated robbery for stabbing Erica Ham. He got sixty years. The same month, Eastridge pleaded guilty to accessory to murder and got ten years. As part of the deal, they agreed to testify against Louis Bressler. But when the trial started in November 2008, Bastien refused.

Without Bastien's testimony, prosecutors were unable to prove their case against Bressler. Defense attorneys argued that Bastien did the killing and Eastridge was helping cover it up. After deliberating for twenty-two hours, the jury found Bressler guilty of a lesser charge: conspiracy to commit murder. The judge sentenced him to sixty years. Ultimately, no one was ever found guilty of killing Robert James and Kevin Shields.

At the trial, local district attorneys tried to argue that the three soldiers murdered Shields because he knew too much—because he had overheard their robbery plans so they had to bump him off. But if anything, Shields was murdered because everyone else knew too little—too little about war's true effects, too little about Fort Carson's hospital with its long waits and copious prescriptions, too little about the shadowy neglect of the Rear D, too little about the senseless horror of Iraq, too little about how, over and over, troubled infantry soldiers with no one to reach out to were sent to self-destruct on home soil.

CHAPTER 11

"EVERYBODY DOES STUFF IN IRAQ. EVERYBODY."

The victims of Bressler's Colorado Springs murders were not the only ones who did not receive the justice that a murder conviction would have provided. There was also no justice for the victims in Iraq. An agent from Fort Carson's Criminal Investigation Division (CID) named Kelly Jameson watched the six-hour confession Bastien made to the Colorado Springs police on December 10, 2007. The CID is in charge of investigating any crime that happens in the military, whether on post or in a war zone. At the end of his confession, when Bastien detailed how Eastridge had killed people in Iraq using Iraqi AK–47s to disguise the murders, Jameson perked up. This was a job for the army.

When Jameson stepped into the room after the police were finished interrogating Bastien, the twenty-one-year-old medic seemed broken and defeated. He had just learned he was being arrested for murder and seemed resigned to his fate—tired of trying to belong, no longer willing or even able to concoct lies. Jameson could have probably gotten him to speak honestly about anything.

The investigator wore a black leather jacket and had a chubby shaved head that gave him an overall shiny appearance. He had pale skin and bad grammar.

He had never been to Iraq. He had not done any homework on Bastien's case. He was unaware that the 3,500 soldiers in the brigade were still deployed. And he did not have much patience. To learn about two murders in the city, the police had interviewed Bruce Bastien three times for a total of more than twelve hours. To learn what the soldier knew about a series of killings by American soldiers and the systematic breakdown of command that allowed it to happen, Jameson interviewed Bastien for just under thirty-nine minutes.

The investigator sat down next to Bastien, pulled out a pen, clicked it three times and began a fast, nervous pitch. "You are in the military," he said.

"You know how much serious stuff happens over there. You know the Pentagon pays attention to it. You know President Bush is on the warpath about it and told Secretary Rumsfeld to look into it, so when I was watching your interview it perked me [sic] ears up. As you know we have many, many, many unsolved crimes over there. And you know if Bressler and Eastridge are doing those activities over here, they are doing it over there, and it is much, much easier to do over there. We get so many complaints over there—some of it is false and some is true and there is no way for us to piece it together. We have a lot of open cases. It is soldiers like you who come forward and say this is what I saw and what I witnessed that allow us to say this is what really happened."

He finished his prepared opener and looked at Bastien. "So you want to share what happened?"[1]

"I guess, if it is going to help you guys," Bastien said calmly. "I mean, I'm fucked anyway so I don't really care. There are a whole bunch of things . . . most of it is all murder, not all of it. . . . Some of them were innocent civilians that, you know, got blown up. You know, pulling security, trying to get the truck out and oh fuck it, let's just kill them. Cause, like you said, it is easy to get away with that shit over there. You can just do it and say 'Oh, he had a gun, I don't know.' No one looks into it. It is just like, fuck it, just another dead hajji."

Bastien leaned back and crossed his legs. He seemed relaxed, almost as if he were talking to a therapist. "And then there was just straight killing. Driving down the road, fuck it, shoot somebody. That kind of stuff."

Bastien explained that he had seen Kenneth Eastridge kill a number of civilians from the driver's seat of a Humvee. "We used to drive down Route Jackson," Bastien said. "We'd always steal [the Iraqi's] weapons, so every truck had one or two AKs with a good amount of ammo, and Eastridge would just drive down the road, take the AK and lean it on his arm and start shooting at people on the street." Bastien mimicked Eastridge holding a steering wheel with his left hand, then laying a rifle across his left forearm and shooting with his right.

"You know this information is not going to help you, right?" Jameson interrupted. He seemed suspicious.

"Oh yeah. But fuck it, I'm fucked anyway," Bastien replied.

"You know making up this stuff can get you in more trouble so you better not lie to me," Jameson said, clicking his pen with what seemed like increasing agitation. He started pushing Bastien for specific names, dates, and places. Like many Lethal Warriors, Bastien's memory of the tour was an endless Groundhog Day. He could not recall specific dates. Whenever Bastien would start into a story, Jameson would cut him off, asking for fine details, or injecting a tangential question so that they kept dallying on the surface of the allegations.

"You don't have dates and names?" Jameson asked incredulously.

"Not for all of them. But, um, I got locations, I don't know how familiar you are with southwestern Baghdad," Bastien said. He started talking about the roads and even drew a map. Jameson interrupted him.

"So did anything get reported higher up?" Jameson asked.

"No, everything we did stayed with us. We had truck unity," Bastien said. No one in the squad would snitch.

But soldiers traveled in convoys of Humvees, Jameson said, so it would be impossible to shoot and not get caught by the other trucks.

"No," Bastien retorted. "Usually we were the rear truck. Everyone in the truck knew we were going to shoot before we did it. . . . If anyone ever called it up and said 'Hey what was up?' We would say, 'I don't know, we took fire.' Because you can tell distinctly the sound of an AK compared to our weapons. So we would just play it off."

Bastien's explanation only seemed to frustrate Jameson. "So did you ever hear Eastridge talk about killing somebody?" he asked.

"Oh yeah, he talked about it all the time, bragged about it all the time," Bastien said.

"Are there any situations where there was an investigation over there?" Jameson asked.

Bastien started to tell the story of the day Eastridge got in trouble for killing the dogs and the goats and the cow and the horse.

"Hold on, hold on," Jameson said, apparently confused. He began speaking in a slow and stern voice. "DID. YOU. WITNESS. EASTRIDGE OR BRESLER OR ANYONE ELSE IN THE UNIT. COMMIT. MURDER. THAT HAS BEEN REPORTED?"

"No," Bastien replied, starting to get offended. "I witnessed it. But not that has been reported. They murdered people and then they got away with it because it was never reported."

Jameson gave him a sarcastic look. The interview started to devolve into something resembling a Samuel Beckett play, with both characters talking but no communication. Jameson clicked his pen three times. "So Eastridge knows you witnessed him killing people but it just was not a big deal at the time?"

"Yeah," Bastien said. It happened all the time, but there was no record of these crimes. That was the point. "I was there. I witnessed it, so did other people in the unit. But when it happened, we wouldn't kill somebody and then call up on the radio saying, 'Hey I just killed this guy. There is a dead guy in the street.'"

The conversation went round and round. Jameson could not understand why Bastien would not know names of victims. Bastien could not understand why he would. Jameson could not understand how killings could just go unnoticed. Bastien could not convey how Al Dora made that so easy.

Jameson seemed to grow more and more annoyed. "So what is the purpose of you telling me all this about Eastridge?" he asked.

"I don't know, you asked," Bastien replied, crossing his arms. "The only reason I was telling Graham anything about it was I was showing him the pattern. Shit happened over there and then they came back here in the States and it is happening here. . . . You said you heard it and you asked me, so I was telling you, trying to explain to you what it was like. So I don't have any dates for you—any specific locations, anything like that. But maybe if you talk to people from the unit, they'll say the same thing. There were times when he was pulling security and he would just start shooting and people would tell him to stop shooting and he would keep going. Other people saw that."

"Well," Jameson said, clicking his pen. "By your demeanor, I think you are either filling me with gas or making stuff up. Because the way you are talking to me, I think you are trying to make me run in circles with this crap."

"No," Bastien said, as calm as ever, as if the disbelief made it easier to say what needed to be said. "No . . . No . . . Everybody does stuff in Iraq. Everybody does stuff. You know, there are some people who follow the rules and never do stuff like that, but the majority of them do . . . and if it ever got called up on the radio, we would call it up as a legitimate kill—a legitimate reason to fire. Because you know our battalion [command] always listened in on the radio, so we would never say, 'I accidentally killed a guy.' We would say, 'Hey, I saw a guy pop up on a roof with a weapon.' There was no way to prove it. . . . It was just a bad guy, who cares?"

Jameson cut Bastien off. He seemed to have walked into the room hoping to close cases. Bastien was suggesting there were dozens of new cases that needed to be opened. "And the soldiers in your unit covered it up?" Jameson asked.

"Yeah, everyone covered it up. No one would ever say anything. I don't know anything about Bressler, I never went out on patrol with him, but in our guys . . ."

The two went back and forth for five more minutes, Bastien trying to explain, Jameson interrupting him. Eventually, Jameson abruptly closed his notebook and clicked his pen.

"You have been sitting here lying the entire time," he said, pounding the table as he made his point. "And when you come in and tell Graham this Iraqi crap and I come in and question you and you basically have no idea because you have no dates, no times, no locations."

"I'm just saying I don't have dates. Now you are saying I'm lying because I don't have dates," Bastien said.

He offered names of soldiers and sergeants who were in his Humvee and would be able to back up his story. Jameson wrote the names down, clicked his pen a final time, jammed it into his shirt pocket, and left the room. A few minutes later, the police led Bastien away to a cell.

———

Was Bastien telling the full truth, exaggerating, or flat-out lying? Initially it is easy to dismiss his claims because he had lied about practically everything in the past, but there are also a number of reasons to believe him. That day, he told the police the truth about all the crimes in Colorado Springs. He later told similar stories about what happened in Iraq to two cellmates, who then brought them to the attention of the police. Other soldiers, notably his roommate and fellow medic Robert Forsythe, gave similar accounts of what the platoon did. And Bastien had no reason to lie. He had already been charged with murder. None of the information about Iraq was going to hurt or help him.

Sitting at a table in a small, windowless room at a prison years later, Eastridge gave hints of what happened but would not go into detail. He would only say things went down in Iraq, "Things that can never be told, but that everybody knew about and approved of—basically war crimes."

The only way to truly uncover what happened in Iraq would have been through thorough, expert interviews of the Lethal Warriors and their Iraqi counterparts. Little of that likely ever took place. Eastridge's squad leader, Sergeant Michael Cardenaz, said he was asked by the army about Bastien's allegations and simply replied, "That never happened." He was never asked again. Whatever follow-up investigation the CID did, agents never spoke with Kenneth Eastridge or his close friends.[2] No findings were ever made public. No other soldiers were ever charged. A door that Bastien opened that day in December 2007, letting the rest of the world peek into what he and some of his fellow soldiers had seen and done in Iraq, was allowed to slam closed.

Detective Derek Graham watched the CID's brief, disjointed interview from a nearby room. He said, recalling the scene, that the army dropped the ball. "You know Eastridge and Bressler were doing the same stuff in Iraq that they did here. They were doing drive-bys here; of course they were doing them in Iraq. Imagine the difference if they had really interviewed Bastien. I would have had him another eight to ten hours to flush that out. Not just a few minutes."

If the CID had conducted an effective investigation, if its agents had talked at length to other Lethal Warriors and uncovered the pattern of killing above and beyond the rules of engagement in Baghdad, they might have stopped other violence before it hit Colorado Springs. They even might have been led to a battle-scarred two-tour veteran Lethal Warrior from their platoon named Jose Barco.

Jose Barco arrived home from Iraq in December 2007, just after Bastien made his confession. The twenty-two-year-old's hands were still mottled with scars from a car bomb. His body was still packed with tiny bits of metal shrapnel from the blast. But, amazingly, Al Dora had barely left a mark. The five IED blasts that had hit him in the fifteen-month deployment had left him with a few concussions. But the mentality of the war—the violence and frustration, the habit of resolving conflicts with violence—had embedded itself like so much shrapnel. All the warning signs were there. When he went back home during the deployment for a brief bout of leave, he assaulted a police officer near his mother's home in Miami.

The first few months back from Iraq, he was jubilant. Not only had he survived, but the battalion had made a real difference in Al Dora. They had fought the enemy and won, and now he was home with a pocket full of money. He lied his way through the postdeployment health screening and went to visit his mother and brother in Miami for a few weeks. When he returned to Colorado Springs, he bought a brand-new purple Dodge Charger with a spoiler and a black racing stripe.

But as he settled back into civilian life, he began to feel like he did not belong anywhere. The simple, often gratifying intensity of surviving in Iraq curdled into a vat of civilian situations where Barco did not know how to react. In Baghdad he had been one of the platoon pit bulls, a crazy guy willing to do what others would not, whether it meant punching a detainee in the face or machine-gunning unarmed Iraqis that the platoon suspected of being spotters. What had been an asset in Baghdad became a severe liability at home.

"In Iraq we were the law," Barco said later, remembering how he felt when he first returned. "In Colorado Springs, the police were the law. That was hard to get used to."

Barco had left Iraq, but it had not left him. He couldn't sleep. He was haunted by visions of the violence. He no longer enjoyed the things he used to. He did not even like hanging out with the Lethal Warriors anymore. Most of the time, he just kept to himself. He began to withdraw from friendships— a common symptom of PTSD. He had a short temper and he always carried a gun. He found himself going out to the bars on Tejon Street all the time. When he drank, he often got in fights. When he got into fights, he often pulled out a pistol.

One night, after drinking at Rum Bay, other soldiers said, Barco got into a fight on the street. He went to his car, where he kept a massive .50 caliber Desert Eagle, then drove past the bar, squeezing off shots.[3] No one was hit, and Barco was never arrested for the drive-by, but he kept heading down the same path of violent behavior. First he was arrested for hitting his wife in the spring of 2008. Then drunk driving. Then burglary with a deadly weapon. Then, at last, attempted murder.

On Friday night, April 25, 2008, while his smaller cases were pending, Barco tagged along to a birthday party at the house of a friend of a friend. By midnight he was by the keg in the basement, drunk and obnoxious. The guy throwing the party told him he couldn't have any more beer and should leave. Barco told him to get out of his face. The host told him to get out of his house. They started shoving each other and Barco pulled out a big .357 revolver and fired a shot through the ceiling.

Chaos erupted in the basement and Barco's friends pushed him up the stairs and out the door. As he left, Barco threatened the guy he was fighting, saying they should not mess with him. He was not just some punk wannabe making threats. "I'm not a fighter. I'm not a gangster," he said. "I'm a killer."[4]

The crowd from the party followed the melee out onto the lawn and watched as Barco and his friends piled into his new purple Charger and drove away. A block later, Barco told his friend, who was driving, to make a U-turn and speed back past the party. As they whipped past, Barco emptied the remaining bullets from his gun into the crowd. One of the bullets ripped through the thigh of a nineteen-year-old woman named Ginny Stefancic. She was seven months pregnant.

Because of uncooperative key witnesses, it took the cops eight months to track down Barco and arrest him. By that time, he had gotten divorced and been arrested on a separate charge for confronting his ex-wife with a gun and shooting a bullet through her pillow. The court had ordered him to seek mental health care and substance abuse treatment at Fort Carson.

Barco was diagnosed at Fort Carson with PTSD. He was given medication and counseling. He had seen some of the worst fighting in the war, had been seriously injured, and had then volunteered to go back for another tour. Given what he had been through, one might have expected some leniency from the court. Instead, in November 2009, a 4th Judicial District judge in Colorado Springs named Larry Schwartz sentenced him to the maximum, fifty-two years in prison, saying "I expect young gang members who are at war with each other to do drive-by shootings. Somebody who has been in Iraq and who is a military veteran, I don't expect that type of behavior from. In fact, it brings considerable discredit upon the uniform that you wore to be engaged in that type of activity."[5]

The most vexing aspect of soldiers like Jose Barco is deciding whether what happened in Iraq was really the primary factor in them ending up behind bars, and whether that should be a mitigating factor in their punishment. It is difficult to untangle the threads that make a killer. Jose Barco had a rough childhood and ran with a tough crowd as a teen, but so did thousands of other soldiers who never shot anyone. Barco saw the worst Iraq had to offer, but so did others who did not come home violent. There is an understandable aversion to granting criminals an excuse, especially one that might get them out of a murder conviction. More than anything, people fear that PTSD will be used as a cover.

Soldiers must be held accountable for their crimes, but that does not mean society is free to dismiss the issue of PTSD. Empathy for these veterans does not necessarily mean leniency or even exoneration; it means striving for prevention.

In the case of the Lethal Warriors, at least legally, PTSD is a moot issue. None of the soldiers' lawyers ever argued that their clients were not guilty by reason of insanity. None of them said their clients should be let off the hook because of their afflictions. It is a legal defense that does not apply to crimes like theirs. In order to be found not guilty by reason of insanity, a person has to lack the ability to know the difference between right and wrong. Most of the Lethal Warriors arrested arguably knew the difference between right and wrong. They just no longer cared.

Sitting in jail after the sentence, Barco said he did not think PTSD was real, but Iraq was undeniably a factor in what happened to him. "It has changed me for the worse," he said. "I talk less. I'm less outgoing. I just want to be left alone to do my own thing. I didn't want to hang out with many soldiers when I returned."

When Barco first heard about his friends Louis Bressler and Kenneth Eastridge being arrested for murder, he said, he could not understand what had happened, but once he was sitting in a cell for the same reason, he started to see how easy it was. "All these arrests have to do with PTSD or whatever you want to call it," he said. "The more I learn, the more I see that. After being in combat so long, you don't think a lot of times. You just react. It is like you black out. I can't speak for the rest of the guys—Bressler and Eastridge—but I think if they had never gone to Iraq, they would have never done those killings."

CHAPTER 12

"READING IS FOR THE LAME, GO SHOOT SOMEONE"

Nataly Cervantes and Cesar Ramirez met while taking night classes in Colorado Springs to learn English. Cesar, who grew up in the mountains of Guanajuato, Mexico, and had been in the United States only about a year, was in the beginner's class. Nataly, who moved to the United States from a village in the desert near the U.S. border when she was fifteen, was in the class above. Both had illegally crossed the border looking for a better life, and were now in their twenties and worked long hours at low-wage jobs. It was not long before they fell in love.

Cesar was thin, muscular, and handsome with large, brown eyes, short hair, and a thin goatee. He worked construction about sixty hours a week so he could send money home to pay for school for his two younger sisters. He never drank or smoked, but loved to put on pointy boots on Saturday night to take Nataly and her younger sister Mayra out to dance to Mexican Duranguense bands.

Nataly, who had long brown hair and delicate features, was just as hard-working as Cesar. She spent twelve hours a day at two jobs cleaning offices so she could provide a better life for her two-and-half-year-old son, Fabian. While she worked, nineteen-year-old Mayra watched Fabian. Mayra was bigger than her older sister in every sense. She was chubby where Nataly was thin, and loud, outgoing, and opinionated where Nataly could be shy. Mayra hung out with Cesar and Nataly all the time. She told Nataly that Cesar was the only one of her boyfriends she ever liked. He was a good man, and she wanted them to get married. Mayra would tease Cesar constantly in English because he had trouble understanding it. He would smile and retort by always calling her Gordita, "little chubby girl."

The three young Mexicans were a small part of the vast but largely anonymous army of undocumented workers who form the backbone of the economy in Western cities like Colorado Springs. They could not vote. They rarely talked about politics. They worked too hard to worry much about the war in Iraq and its indirect consequences.

On Friday, June 6, 2008, Nataly got home from cleaning offices at 8:00 P.M. Caesar called on his way home from his construction job to see if she and her son wanted to go out for a quick dinner. Nataly and Mayra planned to have a yard sale the next day, so after grabbing a bite at a nearby restaurant called Burrito Express, they picked up Mayra and a bunch of yard sale signs and went to plaster key intersections. They lived less than a mile from where Erica Ham was stabbed, in the same working-class neighborhood of aging split-level ranch houses. Cesar drove his pickup down the main road, stopping at every intersection so the girls and little Fabian could jump out and tape a poster to each street sign.

By the time they got out to put up the last sign, at the intersection of Monterey Road and Carmel Drive, it was almost 11:00 P.M. Fabian was too tired to help put up signs anymore so Nataly stayed in the truck with her son. They watched Cesar and Mayra get out and walk over to the closest street sign. It was dark except for a lone streetlight. Through the window, Nataly saw Cesar say something to Mayra and grin. Mayra laughed her loud laugh. Then they were shot.

Nataly did not know what happened. She heard a loud chorus of bangs and thought someone had lit off a string of firecrackers. At the first crack an instant unfolded in slow motion and stark detail. She spun her head toward the noise and saw the flash of a rifle muzzle from the window of a dark blue SUV at the stop sign a few feet away. All the windows were down. She caught a brief glimpse of four guys who looked like Mexicans. Then she followed their gaze and the blazing muzzle of the rifle, and saw Mayra and Cesar crumple to the ground.

The SUV peeled out around the corner. Nataly thrust herself out of the passenger seat and chased the SUV for a dozen steps, trying to get a look at the license plate, then she looked back. Fabian was kneeling over Cesar. She rushed to them and found Cesar struggling to breathe through a throat torn open by bullets. Another cluster of bullets had hit him square in the chest. She looked over at her sister. Mayra was lying facedown. She had been shot six times in the center of the back. She wasn't moving. Nataly whipped out her phone and dialed 911. As the dispatcher picked up, Nataly watched Cesar take his last breath. Myra died a short time later. Fabian started crying. Nataly pulled him away and carried him kicking to the car. Through his tears he was yelling, "Por qué, Mama, por qué?" Why, Mom? Why?

"No sé," Nataly said. "No sé." I don't know. I don't know.

———

Detective Derrick Graham was on homicide call that night in June 2008. When he ducked under the yellow tape to inspect the late-night scene lit by the flickering lights of squad cars, he was half expecting to find the aftermath of a gang fight. It was not unheard-of in the neighborhood. But when Graham talked to Nataly Cervantes, she told him her boyfriend and sister were just innocent bystanders putting up signs. They were not in gangs. There was no fight. They had not said anything to the shooters, or even looked at them. They had no idea who the shooters were.

One of the patrol cops on the scene pulled Graham aside and said, "Just so you know: this is not the first one. Two weeks ago we had a shooting just like this right around the corner."[1]

The other shooting had occurred at 2:00 A.M. on May 26, six blocks away. An army lieutenant named Zachary Szody was smoking a cigarette with one of his sergeants, whom he was dropping off after a Memorial Day party. They stood on the lawn of the sergeant's house talking about their upcoming deployment to Iraq when shots rang out. One of the bullets punched through the lieutenant's buttocks and shattered his hip. Another ripped into his knee. He stumbled and fell. The sergeant saw a white Chrysler 300 suddenly accelerate and disappear into the darkness. He instinctively dropped to his knees and put pressure on the wound while the bleeding lieutenant called 911.

Szody knew from the sound of the shots that he had been shot by an assault rifle. The bullet pulled from his pelvis later confirmed it.[2] Bullets and shells recovered by the bloody yard-sale-signs scene showed the same was true in the second shooting. Graham immediately suggested that the investigators compare the bullets. If the shootings were related, forensic evidence could help prove it.

Five days later, the police lab came back with a match. Slugs at both shootings had come from an AK–47, the same kind of assault rifle some in Eastridge and Bastien's platoon had used to kill civilians in Iraq. Not only were the bullets from the same kind of gun, unique markings on the bullets suggested they had come from one specific gun.

Other details from the crimes were almost hopelessly sketchy. The lieutenant saw a white car fleeing the scene. Nataly Cervantes saw a dark SUV. Neither saw a license plate or a clear face. Searches of the scenes turned up nothing of use. Police still did not know if they were looking for one shooter or two, but at least now they knew they were looking for one gun.

A homicide detective named Bradley Pratt was assigned to the two cases. Pratt had the look of the quintessential hard-boiled cop. He was a broad-shouldered, deep-voiced former infantryman with eight years on the force. He had a shaved head and stern brow right out of a Kojak rerun. He had a bristly mustache, a barrel chest, and an unwavering baritone. His steady green eyes advertised a laconic expectancy that only comes from years of standing over dead bodies. They seemed to say nothing in this world would surprise them, not even two random shootings in two weeks, six blocks apart, with one gun.

From the beginning, Pratt was not optimistic about solving the case. There were no witnesses other than the lieutenant, the sergeant, and the Mexican woman, and they had each only really seen one thing, a fleeing vehicle. It was not the same vehicle. There was no way to identify the shooters, even if the cops somehow found them. Victims of shootings almost always know the person who shoots them. But not this time. The only thing Pratt really knew was that someone out there was capping random pedestrians with an AK–47.

Pratt started obsessively sending out mass emails to the rest of the force that the cops called BOLOs, short for "be on the lookout." "Be on the lookout for a group of Hispanic males in a dark-colored, full-size SUV with an AK–47." "Be on the lookout for a similar group in a white Chrysler 300." The BOLOs were short and almost absurdly vague, but Pratt did not have many other options.[3]

On Saturday, July 6, a month after the yard-sale-sign shootings, Pratt caught what would end up being a critical break. That night, a group of four Lethal Warriors went out drinking and singing karaoke at a Colorado Springs bar. By 2:00 A.M. the soldiers were thoroughly plastered and got into a brawl with another group of guys at the bar. The fight spilled out into the parking lot where one of the soldiers pulled out a gun and fired several times into the air. A police officer named Nate Gabriel, who was in the neighborhood, got a call about shots fired. He was cruising the area, looking for the shooters, when he heard more shots. He turned the corner and saw a white Chrysler 300 full of soldiers driving away. He flipped on his lights and pulled them over.

Backup officers arrived and pulled the Lethal Warriors out of the car one at a time, at gunpoint. The first one out was the driver—Rudy Torres, a short Mexican with a thin vato mustache. Most of the soldiers were drunk but fairly cooperative, but one soldier—the one who had shot his gun in the air, a twenty-year-old private named David Ross who had watched his best friend be blown up by an RPG in Al Dora—started struggling, then went into what Officer Gabriel later called a "full-on PTSD meltdown."[4] At first he started fighting with the police, but then, Gabriel said, Rosas started thrashing un-controllably, calling the police hajjis and towelheads and "every other bad name for an Iraqi in the book."

"He was having a true flashback. He was back in Iraq," Gabriel said.

They stuffed the thrashing soldier into the back of a squad car. Gabriel went to search the Chrysler for weapons. He found the gun the soldier had shot into the air. Then he spotted Torres's digital camera in the center consul. He thought there was a good chance the guys now cuffed in the squad cars would be stupid enough to snap off a few photos of themselves committing the crime. That would be helpful in court. The officer thumbed through the pictures on the tiny screen. The images had not been downloaded in months, and there were dozens—pictures from barbecues, pictures from training at Fort Carson, pictures from Rum Bay, pictures from going out to brunch. There were a ton of pictures of Torres and other soldiers at an unofficial shooting range in the foothills above town. In some they were shooting. In some they were just posing in front of a big blue GMC Yukon with their guns. In one of them a huge bear of a man in a do-rag brandished a black AK–47. But there were no pictures of them shooting off the gun outside the karaoke bar. Gabriel did not see what he was looking for.

Suddenly Gabriel heard a loud thud. Then another. Rosas had started to bash his head against the squad car window. Another officer yelled for help. Gabriel and the others pulled the soldier out onto the pavement where he started bashing his head on the ground, still in the throes of an incoherent flash-back. Gabriel had to run to his car for a protective helmet for the soldier. Rosas was ticketed for unlawful discharge of a firearm—a petty offense. (Just over a year later he killed a fellow soldier in a drunk driving crash.) The others were let go and drove away. The camera was forgotten.

Gabriel got off his shift at 2:00 A.M. and went home to get some sleep. Sunday he woke up and realized what he had seen: the Hispanic males, the dark SUV, the white Chrysler, the AK–47—everything mentioned in the BOLOs was right there in the camera. He immediately called Pratt. The next day Pratt and Gabriel drove down to Fort Carson and found Rudy Torres in the Lethal Warrior's barracks. His white Chrysler 300 was parked out front.

Pratt handed Torres his card and said in his deep monotone that he wanted to see his camera because he was investigating a crime. The detective thumbed through the images on the camera. When he got to the photos of the shooting range, he stopped. "Who's this?" he said, pointing to the big bear of a man wearing a black do-rag and aiming a black AK–47 with a dark blue GMC Yukon in the background.

"Jomar Vives," Torres said.[5]

"He a soldier, too?" Pratt asked.

Torres nodded.

"And whose AK is that?" Pratt asked.

"Vives's," Torres said. "Same with the truck."

Pratt still did not have any solid leads, but he knew he was going to have to meet this Jomar Vives.

———

By the summer of 2008, Jomar Vives's life was falling apart.

In Iraq he had spent twelve months in one of the scout platoon's small kill teams. The teams of four to six soldiers would set up someplace with a view so snipers could lie in wait for targets, then shoot them from a distance. Military psychologists have noted that snipers, with their distance from the gory reality of killing, often don't develop the remorse and aversion to violence that other soldiers do. Vives was not a sniper. He manned a heavy SAW used to defend the team's perch from attack. Still, he likely watched each kill and aspired, like most scouts, to become a sniper. In the small kill teams, each successful shot was a victory, a cause for celebration.

At the same time, the scouts often went on normal infantry missions—picking up bodies, getting ambushed by grenades and suicide bombers, and sweating through the constant deadly threat of IEDs. Other scouts said Vives was a good guy to have in a fight and that he had killed several Iraqis during the tour. The now twenty-three-year-old private had come back from Al Dora in September. Once he was home, he was assigned to the Rear D with Eastridge, Bressler and Bastien. He was sitting in the Rear D in December 2007 when the police came asking about Kevin Shields.

Because Vives came home early, he never got the postdeployment health screening to check for PTSD. Back home, he loved to play shooter video games and go to the firing range to ease his nerves. He seemed to love being a soldier.

"Jomar was still the same old Jomar," his former brother-in-law, Josh Bahrir, said, recalling the months after the tour. "He just put a little more Crown in his coke, that's all."

But under a calm façade, all was not well. After twelve months as a scout in Al Dora, Vives seemed to have little patience for Colorado Springs. He and his wife got into vicious arguments. She said he would go into "combat mode" and seem to lose all control. At one point, she said, he put a loaded .45 in her mouth.[6] She called his sergeant in the Rear D, telling them he was violent and was likely to "take someone's life."[7] But the army has no policy requiring commanders to take action after such claims, and they had little training in how to deal with domestic disputes, so just as they had done when Anthony Marquez's mom called warning that he was a time bomb, the sergeant did nothing.

Vives's court records read like a timeline of his downfall. In October 2007 he filed for divorce. In December he was arrested for domestic violence and lost custody of his son. In January 2008 he was taken out of the prestigious sniper platoon and sent to a normal infantry company in the Lethal Warriors. In March he was found in contempt of court for not paying child support.[8] In April he bought an AK–47. He carried it everywhere. He called it his baby.[9]

That month Vives brandished the rifle during an argument in the parking lot of a steakhouse, where his new girlfriend worked.[10] In May, Lieutenant Szody was shot. In June, Mayra Cervantes and Cesar Ramirez were murdered by the same gun. On July 13, police responded to reports that an AK- 47 was fired during a fight outside of a Cuban restaurant two miles from Vives's apartment. The shells they collected matched the other shootings.

By July 18, when Detective Pratt knocked on Jomar Vives's apartment door, Vives seemed to have an almost total disregard for life, even a blood lust. Under the favorite books section of his MySpace page, he had written, "Reading is for the lame, go shoot someone."[11] On Vives's porch, Pratt found the carcass of a deer that Vives had spotted while driving by a vacant lot near his apartment a few days before and had gunned down with a .45 pistol he always carried. He had dragged the bloody carcass into his SUV and hauled it back to his apartment, where he butchered it in the bathtub. Days later, the bathroom and car were still covered with dried blood. The stinking, fly-covered remnants of the carcass were sitting on the deck when the detective knocked on the door.

Pratt knocked but no one answered. Pratt noticed one of the apartment windows was broken. He called Vives on his cell phone. Vives picked up and Pratt introduced himself. The detective did not mention that the cops had a match on the bullets from the two shootings or that they knew Vives owned a gun and an SUV that matched the witnesses' statements. He just said he needed to talk to Vives. Vives explained that he was in Texas visiting his mom and would not be back until the next day. No problem, Pratt said they could talk later. Then he mentioned that one of the apartment windows was broken and asked if Vives wanted him to take a look inside.

Vives told him he did. He said he had guns in his apartment, and someone might have stolen them. Pratt tried the door. It was unlocked. Inside, nothing appeared to be out of order. The flat-screen TV and Xbox were still sitting in the living room. Vives's .45 was sitting loaded on his dresser in his bedroom. All the drawers and shelves were neat and closed. As Pratt was turning to leave, he noticed the closet door was open, and on the top shelf sat a black AK–47, fully loaded.

Pratt called Vives back and told him his apartment was secure. Both of his guns were safe. Then he asked if Vives minded if he took his assault rifle to be tested?

Vives said he did mind. The detective could not take his gun. By that point, though, Pratt had enough evidence to get a search warrant. He called a few other cops over to watch the apartment while he filed the papers with a judge. A few hours later, the AK–47 was on its way to the police testing lab. Seven days later, on July 25, Pratt had the lab results. It was a match.

———

Matching the assault rifle to Vives did not close the case. The police knew his gun was behind both shootings, but they had no way to prove Vives had pulled the trigger. The detectives knew if they started nosing around, asking his friends, it would just show the cops' hand and give the soldiers time to collaborate on a story. The homicide squad wanted to catch them off guard, so they used a tried-and-true cop trick. They rounded up all of Vives's friends and questioned them all at once. Not only that, they questioned almost every soldier in the battalion at the same time.

At dawn on July 29, the police arranged for a mass interview in which they literally sent a vanload of cops to Fort Carson to meet the Lethal Warriors. Most of the interviews took just a few minutes. If a soldier said he did not know Vives or Torres, he was sent on his way, if he did, he was asked about them. The cops already had a list of Vives's and Torres's closest friends and singled them out for more thorough questioning at the same interrogation rooms downtown where Bastien had spilled his guts.

Detective Pratt took Jomar Vives into the first room and told him he had better come clean, while Detective Graham told Rudy Torres the same thing in the room next door. At the same time, five other detectives questioned five different friends of Vives from the Lethal Warriors. At first, no one said a word.

Vives hunched his hulking bear frame over the interview table, leaning on his elbows, and politely answered questions, but denied he knew anything.

"We know without a doubt that the bullets recovered from both shootings were fired from the same weapon," Pratt told Vives. "We tested your weapon, and what do you think we found?"[12]

"That my weapon is matching?" Vives said.

Pratt nodded.

"That's bullshit," Vives said.

Pratt, with his thick shoulders, shaved head, and stern brow did not play the nice cop like Detective Graham, especially since he knew Vives was lying.

"So you are telling me my firearms examiner is wrong?" Pratt said. "This is a one-hundred-percent match. So you need to give me an explanation."

"I totally understand," Vives said. But then he stared silently, offering nothing more.

"Look, you seem like an articulate, well-educated, well-spoken young man," Pratt said. "Not only do we have the match of the gun, but we have physical descriptions of the guys involved and the vehicle description. We've got seven guys in here right now getting interviewed. One of them is going to be smart enough to help himself out. I want you to be that person."

Vives shook his head. He said he had seen something on the news about a man and woman getting shot a block from his apartment, but that was all he knew.

"Double homicide, your gun," Pratt growled.

"Fuck no," Vives said.

"Your gun, your goddamn gun!" Pratt said, but Vives just shook his head and stared in silence.

"The clock is ticking," Pratt said. "And time is not on your side right now. I don't know what the other guys down the hall are saying, but I do know at some point somebody is going to tell us what happened."

In the next room, Rudy Torres was getting the same kind of shakedown from Detective Graham and being just as stubborn. Graham had started his interview easy, with a long parable about how everyone wants to protect their friends, but sometimes friends do something stupid, and then it is not OK to lie to protect your friend, even if you have gone to Iraq with them. Their issues are not your issues.[13]

Torres grudgingly agreed one mumble at a time, but at the same time he did not offer the truth. He said he did not know about any shootings. He said he did not know why his car was seen at one of the crime scenes.

Graham started to slowly twist the screws into Torres. Graham said he could test Torres's car and find out if anyone had shot a gun out the window. Graham said he could call Torres's cell-phone provider and find out if he was in the area at the time. Graham said if he found out Torres was lying, there would be serious trouble. Graham said the other guys were talking to the police right now. "Maybe they'll try to blame you for something you didn't do. Now is the time to talk."

Torres kept shaking his head, swearing he did not know anything.

Graham got up and left the room, saying he needed to talk to his boss. A few minutes later, he came back in.

"So, you're responsible for the shooting?" he said calmly.

"No. I never shot anyone. Why would you ask me that?" Torres said.

"Because others are talking. Were you the one shooting?"

"Fuck no."

None of the soldiers actually were talking. It was a trick the detectives used all the time. If you want to get a guy to sell out his friend, just convince him that the friend had already done the same. Torres would not take the bait. Graham went around and around for hours with the soldier, telling him he wasn't being honest, warning that the others were talking, and confronting him with the facts of the crime. The gun. The car. The bodies. Torres never flinched.

Next door, Pratt was running in the same circles. He put up huge digital photos on a flat-screen TV of the bullet-riddled corpses of Mayra Cervantes and Cesar Ramirez and said, "Look . . . all the shots are in the dead center of mass," Pratt said. "That's an expert shooter, just like you! Torres isn't a good enough shot to do that. Torres is too stupid to do something like that."

Vives shook his head. "We are all infantry," he said. "We all qualify as experts." He looked at the blood-crusted face of Mayra Cervantes on the screen for several seconds, then looked down and said, "That's sick."

"Yeah," Pratt said. "And you did it."

"You know any soldiers named Bressler, Bastien, and Eastridge?" Graham asked Rudy Torres, hours into the interrogation. "They were guys in your unit. Got back from Iraq about a year ago and were going around shooting people.

You want to know what happened to the nonshooter who was just driving and tried to cover it up? He just pled to sixty years. Sixty years." Graham looked at Torres silently for emphasis. He waited, letting the silence hang in the air for Torres to fill. Torres said nothing.

Graham sighed. "You know what . . . I don't have to talk to you anymore. Vives already told us everything."

Torres seemed to deflate. By then it was almost midnight. He had been in the interrogation room for four hours. Graham was ready to give up, but he tried one more time. "Look, I know you were just driving the car . . ."

"Yeah," Torres mumbled almost imperceptibly.

Graham felt a small jolt. There it was. An admission. It was just one word, but that was all he needed. Just like that, Torres had broken.

"You were driving the car. And who did the shooting?" Graham said.

Torres paused, "It was Vives."[14]

With all the physical evidence, the case was now a lock. Both Jomar Vives and Rodolfo Torres were arrested that night for the attempted murder of Lieutenant Zachary Szody. Through interviews with other witnesses and soldiers in the following weeks, the police were able to also tie the two to the murder of Mayra Cervantes and Cesar Ramirez. The *Colorado Springs Gazette* noted in an article about the arrests that Vives and Torres were the second group of Lethal Warriors arrested for murder in less than a year. It was the first suggestion that something had happened to this infantry unit that had turned men violent.

According to what witnesses told police, Rudy Torres and Jomar Vives had become as tight and mutually toxic as Bruce Bastien and Louis Bressler after the tour in Al Dora. The loyalty and fidelity nurtured by the Lethal Warriors became warped into a twisted code of silence that enabled the soldiers to slip deeper and deeper into destructive habits.

The night the army captain was shot, Rudy Torres and his girlfriend met Jomar Vives at another Lethal Warrior's house for a barbecue. As always, Vives brought his AK–47 with him, fully loaded and ready to go. He put it in the trunk. After the barbecue, at about 8:00 P.M., the three went to play pool at a bar. By the time they left, sometime after 1:00 A.M., Vives was wasted.[15]

Whenever Vives got drunk he turned mean. On the drive back from the pool hall, Torres said, Vives was so wasted that he kept saying they should go to the shooting range, even though it was the middle of the night. Vives then got angry and started saying what Torres would only describe as "stupid shit" about his divorce and his ex-wife.[16] As he drove, Torres heard Vives fumbling around in the backseat. Vives pulled back the backrest, grabbed his gun out of the trunk and set it on his lap. Torres was used to Vives carrying the gun with him at all times, even when driving, and did not think much of it. It was something they were used to from Iraq. When they were only two blocks from Vives's apartment, Vives spotted the two men smoking in the front yard of a house, lifted his rifle, and squeezed off several shots.

"What did you just do?" Torres said.[17]

"I just shot up a bunch of houses," Vives said, laughing.

Torres was freaked out and dropped Vives off at his apartment without saying a word. The next day, Torres and Vives grabbed lunch at a Pizza Hut. Torres asked Vives if he thought he had shot anyone. Vives said, "I don't think so."[18] But Torres knew that Vives was so wasted that night that he could not be sure.

"Why'd you do that shit?" Torres said.

Vives smiled and said he did not know what Torres was talking about. It was like he did not really remember. Torres eventually let it drop.

Ten days later, on a Friday, Torres and Vives were hanging out drinking at Vives's house when two of Torres's friends, Leo "Turtle" Robledo and Alonso "Gordo" Hernandez, called saying they had just almost gotten into a fight with some Mexican thugs in the parking lot of a nearby bar called the Workers Lounge.

Turtle was a medic in another unit at Fort Carson. He was about to deploy to Iraq. Vives met him through other soldiers and started hanging out with him regularly that summer after Turtle reportedly introduced Vives to cocaine.[19] Gordo looked like a straight-up gangster, often wearing a tight wifebeater and covered with tattoos, including a big dollar sign on his bicep. He was the little brother of a member of the Sureños prison gang and had started hanging out with Torres and Vives because Torres, who also wore the clothes and markings of the Sureños, was dating his sister.

After the standoff at the bar, Turtle and Gordo came over to Vives's apartment. All four sat on the couch watching TV over beers while talking trash about how Gordo would have shot those other dudes if he had had his gun. They often talked that way, Torres later told police, but it was just bravado and chest puffing. No one ever shot at anyone.[20]

They drank more beer and did a few lines of coke. They started talking about inviting a bunch of people over for a party that night and Vives started making calls. At around 9:00 P.M. all four piled into Vives's GMC Yukon to get more beer and liquor for the party. As always, Vives took his pistol and AK–47.[21]

Halfway to the liquor store, Gordo started talking about how they should go find those guys that had gotten in his face at the bar. Turtle said they should go get his shotgun, so they rolled to his friend's house to pick it up. Then they went to Wal-Mart and bought some bandanas. When the police later asked why they bought bandanas, Torres said, "I don't know. Jomar thought he was a cowboy."[22]

They went back to the Workers Lounge to hunt down the guys Gordo had fought with that afternoon. They were going to "scare the shit out of them" with the shotgun, Turtle told the police.[23] But they never found them.

After the bar, the four picked up a load of beer and Crown Royal for the party, but instead of going home they started slowly driving around through the humble split-level ranch neighborhoods near Vives's apartment. Gordo, Turtle, and Torres all told police they were "just cruising" to kill time before the party.

Vives drove with his AK–47 cradled in his lap. Sometime after 10:30 P.M. he came to a stop sign and saw a lone man walking down the dark sidewalk. He lifted the rifle with both hands and brought it up to his cheek. Just as he was sighting down the barrel, another car pulled up to the intersection and Vives let the gun drop into his lap. "That car just saved your life," Vives said out loud, looking at the pedestrian disappearing down the block.[24]

A few minutes later, at 10:50 P.M., Vives pulled up to a stop sign on Monterey Boulevard, just four blocks from his apartment and six blocks from where he had shot the lieutenant ten days before. Just a few feet to his right, Mayra Cervantes and Cesar Ramirez were taping up a yard-sale sign. Vives looked silently at them, then said, "Fuck it!"[25] He lifted his AK–47 to his cheek, pointed it through the open passenger window, and squeezed off about a dozen quick rounds. It was not just a gangster-style spray of bullets. He took careful aim, hitting Mayra six times and Cesar five. The flash of the muzzle and shower of hot shells hit Turtle's face in the passenger sheet. He shielded his face with his hands and glanced over as the two bodies dropped, then yelled, "No!"[26]

"What the fuck?" Gordo said from the backseat.[27] Torres, sitting next to him, was silent. He knew Vives often went into a rage when he was drunk, but this time his friend had gone off the deep end. He kept thinking that a normal person who had shot two people would act shaken up, but Vives just acted calm, as if nothing had happened.[28]

Vives said nothing. He just pressed on the gas and took off from the intersection, making a quick loop through the neighborhood and back to his apartment.

Turtle felt sick to his stomach. He knew as a medic he should have jumped out and tried to save those people. "You shouldn't have done that," he said. "Them people didn't have nothing to do with anything."[29]

Vives did not respond. "He was like hi, bye, nothing," Torres later told the police.[30]

Gordo and Turtle were not charged in the crimes because they agreed to cooperate with prosecutors.

Vives's friends never offered any theories as to why he shot three people, other than that he was "a nut" and "crazy." Torres told the cops his friend probably had PTSD, but had never asked for help. He had never gone to see a doctor or taken medications. By the time he gunned down Myra and Cesar, Torres said, "Jomar was in a different world. It was like a fuck-the-world thing. Like 'I don't care about anything or anyone.'"[31]

Back at his apartment, Vives walked out on the deck and looked out at the dark city. He saw the lights of an approaching ambulance and heard the distant wail of the siren. "Do you hear that? You hear it? You hear that?" he said, then he laughed out loud. "I love that sound."[32]

Jomar Vives was found guilty of two counts of murder and one of attempted murder in November 2009 and given two life sentences plus 140 years. Torres was given twelve years in a plea deal in which he testified against his friend. When the judge read Vives's sentence, Vives said he understood what was happening, but he never admitted guilt or apologized. He only said, "I'm a soldier and I've always been a soldier. And I'm ready to take the road which you are going to set before me. Sorry."[33]

Jomar Vives's mother, Marta Vives, was the chief of a six-person mental health team in Iraq and one of the people who, perhaps better than anyone, could see the shortcomings of mental health care in combat that may have contributed to her son's murders.

When Jomar was stationed in the Al Dora neighborhood of Baghdad in 2006, Marta was stationed just eighteen miles away at the notorious Abu Ghraib prison, then at another prison called Camp Cropper that was even closer. She was able to visit him once during the tour by helicopter.

For most of her tour, she and her six-person team were expected to offer confidential counseling to hundreds of soldiers out of one small room. Eventually, they got a double-wide trailer with a few private rooms and a large meeting room where they could hold group therapy sessions and anger management classes. They also tried to offer little stress breaks by hosting weekly movie nights. But infantry soldiers like her son often could not go to things like counseling or movie nights; they were out on missions all the time, day and night. Snipers would often stay in their tiny outposts for days on end. "They were going twenty-four hours a day for days at a time," she said.

Even if they had time to visit, she said later, soldiers would often avoid the services she offered because they did not want to be ostracized by other soldiers or by the command. "There is still a stigma behind getting help," Marta said. "That is the hardest part. It is still seen as a sign of weakness."

In an interview before Vives was found guilty, his mother said she spoke to her son often in Iraq and after they got back but she never saw evidence of his having serious problems. She is not alone. The wives of Bressler and Bastien both expressed shock when police first told them what their husbands had done. "I don't even know you anymore!" Jackie Bastien shouted through tears in an emotional call to her husband in jail.[34] But even Marta Vives, with all her training, could not see trouble coming.

"My son is my son. I did not look at him as my patient," she said, recalling his return from Iraq. "Did he change over there? We all changed over there. We all changed. It's a life-changing event. The vigilance, the sleeplessness—the symptoms that kept us alive over there are bad here." Because he came home early, she said, he did not get any of the reintegration training that the battalion had received when it returned. "He just came back to family problems and divorce and court and a whole bunch of mess."

She knew her son was stressed out over his divorce and his legal problems but she did not think to add combat stress injuries to the mix. "I know he had problems with his sleep. But I honestly can't say I saw clear evidence of other symptoms," she said. His nightmares persisted, but Marta never for a moment suspected that her son would shoot three people at random. He had no history of violence. He was always a good kid. She still doesn't believe he is a killer. She thinks Rudy Torres pulled the trigger and framed her son. "He isn't a criminal," she said. "He never killed a fly—except when it was his job."

Soldiers in Vives's platoon also did not notice he was struggling. That may be because a few months after the tour his platoon was dismantled. The new leadership of the battalion wanted to dissolve the scout platoon thrown together right before the Al Dora deployment and build a proper platoon using tryouts to pick the cream of the crop. Vives and Torres were both removed from the scouts and sent to Alpha Company. In Alpha, new leaders unfamiliar with these soldiers' baseline behavior, may have been ill-equipped to decide who needed help. Besides, as in the past, they were primarily focused on training to deploy again. If Vives was having problems, none of his command noticed, or at least none of them did anything.

Vives is one of the hardest killers in the brigade to figure out. He has never given interviews or said anything illuminating to the police or in court. While he was in a few IED blasts and firefights in Iraq, he was not seriously injured in battle. He did not see any close friends die. No obviously damaging events emerged from his tour in Al Dora, except for Al Dora itself. Maybe that was sufficient.

Dave Grossman, the author of *On Killing,* writes that the act of killing the enemy, combined with the training in reflexive fire that soldiers receive, may be enough to cause major damage to a soldier. Two barriers in the human brain normally keep people from shooting others, he writes. One is in the prefrontal lobe, or forebrain—the logical rider, our humanity. The other resides in the limbic system, or midbrain—the instinctual beast that decides right from wrong without necessarily knowing why. "A hundred things can convince your forebrain to put a gun in your hand and go to a certain point: poverty, drugs, gangs, leaders, politics, and the social learning of violence through the media," he writes. The only thing that can overcome the barrier in the midbrain is repeated conditioning similar to what soldiers get during training. "If you are conditioned to overcome these midbrain inhibitions, then you are a walking time bomb, a pseudosociopath, just waiting for the random factors of social interaction and the forebrain rationalization to put you at the wrong place at the wrong time."[35]

Is that what happened to Jomar Vives and other members of the Lethal Warriors? It is a difficult question made even more difficult because the vast majority of the soldiers in his platoon were never arrested for violent crimes. If they all got the same training and endured the same tour, why did they all not come to the same end? That is the most perplexing aspect of combat stress injuries: figuring out who is vulnerable and who is not, who is truly injured, and who needs help.

The victims are difficult to spot, which can encourage people to dismiss the whole phenomenon. But these injuries are real. The surge in arrests and violent crimes in Lethal Warriors returning from combat is undeniable. Fake injuries do not cause the arrest rate of soldiers to triple in a city. The number of murders, while perhaps still small enough to be a random confluence of events, offers a rate so much higher than the population at large that it is foolish not to search for an underlying cause, especially for anyone familiar with the ordeals of the men arrested for murder. The lives of these soldiers seem to make one thing clear: combat can mess guys up. Increased exposure can mess them up even more. Modern warriors are not immune, even when provided with welcome home parades, combat stress teams, and mood-stabilizing drugs.

Combat exposure is one way to gauge the potential risk, but it is not a sure bet for diagnosis. Even within the scout platoon there was a range of reactions. Some soldiers, years after the tour, have successful army careers. Some believe in the mission more than ever. Some were disillusioned and left the army but lead stable civilian lives. Others are unemployed and adrift. Some are struggling with the same issues as Jomar Vives.

Paris Taylor, another private in the scouts and one of Vives's friends, went home to rural eastern Kentucky after the Al Dora tour and felt fundamentally out of place. His wife had left him during the tour and he was unemployed. He could not qualify for work that seemed to have any meaning or importance after Iraq. "We did everything in the world over there and now we are qualified to do jack shit," he said, remembering his return. "I still don't feel like I belong anywhere. [The employment agency] told me to work at Subway and I wanted to choke the bitch behind the counter."

Taylor felt betrayed. He had been through so much in Iraq—killing people and seeing others blown into bits so small "you could have picked them up in a Ziploc,"—but he felt that the society he came home to did not care. He began drinking too much and getting into fistfights at bars. In 2009, more than a year after returning from the tour, the crash of a mirror falling off his living room wall one night sent him into a rage. He smashed up his mother's house and his car with a piece of lumber, then ran into the street, yelling. When a neighbor told him to keep it down, he went after the neighbor with a knife.[36] After getting out of jail, he went to get help at the regional VA hospital. The doctors gave him the antidepressant Trazodone. A few days later he tried to kill himself with an overdose of the drug. He was in a straitjacket in the hospital for days.

"When we got back, we all seemed fine," he said. "But it is hard. It is a struggle. And everything I saw, Vives saw."

CHAPTER 13

FUEL TO THE FIRE

One night in late July 2008, just a few days before Jomar Vives was arrested for murder in Colorado Springs, Mike Needham awoke to a crash in his town house in Southern California. It was dark. Two of his grown sons, who lived with him, had gone to sleep, so he slipped out of his bed on the third floor and padded down the stairs in bare feet to investigate.

Almost a year had passed since the fifty-four-year-old father learned his once easy-going surfer son, John, was under armed guard in Baghdad for firing a pistol in the barracks. The Warriors' commander and the soldier's father differed on whether he had been drunk and reckless with a pistol or trying to kill himself because of the stress of combat, but either way, after the gun went off, doctors in Baghdad found the soldier had serious combat stress injuries, as well as physical injuries, and he was flown to Walter Reed Army Medical Center in Washington, D.C. At Walter Reed, doctors diagnosed Needham with PTSD and major depression. He was jittery and afraid, but he was in a locked mental ward where his father at least knew he was safe and getting help. His family expected him to stay at the hospital for several months until he stabilized and was medically retired from the army, but less than three weeks after he arrived, in October 2007, the soldier got notice that he was being shipped back to Fort Carson for a possible court-martial.

Mike Needham, a successful electrical engineer who had worked in army intelligence during the Vietnam War, packed up his car the day he heard the news and drove more than a thousand miles to Fort Carson to find out what the heck was going on. When he got there, he almost did not recognize his son. The stereotypically mellow California surfer was now tense, dark, and sullen.

Mike Needham had always been a little skeptical about veterans' flash-backs. He thought there was some truth to them, but stories of full-on hallu-cinations in which the guy thought he was back in the jungle were probably a little exaggerated. Then he took John to stay with him in a hotel suite after he arrived at Fort Carson in 2007 and woke up to find him hiding behind a cof-fee table, completely naked.

"What are you doing?" Mike asked, cocking is head and peering at his son through the dark.

"Get down," John hissed. "They are right there. Right there!"

He motioned to a fan whirring quietly in the corner of the room. He was convinced it was a machine-gun nest.

"What?" Mike said. He looked around the empty sitting room of their suite. "John, it's me. It's dad," he said. "John, we're in Colorado Springs. We're in the United States."[1]

Slowly he was able to talk his son out of the delusion, but over the com-ing months the flashbacks returned again and again. They almost always came at night. Alcohol often set them off, as did emotional distress, but sometimes they would take over without warning. In every case, John would take off all of his clothes. And in every case, when his father tried to talk to him about the bizarre episodes the next morning, John would glance at him with an odd look and say he did not know what his father was talking about. In many ways, his behavior resembled the actions of Louis Bressler or Jomar Vives—bizarre acts late at night, usually after drinking, and without a clear sense the next day of what had happened.

His father started to asked him what in Iraq had done this to him.

"Dad," John said, "there is no way you could understand." He started trying to describe Al Dora. It was more than just the endless raids, the near-death experiences, or digging giant IEDs up by hand. It was more than being hit by explosions again and again or seeing buddies killed. It was the killing. Guys in his platoon would kill people for no reason, he said. Sometimes they would then mutilate the bodies, he told his father, and sometimes plant weapons on them to make it look like they deserved it.

"John," Mike said, a bit shocked, "you have to tell someone about this. You have to. If you don't, you could be punished for not speaking up."[2]

A few days later, John's father had him sit down with a tape recorder and Georg-Andreas Pogany, the veteran's advocate. Out of the session came a let-ter to the inspector general's office—the branch of the army that investigates the army—that began "The purpose of my letter is to report what I believe to be war crimes and violation of the laws of armed conflict I personally witnessed while deployed to Iraq." In three pages, John detailed five instances where he said members of his platoon of Baker Company needlessly killed civilians in Al Dora. A kid on a bicycle was shot without cause while riding past a spot where soldiers were waiting for an IED planter, John said. When John tried to render aid, a sergeant told him to just "let him bleed out." During another mission, John said, he responded to a radio call of a firefight and found a bleeding Iraqi next to what looked suspiciously like a "drop weapon." The man was still alive. He said he watched one of his sergeants shoot him twice to kill him. On another day, he said, he saw the gruesome aftermath of a soldier in his platoon who detained a man, bound his hands, and skinned his face.

"In June 2007," he wrote detailing his last allegation, "[my sergeant] caused an Iraqi male to be stopped, questioned, detained, and killed. We had no evidence of the Iraqi being an insurgent or terrorist. In any event, he posed no threat. Although I did not personally witness the killing, I did observe [my sergeant] dismember the body and parading of it while it was tied to the hood of a Humvee while driving around the *muhalla* [neighborhood] while the interpreter blared warnings in Arabic over the loudspeaker. I have a photo that shows [my sergeant] removing the victim's brains."[3]

He ended the letter by saying, "My experiences have taken a terrible toll on me. I suffer from PTSD and depression. I had no way to stop the ugly actions of my unit. When I refused to participate they began to abuse and harass me."[4] Needham met with army investigators, but nothing further came of his letter. Investigators were unable to substantiate his claims. A handful of the soldiers he named were later awarded bronze stars.

A doctor's note Needham carried when he arrived at Fort Carson from Walter Reed in November 2007 said he needed treatment for his PTSD and a screening for traumatic brain injury. The attention he received at Evans Army Hospital did not amount to much. He was kept on a half dozen medications that made him drowsy and listless, but never had regular sessions with a psychiatrist. Instead, he was required to sit in the Rear D with Shields, Bressler, Bastien, and Vives. When he fell asleep from his medications while sitting with the other shelved soldiers, a sergeant barked, "This is no time to sleep!" When Needham stared at the sergeant in confusion, the sergeant called him a pussy and yelled at him, "I will break your face."[5]

Late in November 2007, just before Shields was killed, Needham was given permission to go home for Thanksgiving. His father was afraid of what would happen if his son went back to Fort Carson. He thought it was entirely possible that he would kill himself or someone else. He was also afraid that fellow soldiers might hurt him if they learned about his letter to the inspector general.

So Mike Needham checked his son into Balboa Naval Hospital in San Diego, not far from their house, claiming he had reinjured his back. "We basically kidnapped him," his father said. "I could not let him go back."

Eventually, John Needham had his place of duty officially changed to the navy hospital in San Diego. He spent months there going through mandatory drug and alcohol abuse classes because he had been caught drinking in Iraq, and going to occasional sessions with a psychiatrist. He was given a few light work details, such as moving beds to different rooms, but most of time he just sat around in his room, heavily medicated, waiting for his medical retirement process to be complete.

He was put on powerful antipsychotics, an antidepressant, an antiseizure drug used to calm PTSD, and a potent blood-pressure drug used to silence nightmares. According to the drug makers, side effects of the cocktail can include hangover-like symptoms, short-term memory loss, irritability, aggression, hallucinations, sleepwalking, paranoia, and panic attacks. So many of the side effects resembled the symptoms of his disorders that it was hard to know if the drugs were making him better or worse.

John got out of the army on July 18, 2008—the same day police seized Jomar Vives's assault rifle. John was medically retired for PTSD and injuries to his back and given an honorable discharge. But when he came back to his father's house near the beach in San Clemente, California, he was a different person from the surfer who drove off in a recruiter's car two years before.

"I saw almost nothing of the son I knew," his father said. "He used to smile all the time. Now he never smiled. He could not hear very well because of the IED blasts. He was in constant pain from his back. I just saw a hopelessly fucked up individual."

John could not go out to restaurants because the crowds made him too jumpy. He did not like to drive on the highway for fear of IEDs. He had little interest in surfing anymore, and even if he did, the cracked vertebrae in his back crippled any chance of carving a wave like he used to. He readily admitted he had been shattered in Iraq, but at the same time he yearned to go back. He said he felt like a ghost. He was living in the civilian world but haunted by Iraq, and part of neither. When he got out of the army, one of the few things he told his dad he really wanted to do was buy a gun—an M–4 assault rifle like the one he used to carry in Iraq. Mike Needham was against having guns in his house, especially given his son's state. When he said no, John kept hounding him like a junkie angling for a fix. If not an assault rifle, he said, then a pistol. He needed something to protect himself. They eventually compromised on a harmless toy Air Soft pellet gun. John carried it constantly.

Mike had always been able to offer his three boys a good life. They grew up on the beach and traveled extensively together. They golfed together all the time. When twenty-five-year-old John came home unable to live on his own, Mike rented a handsome, stucco, 2,500-square-foot town house next to a golf course in a community called Talega on the steep, grassy hills above San Clemente and moved in with John, his younger brother Matt, and Matt's girlfriend, Jen, to try to give John a quiet, stable place to live.

———

When Mike reached the bottom of the stairs that July night in 2008, he looked around in his dark townhouse for the noise he had heard from his bedroom. He walked down the hall and clicked on a lamp. In the corner he saw the blond curls of his son's head sticking up from behind a sofa that had been pushed out from the wall.

"John. John," Mike said softly, as if waking his son from a deep sleep. "John, it's me. It's your dad, John . . . John? . . . Listen to me . . ."

Mike never wanted to be abrupt while trying to bring his son out of a flashback. John was big, he was strong. And he was a trained killer. If Mike grabbed him and shook him while he was battling Iraqis in his mind, there was no telling how he would react. Instead, Mike had learned he could bring his son out of a flashback gradually with calm, soothing reassurance.

"John . . . John . . . ," he said.

John's brow rose above the couch. All around his intensely focused eyes, he had smeared his face with dark lines. He had rifled through the bathroom and applied his brother's girlfriend's makeup like camouflage paint.

"John . . . It's OK . . . John . . . It's me . . . It's your dad," Mike said, taking a step forward.

John rose slightly from his crouch behind the sofa. He was bare-chested and in his hand he held a broomstick he had somehow sharpened. He was trembling.

John's nineteen-year-old brother, Matthew, came downstairs to see what was going on.

"John, you're at home," Mike said. "It's your dad. I'm here with your brother. It's OK. No one is going to hurt you."

"Come on, John," Matthew said. "You're OK."

Mike and Matthew kept coaxing John until finally he stood up, stark naked, and shook his head as if coming out of a trance. He looked around, and, without even really acknowledging his brother and father, walked out of the living room and fumbled downstairs to fall asleep in his bed. The next morning at the breakfast table John acted like he had no knowledge of the whole ordeal.[6]

"John, we really need to talk about what happened last night," his father said.

John smiled and gave his dad an odd look and said, "What are you talking about?"

———

Mike Needham did not know what to do. Unlike Jomar Vives, it was clear that his son needed help. John was now out of the army, and because he was disabled and honorably discharged, he was eligible for counseling and continued care at a Veterans Administration hospital, but his father worried that it would be too little and too late.

The VA had told him it would take months to get John into an intensely supervised treatment schedule. Like Evans Army Hospital at Fort Carson, the VA system was overwhelmed by the sheer number of psychiatric cases. It had been so even before the war started. As early as 2002, the American Psychiatric Association was warning Congress that the VA had a shortage of psychiatrists and that patients were waiting up to four months for an appointment.[7] That was before years of war in Iraq and Afghanistan had churned up a whole new generation of psychiatric casualties.

By 2006, a study by House Veterans Affairs Committee found that a quarter of all VA centers surveyed said the flood of patients had already forced them to limit services and institute waiting lists, or were on the verge of making them do so. The same survey found that half of VA hospitals sent patients to group therapy when they needed individual treatment and a third of hospitals said that they needed more mental health staff.[8] It was the same wave that had crashed on a short staff at Evans Army Hospital, but this was not just at one army base in Colorado, it was nationwide.

By late 2008, more than 134,000 veterans of the wars in the Middle East had been seen at VA health care facilities for "potential PTSD."[9] Almost 390,000 veterans were receiving benefits for PTSD, making it the fourth-most prevalent service-connected disability.[10] John was just another face in a vast, desperate crowd.

John's father had pushed for his son's medical retirement because he thought Fort Carson and the army as a whole were too overwhelmed to give his son anything but strong medication and long waits for appointments. He thought the VA, whose job it is to care for ex-soldiers, would be better equipped. Instead, he found more of the same lack of resources.

John Needham in many ways was a success story for the army, even though it was largely because of his father's frantic lobbying. He was properly diagnosed with PTSD. He was treated in the army for PTSD. He got the drug and alcohol classes he was ordered to receive. He was correctly medically retired instead of being chaptered out. He got his benefits. But the problem of returning veterans does not end when they take off their uniforms, and it is not limited to military towns like Colorado Springs. Every year, thousands of soldiers like Needham leave big military bases and disperse throughout the country to suburbs and small towns where they are haunted by the same problems. Often these communities are even less prepared to deal with them than places like Fort Carson.

The army kept John on a regimen of strong drugs and treatment, but when he was discharged it did not give his family any kind of guidance in how to take care of him. His father was left to figure out the confusing landscape of the VA and the shadowy realities of complex PTSD on his own.

"John was so messed up that he needed to be committed," his father said, looking back. "He needed serious psychiatric help. I tried to put him in the hospital, but the VA said they could only treat him as an outpatient. He was slowly getting better, but then he started drinking. I could see a train wreck coming."

In July 2008, John spent the money he had saved up in the army on a new Infiniti G35 sport coupe—a low, sleek two-seater packing 280 horsepower. Two weeks later, Mike was driving to work down the twisting road from their town house in the hills to the freeway along the coast. It was just after 7:00 A.M. He came around a curve on the steep road and saw his son's new Infiniti tipped over on the edge of a ravine at the end of four long black skid marks. Mike pulled over and jumped out, expecting to pull his bloody son from the car, but there was no one inside.

"John!" Mike yelled. He scrambled to the edge of the ravine and scanned the dry California scrub for any sign of a body. He saw nothing but thickets and golden grass. "John! John!" he yelled into the ravine, but no one answered. He sped home and asked Matt if he knew anything about where John was. Then they called his oldest son, who lived in San Diego, to see if he had heard anything from John. They called everyone that could think of. No one had seen him. Finally at about noon Mike called the police. He told them he did not know where his son was, but that he was an Iraq war veteran with PTSD and the police should be very cautious if they spotted him. The police said they would send some officers over.

A few minutes after Mike hung up, John walked through the door. He was wearing jeans but no shirt or shoes. He told his dad he had gotten drunk late the night before and taken his car out. On the drive down the hills, an urge had hit him. He was going to drive off the side of the road into the ravine and kill himself. He was taking drugs similar to the ones Louis Bressler was taking when he tried to kill himself—the ones that warn of increased suicidal behavior in young adults. John careened down the winding road at breakneck speed, screeching around the corners. Ahead of him he saw the curve where the asphalt jerked away, leaving only the airy abyss of the ravine. With enough speed he would hurtle over a hundred feet to the bottom. He pushed the accelerator and centered the wheels on the open darkness beyond the road. Then, suddenly, he changed his mind. He jammed on the brakes and yanked the wheel to the side, going into a screaming spin that ended just before the cliff. John clambered out of the wrecked car and started running down the dark road. He ran and ran for miles, weeping, until he reached the sea.

He stayed there by the crashing waves for hours. In the morning, John told his father, he had been picked up by two women his age and given a ride home. He was just finishing his story when a police officer responding to his father's call knocked at the door. His father told the officer his son had just been medically retired with PTSD and recounted the story of the night before. Perhaps because he could see John was struggling, the cop did not cite John for drinking and driving. Instead, his father remembers the officer saying he respected and honored his son's service, but John needed to get help. Mike and John agreed, but with the backlog at the VA, Mike was not sure how to make that happen.

―――――

Around that time, John met a beautiful young woman named Jacqwelyn Villagomez at a mutual friend's birthday party. John was immediately drawn to Jacque's outgoing friendliness and vivacious smile. The nineteen-year-old had moved to the San Clemente area a few years before from California's Central Valley, where she had grown up with her grandmother. Her mother had died when she was young, and her father, who lived in Guam, showed little interest in raising her. Neither had her grandmother, so she came to the San Clemente area to be with a boy she later broke up with and stayed in the beach community to finish her senior year at El Toro High School in Laguna Hills. While in school, she was taken in by a fellow student's family and given a room. "She had a hard life, but she was never angry about it. She was always smiling," said Sarah Sevino, the daughter of the family that took her in.

Jacque's beauty and friendliness made her popular at school. She was five feet seven inches tall and weighed just 95 pounds. Her skinny frame made her a natural at track, and she broke a number of school records in hurdles. After she graduated, she worked at a local Chili's while she dabbled in singing, acting, and modeling. She was taking classes at a local community college. Photos from 2008 show a woman with smooth, dark skin, inviting eyes, a captivating smile, and a slim model's build.

Jacque started staying with John less than a month after meeting him. First she would stay for the night, then a few nights. Then, without ever officially moving in, she was practically living there. She told John's father that she was homeless and had no family, and he told her she was welcome to stay. Within weeks he was regretting his decision. Jacque had a troubled past and had been arrested for drunk driving a few months before. Too often Jacque and John got wasted together. They would lounge by the pool when he was supposed to be going to the VA. She would say she was going to take John to his medical appointments, then they would blow it off. Even worse, his brother suggested to his father that Jacque ran with a crowd associated with hard drugs. Mike was afraid that in that company his troubled son would start shooting heroine.

"It was a bad situation with the two of them together," he said later. "Jacque was just fuel to John's fire."

Mike called a family meeting with his three sons at the kitchen table near the end of August 2008. They discussed what was going right and wrong and decided together on three courses of action. One, there would be no more alcohol. Two, John would start seeing a civilian psychiatrist to augment the care he was getting at the VA. Three, Jacque had to go.

"Yeah, I know, Dad. I agree," John said. That day he broke up with her.[11]

She cried and yelled, but after a few hours agreed to leave. She said she just needed a few days to find a job and a place to live. But a few days turned into a week. To Mike it seemed like Jacque kept finding excuses to not leave. She was still in love with John. On Friday, August 29, four days after he broke up with her, she left a message on John's MySpace page saying, "You walked out on the only thing that cares about you more than themselves. You're walking out on love."[12]

By September 1, Mike began to think that his son's ex-girlfriend would never go. He did not want to throw her out on the street, but he could not let her stay either, so that day he called a friend who owned a restaurant and asked him to give Jacque a job. Then he made a reservation at a motel for her. At about 8:00 P.M. that day Mike put about $400 in an envelope and gave it to Jacque. He told her to it would pay for the motel, and that the next day she should go to the restaurant and ask about a job. Then he told her Matt's girlfriend, Jen, was waiting outside to drive her to the motel.[13]

John knew about the plan to move Jacque to a motel. He said goodbye to her and watched her pull away. After she left, Mike went up to the third floor to take a shower and John called a friend named Renee and invited her to come over and play video games.

Jacque did not take the breakup well. As Jen drove her down out of the hills, she made an angry call to one of her friends. When Jen stopped at a traffic light, about a half mile from the town house, Jacque suddenly jumped out of the car, saying she was going to go back and confront John. She walked in the door of the town house up in the hills at about 10:30 P.M. and found John and Renee sitting in the bedroom. Jacque attacked Renee, according to police, pulling her hair. John pulled the two apart and pinned Jacque down. He told Renee to call 911. Renee went out to her car to get her cell phone, then called the police saying there had been a dispute and she wanted to go back in the house to get her shoes.[14]

A squad car with two Orange County sheriff's deputies pulled up to the town house just before 11:00 P.M., expecting a run-of-the-mill domestic dispute. Renee told them what had happened. She said she just wanted to be able to collect her things and go.[15] The cops knocked on the front door. John answered completely naked with blood streaming from slashes on his head and neck.

The cops said they needed to get Renee's shoes so she could leave.

"There are no shoes here," John said, and slammed the door.[16]

The cops knocked again. After several seconds, John answered, still bleeding, and handed them Renee's shoes and Jacque's purse. Then he slammed the door again. The cops were taking the shoes back to Renee when John's father, who had just gotten out of the shower, noticed the police on the front walk and came downstairs.

"I live here. This is my house. What's going on?" he said.

The cops told him it was "just a cat fight" between the two women.[17]

"What women? What other woman?" he said, turning to Renee. "Is Jacque back?"

She nodded and Mike rushed inside to see.

He knocked on John's door and John came out crying, "She fucked me up, Dad! She fucked me up!"

Over his son's shoulder, Mike could see the body of Jacque Villagomez lying on the floor in a pool of blood. The cops saw it, too. They rushed in and tackled John.

"He's an injured Iraq War veteran! He's an injured Iraq War veteran!" Mike shouted. John and the cops struggled in the hall.

One of the deputies shot a Taser barb into John's back and shocked him again and again. He cringed and yelled and continued to struggle. His father counted eight separate jolts over a period of twenty minutes. Mike started yelling at the cops, demanding that they stop. They put him in cuffs as well.

In the bedroom, Jacque was sprawled unconscious and barely breathing on the floor. Her once beautiful face was badly beaten. Her neck showed signs of strangulation. She was pronounced dead an hour later at Saddleback Memorial Medical Center in San Clemente. John was arrested that night for first-degree murder. Homicide detectives searched his room for some kind of weapon because they did not believe that John could do so much damage with just his fists.[18]

John told his family he did not remember what happened that night.

The next day, Jacque's friends gathered outside the town house, leaving candles and flowers beneath the yellow crime scene tape. Matt Needham, still perplexed about how his older brother could have beaten a girl to death, told a reporter from the *Los Angeles Times,* "He's been no good since he got back, I'll be honest. I mean, he's my brother, we grew up in the same crib together, I love him like no one else, and it's sad to know the person who means the most to me, to completely write them off because they're crazy."[19]

If John Needham had been a physically injured Iraq War veteran who had committed such a violent act as a result of not getting proper care, perhaps there would have been some public outcry, as there was in 2007, when the *Washington Post* uncovered rampant neglect at Walter Reed. There might have been a government investigation and a pledge for more resources to try to keep the same senseless tragedy from happening again. But the suspicion directed toward PTSD—the aversion to acknowledging that it is real—exists well beyond the army. Society as a whole is reluctant to accept that the values and decision-making processes that make us who we are can be bent and broken by combat. It doesn't fit the image most people have that an individual's personality is fixed and incorruptible. To admit that is to admit that none of us truly knows ourselves. Many people instead view PTSD as a pop psychology label that criminals hide behind when they get caught.

And so John Needham's killing of Jacqwelyn Villagomez, and the horrors of combat and subsequent neglect that contributed to the death, did not spark any public outrage or a call for change. If anything, it just offered people a chance to voice their predisposed beliefs.

"To me it seems like a cop-out," said one reader of an online news article that appeared the day after the murder. The comment echoed what many were saying. Others said any suggestion of empathy for Needham's war experience would somehow excuse what he did and disrespect the victim.

But one comment, by a poster who called himself "armycsmith"—a moniker often used by Needham's roommate in Baghdad, Christopher Smith—disagreed. Smith knew what Al Dora was like. He knew the horror of un-earthing IEDs with only screwdrivers. He had seen Needham buckle under the stress of combat. He had seen Needham fire the shot—suicide attempt or not—that sent Needham home. He did not think what had happened to his buddy was somehow a cop-out or an excuse. Armycsmith wrote, "I know Iraq changed Needham into a man that could do something to this extreme."[20]

The story of John Needham does not end with his arrest. Like the other killers, he was thrown in jail. But unlike the other killers, he bonded out. A judge in Orange County set bail at $1 million. John's family mortgaged several proper-ties and scraped together over $200,000 to get a bail bond. They got him out of jail in April 2009. He was scheduled to go to trial in the summer of 2010.

After ten months in jail, John went to live with his older brother, Mike, who ran a car repo business in San Diego. There he went to a civilian psychi-atrist for a while, but eventually the psychiatrist told John's family he did not have enough experience with combat veterans to really help, and suggested John go back to the VA. So John started counseling at the VA again.

In July 2009, while working for his brother tracking down deadbeat car owners, John and another man went into a Newport Beach condominium and got in a fight with a guy whose car they had come to repossess. John, wearing an Arab scarf and the Army Ranger hat of a Green Beret, punched the guy in the face. The guy called 911. The cops later arrested John's younger brother, Matt, thinking he had punched the guy, but eventually, after several months, the victim identified John by the tattoos on his arms.

Before John could be identified, in the fall of 2009, he had surgery on his war-damaged back. It did not take away the pain, but it did help him get hooked on painkillers. In November he checked into a VA hospital in Long Beach, California, to get over his addiction.

When he got out in December, John moved to his mother and grandpar-ents' house outside Tucson, Arizona. There he went through two more sur-geries to try to repair his back. Because of his past, the VA was careful to give him pain medicine only in slow-release patches that he could not abuse.

Mike went to visit John in early February 2010. John was a shell of the 220-pound surfer who ran with a backpack of stones on the beach to get ready for the army in 2006. He was walking with a cane. His weight had dropped to 175 pounds. "But for the first time in years," Mike said, "he had a shine in his eyes, he was not dead in the eyes."

Shine or not, authorities in California were closing in on him for the car repo beating. On February 18, 2010, Orange County investigators filed papers for his extradition from Arizona. That would mean he would forfeit the money his family had put up for bond and would sit in jail until his murder trial.[21]

The next morning, John's family found him dead of a painkiller overdose. At first the circumstances seemed to suggest suicide, but John's father says it's not so. He said John had no knowledge that the cops were coming for him. His oldest brother had talked to John just a few hours before his death about going out that day to a swap meet. John agreed that it sounded like fun, then said he was not feeling very well and wanted to lie down for a few hours first. He went to his room and closed the door. A few hours later a VA nurse making a house call to give John his daily dose of pain medicine found him unresponsive on the floor near his bed. The hospital did not find any pills in John's stomach. The Pima County medical examiner's report said he died of an opiate overdose, but did not rule whether it was a suicide attempt or an adverse response to his prescribed medications. He did not leave a note or offer any other evidence that he was thinking of killing himself, but he never had in other attempts either. His final moments are one more unknown in the story of the Lethal Warriors.

Needham's story, perhaps more than any other in the battalion, should offer pause for skeptics. He did not have a criminal past like Kenneth Eastridge. He was not a liar and aspiring gangster like Bruce Bastien. He did not have a history of violence in Iraq like Anthony Marquez. He did not drop out of high school and score poorly on aptitude tests like Louis Bressler. He came from a loving, supportive family. He was a smart, well-liked, and well-adjusted kid. He joined the infantry in a time of great need, driven by patriotic altruism. He was a model soldier with an instantly endearing smile and a can-do attitude that made him a favorite of commanders. He fought bravely and resisted Iraq's tendency to turn soldiers savage. It is very hard to look at the mug shot of John Needham and believe he would have turned out that way even without Iraq.

At home, John Needham followed a psychiatric care plan that the others arrested for murder did not. He went to his appointments. He took his medications. He had the help of his family. But in the end, the services the army and VA could offer were not enough. They could not counter what Needham had experienced in Iraq. They could not keep him from self-destructing. Neither could his family's love. The story of John Needham is the story of how powerful the venom of war is for some soldiers who saw the worst, and how poorly prepared society is to offer an antidote. It is not a story that is unique to John Needham, or one that ends when he collapsed on his bedroom floor. There are uncounted soldiers in every state in the nation just like him. It is dishonest and disrespectful for society to label these returning soldiers as "crazy vets." Such attitudes do as much to feed the stigma against seeking help as any hard-nosed sergeant at Fort Carson. These men have been wounded. They can recover, but the soldiers and their families have to have the resources they need to heal.

CHAPTER 14

INVISIBLE WOUNDS

General Mark Graham had taken command of Fort Carson just under a year before the news of John Needham's arrest reached the base in September 2008. It hit as hard as the news about Jomar Vives, Jose Barco, Bruce Bastien, Louis Bressler, Kenneth Eastridge, and other Fort Carson soldiers. Graham remembered Needham. He had allowed the soldier to finish his army service in California instead of at Fort Carson, thinking it would be best for him to be near his family. Now he was in jail for murder.

Whenever he got news like this, Graham naturally felt for the victims. But he felt for families on both sides as well, and for the soldiers themselves. He had been through deep, senseless loss. He knew how the grief rippled out through family and friends. He understood what they would be feeling. The sadness naturally forced him to ask questions. What had he not done as a leader? What had Fort Carson missed? Could they have done more? The questioning naturally led him to wonder why one infantry battalion was so hard hit. He could understand how deployments could wear on soldiers and their families, but why so many arrests from one unit? With Bressler, Vives, and Needham, almost half of the homicides at Fort Carson had come out of one battalion that made up only 4 percent of the population. What was unique about it? And was it something he could fix?

A number of things had happened to Mark Graham since the start of the war that made him uniquely equipped to tackle these questions. In the summer of 2005, just as the Band of Brothers was returning from the Sunni Triangle, Graham was promoted to general and made deputy commander of the Fifth Army, in charge of "homeland defense." He and his wife, Carol, moved from

Fort Sill, Oklahoma to Fort Sam Houston in San Antonio, Texas, where he was in charge of a specially trained team responsible for coordinating the response of thousands of Army Reserve and National Guard troops in the unlikely event of another 9/11-style attack, a nuclear blast, or any other disaster on American soil. It was a job that historically had been heavy on planning and light on action, but that was about to change. Two days after he started the job, on August 29, 2005, Hurricane Katrina hit New Orleans.

Responding to the flooding caused by the hurricane was not supposed to be a concern of the U.S. Army, but one by one local, state, and federal disaster agencies faltered, leaving an estimated 65,000 people stranded on rooftops and islands of high ground in the city. So, a day after the flood, Graham's commanding general at Fort Sam Houston, Robert T. Clark, ordered Graham and a team of a dozen trained disaster-relief coordinators to climb into a van for an overnight drive to Louisiana. They arrived eight hours later to find a state of chaos in which thousands of cops, firefighters, troops, and volunteers commanded by dozens of local, state, and federal agencies were scrambling to rescue residents in the flooded wreckage of the storm. Any master plan there had once been had dissolved as the murky water rose. Huge crowds of people without adequate food and water were streaming to places like the Superdome and the New Orleans Convention Center, and no one seemed to know what to do with them.

When Graham arrived, General Russel Honoré, a rough-talking Creole from Louisiana who was the army's commander of the Katrina response, was in a heated discussion with the governor of Louisiana and the director of the Federal Emergency Management Agency (FEMA), Michael "Brownie" Brown, over what was whose responsibility. The general looked up, spotted Graham, paused for a moment, then said, simply, "Mark, evacuate the City of New Orleans."

Whether it was a reflex from years of military service or a sense that there was no time for questions, Graham only said, "Yes, sir."[1]

That night his team called in spy planes to get up-to-the-minute aerial photos of the city, then used the images to map a dry route into the heart of New Orleans. They worked around the clock to identify the resources available to move that many people and ended up asking the governor to order the commandeering of about 1,500 local school and commercial buses. Then Graham helicoptered two-person teams with satellite phones into key junctions on the evacuation route so he could coordinate the armada of buses. On September 1, the evacuation started. The fleet of buses moved 15,000 the first day, 32,000 the second day, and the final 18,000 people the third day.[2]

General Honoré saw the evacuation from the ground in New Orleans. He said that, all things considered, the evacuation team did a stunning job. "It was ugly. Hell, nothing goes smoothly under conditions like that," Honoré, said in an interview years later, "but we got it done."

Graham's coordination of the evacuation expressed something fundamental in his character, Honoré said. He was not flashy. He was not a headline grabber. None of the hundreds of stories written about the hurricane evacuation ever mentioned the general or his team. He was just a man who was able to take in all the information, filter out the turf disputes and petty arguments, see what needed to be done, and pick the simplest solution.

Just as important as what Graham did as a general while stationed at Fort Sam Houston was what he did as a man. Fort Sam, as it is known, is the home of Brooke Army Medical Center, the military's most advanced amputee and burn hospital. The burn center is a horror movie made real—one of the few spots on American soil where the terrible tolls of the wars in Iraq and Afghanistan are truly apparent. Soldiers, often missing arms or legs, lie wrapped in gauze in rooms warmed to over 90 degrees because their skinless bodies have trouble regulating their own temperatures. Soldiers with throats and lungs scorched by the superheated shock waves of bomb blasts wheeze with the help of ventilators and powerful antibiotics. Soldiers with burnt nubs of hands and melted-away ears and eyelids struggle to learn to move again in scarred, painfully tight skin. The young faces are often seared and blistered until they resemble ghoulishly mottled masks. For Graham and his wife, it was one of the saddest places on earth, and one of the most inspiring.

Almost all the patients in the burn center had been hit by IEDs like the Grahams' son Jeffrey. In previous conflicts, most of them would likely have died from infection. But now many survived to face the slow and agonizing process of healing.

Carol Graham cannot remember why she and her husband started visiting troops in the burn center late in 2005. Probably it was as a favor to another friend in their big army family who was commanding a unit in Iraq and asked them to say hello to a wounded soldier. But before long, they were regulars. At first the burned, disfigured faces haunted the Grahams. "It is horrible. More horrible than you could ever imagine," Carol said, recalling her first visits. But she and her husband saw a real hunger for encouragement on the floor. The troops were sad, lonely, and scared. And being there for those young men helped fill the void left by their sons' deaths.

In his free time, General Graham would suit up in a sterile gown and a paper hairnet and go into the ICU to offer whatever support he could to the most desperate patients. Often he would not even mention that he was a general. He would introduce himself simply as a fellow soldier who wanted to lend a hand. Carol spent much of her time sitting with families in the surgical waiting room, doling out friendly reassurance and a seemingly endless supply of hugs. After a while, the hospital began to call the Grahams when a soldier died of his wounds. "By that time they knew our family story," Carol said. "And must have figured we could offer a special kind of understanding."

The Grahams started inviting families into their home to grieve with them when soldiers died. They knew exactly how it felt. Though the Grahams had made a vow to find some good in the tragedy of their boys' deaths and spoke to groups nationwide about suicide prevention, it had not filled the hole in their hearts. At the burn center, something unexpected happened. In comforting those wounded soldiers and their families the Grahams gave them a quiet solace. If they could not help their own sons, at least they could help other families' sons.

"We were just like these families," Carol said. "If Jeffrey had survived that IED, he would have been one of these boys at the hospital. And many of these guys also were struggling with depression, like Kevin. These were our boys. We really looked at them that way. Every soldier became Jeffrey and Kevin."

But beyond solace, the burn unit offered something vital for Mark Graham. It made him confront the very real and horrible toll of war. Even though he had not deployed to Iraq or Afghanistan, he could see firsthand what the soldiers went through. He knew how many struggled when they returned. It made PTSD more than just another army acronym. It made it real. And it made it a priority—one that he would champion at Fort Carson.

Later, in 2006, the general worked with a federal task force to place a military liaison in every federal emergency response team to try to avoid ever repeating the confusion of Hurricane Katrina. His swift thinking and cool head during the hurricane evacuation became instrumental in earning him command of Fort Carson in 2007.

By the spring of 2007, General Honoré was the commander of the U.S. First Army, which oversaw Fort Carson. He had seen Graham in action during Katrina and was deeply impressed. "He looked at how to make things happen, not why they couldn't. His focus was on what needed to go right, not what had already gone wrong," Honoré said. Graham never assigned blame or chose sides, he simply allowed everyone to work together. In 2007, when Honoré learned that Graham was on the list for command of Fort Carson, he heartily recommended him. Fort Carson needed someone to coordinate a rescue, and Graham was just the man for the job.

Honoré personally handed the flag of command to Graham when he took over Fort Carson in September 2007. "He is a team player," Honoré said later. "He never sought the spotlight. He never sought anything other than to help the people of the region, and he did that superbly. That is exemplary of him. He never does anything other than try to be as effective as he can. In Katrina he came in and made the best of a really bad situation, it was the same thing he did years later at Fort Carson."

───────

Arriving at Fort Carson in the fall of 2007 for Graham was a lot like arriving in Louisiana in 2005. The storm had already hit. Four and a half years into the Iraq War, many soldiers on the post were in their second or third combat tours, and the toll on the force was undeniable. Suicide, divorce, drug and alcohol abuse, and rape were at an all-time high. New cases of PTSD on post had skyrocketed from 106 in 2004 to 750 in 2007.[3] As they had been on the hurricane-battered Gulf Coast, the forces designated to rescue people from the aftermath were overwhelmed and in disarray. Evans Army Hospital did not have the resources or resolve to treat all its soldiers. Many commanders of combat units did not have the time, patience, or even desire to encourage troubled soldiers to seek mental health care. Even the soldiers themselves were reluctant to admit problems. Just as in Katrina, many people were pointing fingers instead of offering hands. When Graham arrived, he did the same as he did in New Orleans: he calmly assessed the situation, looked at every possible solution, then set about the work of coordinating the rescue.

The biggest problem was an atmosphere of intolerance toward PTSD.

"Right away I saw that seemed to be the big challenge for the whole post, behavioral health," Graham said in an interview, looking back on his first weeks at Fort Carson. "The force was strained. There was a lot of tension. I think people were not sure why. If you are missing an arm or you have been shot, people can see your wound. They don't think you are making it up. But if someone has an issue like PTSD, you can't see it. Those invisible wounds are just hard to understand."

The general's first course of action was to publicly and repeatedly state that PSTD was real and no soldier, no matter how tough, was immune. Drawing a comparison from his recent experience, Graham said, "PTSD is like a hurricane. If you're in the path, it doesn't matter who you are, it hits you."[4]

It may have been an obvious message, considering PTSD had been on the books for a generation, but it was one Fort Carson needed to hear. When the commanding general gave something a priority, it was an unspoken permission for commanders down the line to do the same.

Graham's two motivators were his sons. He felt he could honor their deaths by treating soldiers at Fort Carson as if they were his own children. He took the issue of suicide most seriously. Six soldiers had committed suicide at Fort Carson by the end of 2007—the most suicides the post had ever had in one year. "Every one devastated him," said Angela Gilpin, his assistant at the time. "It was as if his son was dying all over again." He would ask his assistant to scrub his calendar so he could attend each suicide victim's memorial—something no other commanding officer at the post had ever done—and made it a point to personally offer his condolences to the families.

The general also made it a priority to not let the bureaucratic necessities of his position interfere with things he felt were more important. He flew to the six bases in his command in the evenings to leave his days more open. He had his staff devise a computerized document system that let him review, sign, and forward official papers from his laptop on the go. He wanted to be sure he was not trapped behind a pile of paperwork. He arrived at work at 7:00 A.M. and often left after 7:00 P.M. He often skipped lunch. His strict efficiency offered him the freedom of an officer not forced to play catch-up—someone who could choose what was important.

"He had very clear priorities," said Lieutenant Colonel Nick Palorino, the secretary of the general's staff, recalling his former boss. "He always wanted to be the number-one person to welcome home the troops at the ceremonies. He wanted to be there for the families and soldiers. He made that a priority event. If he was in town, no matter when, he was going to be there to shake their hands." Graham also went to every memorial for the fallen that he could, quietly sitting in the front row of the chapel as the name of each soldier was read.

It was Graham's personal quest to do everything he could to erase the stigma toward seeking mental health care at Fort Carson and stop suicide. But it meant more than just showing that he cared. It meant overhauling the behavioral health system and trying to break down the barriers that left some soldiers with nowhere to go. Just a week after Kevin Shields's murderers were arrested, in December 2007, Graham announced a new plan to let soldiers and their families go to civilian psychiatrists in Colorado Springs. He knew his own son had avoided army counseling because he feared what it would do to his career. Graham did not want any other families to experience the same torment. By the end of 2008, 2,171 soldiers were seeking therapy in Colorado Springs.[5] Graham noticed that the hotline that had existed at Fort Carson for years for

it was not clear what was broken. Some thought the rash of killings coming out of the Lethal Warriors were the result of lax recruiting standards. Some thought it was poor screening for PTSD. Some thought there was no problem—just a random statistical blip that had nothing to do with the army.

Even so, the arrests kept coming, one after another. First Bastien, Bressler, and Eastridge caught Graham's attention. Then Vives and Torres. Then Needham. Then, in October 2008, Robert Hull Marko, a twenty-year-old specialist from the 2nd Battalion, 17th Field Artillery Regiment—a unit in the same combat brigade as the Lethal Warriors—allegedly drove a nineteen-year-old Colorado Springs girl up a winding, isolated dirt road into the mountains above the city, had sex with her, then slit her throat and left her to die.

Marko's alleged crime was slightly different from the others. For years the soldier had suffered from psychotic delusions that had nothing to do with combat, but the news of his arrest, on top of all the others, stoked local public opinion from a smoldering suspicion that something was not right at Fort Carson to a heated demand that something be done.

Five days after Marko's arrest, on October 17, 2008, Colorado's Democratic senator, Ken Salazar, sent a letter to General Mark Graham and Army Secretary Pete Geren demanding "immediate attention to a set of tragic incidents at Fort Carson in Colorado Springs," which, the senator said, "raise a number of troubling questions that merit serious scrutiny and attention."[7]

The senator called for a comprehensive review of all soldiers arrested for violent crimes at the post, specifically focusing on whether the demands of the Iraq war were forcing the army to let in undesirable recruits. "In the Army's effort to meet its target recruiting numbers, the service has been issuing an increasing number of waivers to recruits who may not meet educational or moral standards," Salazar wrote. "Were any of the soldiers involved in these violent incidents at Fort Carson granted any such waivers, including felony criminal waivers, serious misdemeanor criminal waivers, or medical waivers related to mental health?"[8]

Since the start of the killings, the army's response to the murders in the ranks had been essentially to point out that the vast majority of soldiers never commit crimes, but there are a few criminals in every population. Salazar was suggesting that the army, out of necessity, was using waivers to let in too many criminals. Both theories missed a critical point, because neither took into account what role combat played in turning men into criminals or what the army was doing to help them when they came home. Even so, Salazar's letter had one very important consequence. It spurred Mark Graham to action.

"I really don't believe that any of the problems we had at Fort Carson were because we had bad people," Graham said of the failures of commanders and mental health staff. "We just had a lack of understanding." His job as commander was to build understanding—to make sure everyone from soldiers and sergeants to battalion commanders understood combat stress injuries and where to go for help. Graham believed good decisions could only be made if commanders had good intelligence. Just as there was no way to evacuate New Orleans without first getting up-to-the-minute aerial photos, there was no way to effectively address the murders unless you understood their connection to the big picture.

When Senator Salazar wrote to the army demanding an explanation for the rash of violence, Graham was truly stumped. He realized he would have to start by educating himself. In the end, he wound up educating the entire army. In response to the senator's October 2008 letter, Graham immediately gathered all the people at Fort Carson who might have insight into the trend in violence: military police, commanders, military lawyers, substance abuse counselors, and Evans Army Hospital psychiatrists. "It was an informal brainstorming process to try to think of any ideas of how we could go after this problem," one officer at the meetings said.[9]

One of the doctors from the hospital suggested a possibility. A few years before, Fort Campbell, Kentucky, had been hit by a rash of soldier suicides. In response, the army surgeon general sent a team of epidemiologists to comb the cases for trends. Epidemiology is the branch of medicine that seeks to study the factors affecting the health and illness of entire populations. Its findings form the basis for public health decisions. For example, in the case of cholera, an epidemiologist would look not at the bacteria that causes the illness, but at the contaminated wells and unsanitary practices that facilitate the bacteria's spread. By looking at populations instead of individuals, epidemiologists can often uncover the surprisingly obvious but heretofore unnoticed.

Most of the time epidemiologists focus on infectious disease, but increasingly the army has used its experts to look at behavioral health issues. Maybe, the Evans doctor suggested, they could discover something about the murders.

"Right away I was on the phone to the surgeon general," Graham said later. "We were eager to get a fresh pair of eyes on the problem." When a team of epidemiologists set up a preliminary meeting with him in October, he said, "I gave them carte blanche. I told them to go anywhere, talk to anyone, look at anything you want."

A team of twenty-four physicians and PhDs from Walter Reed Institute of Research descended on Fort Carson a few weeks later, on November 3, 2008, and began an in-depth "epidemiological consultation," which became known colloquially around the post as "the EPICON."

Graham asked the researchers not just to look into soldiers who were accused of murder, but also those, like Jose Barco, accused of attempted murder. He figured the factors contributing to those crimes were not so different from the murders, and the more soldiers the team looked at, the more they might learn.

Talking with Graham and his task force, the EPICON team developed six questions the general wanted answered: Are recruitment waivers for criminal convictions and behavioral health issues a factor in the killings? Why is violence seemingly clustered in one brigade? What are the common factors among the murderers? Does Fort Carson have the resources to handle behavioral health needs? Are there barriers that keep soldiers from using those resources? And is there a relationship between deployment and crime?

The team questioned doctors, senior officers, and nine accused murderers already sitting behind bars. They dug through waivers, aptitude scores, medical records, and mounds of other data, comparing the demographic makeup of the Lethal Warrior's brigade combat team, the 4th BCT, to a similar brigade at Fort Carson, the 3rd BCT, and to the army's population as a whole. They had 2,779 soldiers fill out anonymous surveys, and interviewed fifty-six focus groups.

———

In July 2009, the army's surgeon general released a 126-page report detailing what they found. Since the start of the murders five years before, speculation had swirled about the individual killings and the mounting body count in the brigade. Opinion on the causes ranged from a sinister government cover-up to sheer coincidence. The EPICON offered something beyond speculation. It offered real data.

The idea, said Dr. Amy Millikan, the lead author of the study, was to learn as much as possible about the murders, then look at them "in context of community." How did the experience of the whole influence the experience of the individuals? What was the Lethal Warriors' equivalent of the contaminated well? "A lot of times," she said, "We offer detailed facts that support common sense. But sometimes that is what you need."

First, the study made it clear that what happened to the Lethal Warriors was not just the normal levels of crime in the army or society. The murder rate for Fort Carson had doubled since the start of the Iraq war. Rape arrests had tripled and stood at twice the rate of other army posts.[10]

Second, the report dismissed suggestions that the brigade, tucked for years in a strategic backwater along the North Korean border, had been stocked with undesirables—criminals and dimwits let in on special waivers. The study showed that the Band of Brothers and its brigade had the same rates of waivers for crime and prior mental illness as similar units elsewhere in the army. Their aptitude tests, administered when recruits joined, showed the troops were average—not stellar, but not an anomaly. At an individual level, a small minority of the killers had waivers, but most did not. The EPICON made it clear that the murders could not be blamed on lousy recruits.

Third, the study looked at common factors in the murderers—a much stickier web. Here the report failed to find characteristics common to every crime. Some soldiers had come from broken homes. Some had not. Some had taken antidepressants, some had not. Some had started in Korea and done two tours, some had only done one. Some had received mental health care, some had not. Race and marital status seemed to play no roll. The biggest common thread was that the killers were all grunts who had seen serious combat.

The data painted a dark picture of soldiers burned out by intense deployments that finally quantified for outsiders what life in the brigade was like. In the 4th BCT, the casualty rate was eight times as high as for other soldiers at Fort Carson. On their first tour, in the Sunni Triangle, the combat intensity was a hundred times greater than the 3rd BCT had experienced on its first Iraq tour, when gauged by soldiers' own reported combat intensity. The men of the 4th BCT came home with traumatic brain injury and PTSD rates more than three times greater than the 3rd BCT. They had double the cases of substance abuse.[11]

To compound the problems, the study found that returning veterans often were unable to get mental health treatment at Fort Carson, both because of an overwhelmed medical system and a macho military culture that directly and indirectly discouraged soldiers from seeking help. In focus groups conducted by the EPICON team, where researchers asked open-ended questions and let troops guide the conversations, the convoluted attitudes regarding PTSD started to emerge. Officers and senior sergeants complained that it was almost impossible to let soldiers receive mental health care while also preparing to fight in Iraq again. Throughout the ranks, soldiers said troops did not seek mental health care because they feared killing their careers and alienating themselves. They complained that there was an unfair stigma. At the same time, they also thought that many who did seek mental health care were faking it. This contradiction was voiced over and over throughout the brigade, but was strongest among the Lethal Warriors.

The stigma created a "don't ask, don't tell" climate in which combat stress injuries were hidden and treated at home with illegal drugs and alcohol. Officers not trained to handle the out-of-control troops used heavy-handed discipline. Data show that soldiers returning from the first tour were less likely than soldiers in other brigades to be diagnosed with PTSD, but more likely to be kicked out for drug use or bad conduct. The rate of discharges for bad conduct after the tour nearly doubled. The higher numbers suggested that the soldiers were showing symptoms of PTSD, but getting punishment instead of help.

At the same time, Fort Carson's substance abuse program was in such disarray that 80 percent of the soldiers who showed up hot on drug tests never received treatment, and no one from their command or the hospital ever followed up to make sure they did.

Soldiers in the 4th BCT were also more likely to be chaptered out through shady personality disorder diagnoses. Before the first tour, records show none in the brigade were diagnosed with a personality disorder. After the tour, thirty-nine soldiers somehow developed a preexisting condition. It was a rate four times greater than in the 3rd BCT.

Many of the findings likely seemed blatantly obvious to the men who had been in the brigade since Korea. They did not need a team of epidemiologists to explain what had happened to Nasty Nash or Kenny Eastridge or any of the others. Any one of the soldiers could have explained the aftermath of the horrors of Iraq and the dysfunctional indifference of home. But in a strictly hierarchical culture like the army, where nothing is done or said until the top brass give orders, having an official report state the obvious can have an enormous impact.

From a public health point of view, combat seemed to be a contagion. Drug and alcohol abuse, PTSD, violence, and murder were just the symptoms. The more soldiers were exposed to combat, the more they showed the effects. Lethal Warriors who had been on both combat tours were more likely to abuse drugs and alcohol, end up with PTSD, and get into serious trouble with the army and the law. The worst-off were the soldiers who did three tours, starting with Korea.[12]

With the broken mental health system so choked with injured soldiers after repeated tours, the fallout from the EPICON document seems almost inevitable. Of the 2,779 soldiers from the brigade who answered the EPICON survey, 48 percent said they thought they had mental health problems and 26 percent reported alcohol abuse. Just over 40 percent reported choking, beating, kicking, or pointing a gun at someone. That suggests 1,112 soldiers had likely committed some kind of felony assault, which means that even though the number of soldiers booked at the jail in Colorado Springs for violent crimes was staggering, the official arrests were only the tip of an unseen iceberg.[13]

Given how many soldiers were mentally wounded, unable or unwilling to get effective treatment, violent, and constantly carrying personal guns off post, it is not surprising that there were so many murders in the Lethal Warrior's brigade; it is surprising that there were so few.

In the EPICON's search for patterns among the killers, there were outliers, of course. Robert Hull Marko displayed signs of psychotic delusions long before he joined the army. Stephen Sherwood, who shot his wife, then himself, was thirty-five, while all the other killers were between the ages of twenty-one and twenty-five. But once the outliers were removed, a clearer picture of the killers started to emerge.

They were all young infantry soldiers or noninfantry troops who had been used as infantry in Iraq. All were low-ranking specialists or privates. Half said they had witnessed war crimes, including soldiers killing civilians in Iraq. Many said they had also participated in war crimes. More than 70 percent of the Lethal Warriors arrested for murder had been sent home early and not received reintegration training, even though they likely needed it more than anyone else. Eighty percent of those arrested for murder fell into substance abuse after their combat tours. Sixty-four percent had been in trouble with the civilian police for less serious crimes such as domestic abuse, drunk driving, illegal gun possession, and assault. Seventy-one percent were diagnosed with mental health issues and were prescribed psychotropic drugs. Only half found the drugs useful. Thirty-seven percent were given therapy. None found the therapy useful.

Looking at the results, Dr. Millikan said, there was not one factor that explains the massive increase in crime. Instead, the data suggest the murders were the result of two major factors coming together: the pressures of deployment and exposure to violence in Iraq. "Bring a couple of thousand people together with their own pasts, their own issues, their own propensity for violence or mental health problems, and you are going to have some risk of aggressive behaviors. We call that baseline. People are people, and people bring things with them," she said. "What we see here is an accumulating confluence of additional risks that has pushed the entire baseline of the population toward higher risk."

The whole brigade was pushed toward what epidemiologists refer to as "negative outcomes." That means soldiers who would probably otherwise live out life in one risk category were often bumped into the next riskiest population. Guys who might never have been arrested were more likely to be arrested for drunk driving or domestic disputes. Guys who might have been arrested for minor domestic violence were more likely to be arrested for serious assault.

Guys like Kenneth Eastridge or Jose Barco, who seemed to have a propensity for violence anyway, were more likely to be arrested for murder. It is not, in most cases, that war took guys who otherwise would have been Eagle Scouts and Nobel Prize winners and turned them into drug-addled homicidal maniacs. It is that war nudged everybody toward the edge. Guys who might have struggled with minor crime ended up committing something major, like murder.

Dr. Millikan sees the ability of the twin pressures of deployment and combat to affect a whole population as the most intriguing finding of the EPICON. But the one that got the most press when the study came out in 2009 was one carefully worded assertion: "Survey data from this investigation suggest a possible association between increasing levels of combat exposure and risk for negative behavioral outcomes."[14] In other words, the report was confirming a notion that civilian sociologists had long asserted but the army had downplayed: combat contributes to crime. Soldiers come home different. By sending hundreds of thousands of young men to war, the country is unintentionally bringing violence back on itself.

The EPICON team made several recommendations regarding what the army could do to avoid another outcome like the Lethal Warriors. First, they noted, reintegration training must be overhauled and started before soldiers come back from overseas. Even soldiers who return early must get this enhanced training. Second, units and individual soldiers who have been exposed to high levels of combat must be flagged by commanders so they can get better care. The days of letting soldiers lie their way through the Post-Deployment Health Assessment must end. Third, the army should reassess whether entire command structures should change after each tour, since it can interrupt the supervision of soldiers who need help. Fourth, commanders have to ensure that soldiers caught for drugs or drinking get substance abuse care and stick with it. Almost all of the Lethal Warriors who were arrested for shootings were intoxicated at the time of their crimes. Minimizing drinking and other substance abuse is the simplest way to keep soldiers out of jail. Fifth, make sure soldiers are not humiliated by peers or commanders by educating all ranks about combat stress injuries. The prevailing attitude that legitimate stress injuries are a made-up disorder and a sign of weakness has to be broken. And sixth, the army needs to train sergeants and young officers to manage their troops, instead of instinctively punishing soldiers who are acting out.

Months before the EPICON report was released to the public, General Mark Graham drew his own conclusions from the data and used them to institute a number of changes at Fort Carson. The first conclusion was that almost all of the men arrested for murder were initially arrested for smaller crimes. He called this pattern "the crescendo" because it started small, then grew. The general reasoned that if commanders could identify a soldier and get him help at the beginning of the crescendo, he might avoid prison.

To enable commanders to catch the crescendo early, Graham pushed a new electronic database at Fort Carson that would give commanders a computerized, real time, color-coded "risk assessment" of every soldier in a unit and the unit as a whole. He also pushed for changes to army-wide policies so soldiers changing units would have the information on their risk level follow them to their next assignments.

To break down stigma, Fort Carson moved some mental health care services out of Evans Army Hospital and into individual battalions. It allowed soldiers to visit doctors more readily, making it easier for platoons to care for their troops while also preparing for their missions. But it also started to normalize the concept of mental health care; help was no longer an outside unknown tucked away at Evans, it was part of the unit.

The EPICON findings were key in spurring a new army-wide program called Comprehensive Soldier Fitness, which seeks to teach soldiers the coping skills that can help them endure combat by focusing on building strength in five areas of their lives: physical, emotional, social, spiritual, and family strength. The idea is to let new soldiers know what the Band of Brothers never did: that stress reactions in combat are normal and that soldiers together have the tools to address and overcome them.

Before the Comprehensive Soldier Fitness program was rolled out across the Army late in 2009, Graham, working with the new commander of the Lethal Warriors, Colonel Randy George, implemented a local version at Fort Carson. Against the recommendations of the head of psychiatry at Evans Army Hospital, they sent every soldier in the Lethal Warriors brigade to a four-hour class on relaxation techniques that can ward off combat stress injuries—exercises the troops could use after missions to unwind in a positive way.

The head of psychiatry, George Brandt, said he was concerned that the training was not evidence-based and the psychiatric community needed more time assess it. But Graham asserted that there was not time. "If it wasn't going to hurt," Graham said, remembering his decision, "I figured we might as well try it. Maybe it would help."

Graham also pushed for the creation of a storefront in Colorado Springs where soldiers and their families could go for "one-stop shopping" for help, whether it was family issues, substance abuse counseling, mental heath care, financial counseling, or any of a number of other services the army offers. "My goal," he said, "was to make it as easy as possible to get help."

All of the changes were, in part, set in motion the moment Kevin Shields was shot. If he had not been killed, and led police to arrest Louis Bressler, Bruce Bastien, and Kenny Eastridge, the problem of soldiers coming home to Colorado Springs suffering from combat stress injuries might have remained unnoticed. The murders by Jomar Vives and John Needham might have appeared as little more than police-blotter tragedies. The trend in violence in one brigade combat team might have gone unstudied. Fixes might have never been proposed. Shields paid the ultimate price, but a million troops benefited.

Fort Carson's changes did not solve every problem. Despite Graham's high-profile efforts, suicides at Fort Carson in 2008 set another record. Arrest rates of military personnel in Colorado Springs continued to edge upward. What couldn't be measured was how much higher the numbers would have been if Graham had not been there, doing everything he could do to address the problem. "That's the hardest thing," Graham said, looking back at the numbers. "You never see how many you prevented. I have to believe we saved a lot of people."

But once the programs took hold, trends quickly started to reverse for the first time in almost a decade. After a small decline in 2009, Fort Carson's suicide rate in 2010 dropped by almost half compared to 2008, bringing it in line with the rest of the army.[15] Crime has also leveled off, though it has not fallen to prewar levels. The arsenal of small fixes and new programs Graham and his staff devised at Fort Carson did not make headlines like the murders did, but the numbers show that smart leadership can make a real difference.

———

Graham left Fort Carson in July 2009, just after the EPICON report was released, and moved to his next assignment as deputy chief of staff for U.S. Army Forces Command, located at Fort McPherson, Georgia, where he helps orchestrate when and where army units deploy all over the globe. The job is instrumental in making sure no unit is sent to the worst places over and over, as the Lethal Warriors were. Many of the changes he pushed for are now permanent at Fort Carson. Soldiers are screened for PTSD and other problems before they return from a tour, then again as soon as they get home, and again three and six months after their return, in order to minimize the number who lie to hide their problems. Combat commanders can flag soldiers whose experiences overseas have put them at high risk for PTSD or suicide for more in-depth screening when they return.

The military has created a slew of new programs to address combat stress—everything from a new "resiliency campus" at Fort Hood with yoga classes and meditation rooms to a fifty-base tour by a traveling production company called Theater of War that stages two ancient Greek plays by Sophocles, *Ajax* and *Philoctetes,* that explore the themes of what is now called PTSD.

Not everyone saw the value in the changes Mark Graham made. Some at the Pentagon thought he was being too indulgent, encouraging soldiers to grow soft and in the process costing the army a bundle.[16] But Graham had a saying he quietly told close friends when he faced such criticism: "If they think I am being too caring, they can put that on my tombstone."[17]

CHAPTER 15

CHANGING THE MINDSET

Two months before the findings of the EPICON were released in the summer of 2010, the Lethal Warriors deployed from Fort Carson again. As in every previous tour, their brigade ended up in the worst combat zone at the height of the violence. This time it was the mountainous southeastern boarder of Afghanistan.

Some aspects of their third tour were different. They were given extra screening and a series of classes in social skills and relaxation techniques that the army calls "resiliency training" to try to teach them to manage combat stress before shipping out. They had a four-person traveling Combat Stress Team visit them occasionally. But other characteristics of combat were the same as ever. The price of the brigade's one-year tour was steep. The rugged mountain valleys they patrolled became a shooting gallery for Taliban insurgents and fundamentalist zealots streaming over from Pakistan. In twelve months, forty soldiers were killed, mostly fighting to hold remote outposts. In the most intense battle of the tour, in October 2009, an estimated two hundred Taliban fighters attacked a small outpost called Combat Outpost Keating, raking the isolated soldiers with machine-gun fire, breaking through the defenses, overrunning half the base, and setting fire to several buildings, before eventually being driven back by air strikes. Ironically, the army had already decided to abandon the outpost as strategically unimportant, but had not gotten around to it. Eight American soldiers were killed. After fighting for their lives, the remaining soldiers walked away, leaving the hard-won ground to the enemy. A few weeks later, the Taliban posted videos on the Internet of their fighters lounging in the outpost.

Such a tour is bound to produce the same kind of stress, grief, and inner-conflict that Kenneth Eastridge felt in the first tour or John Needham felt in the second. This time around, the combat stress team held debriefings with some of the hardest-hit troops and offered stress classes, but talking about what has happened can only do so much. A number of soldiers said the efforts of the stress teams missed the point. "They are a waste of time for the people giving them and for us here on the ground," one Lethal Warrior sergeant said via email from Afghanistan in the fall of 2009. "There is nothing you can tell us that will help with stress. The reason there is combat stress is 'cuz we are un-dermanned and get only one day off a month."

As in the past, the mission may still trump concerns about mental health. The army is sending fewer and fewer soldiers home for mental problems. Guys like Louis Bressler and Kenneth Eastridge, who were sent home from Al Dora, are now usually treated as close to the combat zone as possible instead. "My mission here is to keep people on mission, keep people in the fight, keep peo-ple in the theater as opposed to having them air-evaced out," Dr. Randal Scholman, the brigade psychiatrist, told the Associated Press near the end of the tour, adding that two soldiers he sent back to the Rear D had already acted out violently.[1] The army says keeping stressed troops in the war zone improves soldiers' likelihood of recovery, which may be true depending on the individ-ual and the quality of care, but the practice also improves troops' likelihood of returning to missions, which for these damaged soldiers could be a dan-gerous move.

The brigade returned to Colorado Springs in May of 2010. By that time, ten percent of the soldiers from one of its infantry battalions were on anti-depressants and a quarter of the brigade—almost 1,000 soldiers—had been flagged by command to get enhanced mental health screening for possible PTSD.[2] Colorado Springs has yet to see another murder from the brigade, but it may just be a matter of time.

Almost as unnerving as the uncertainty of violence from the brigade in the fu-ture is the failure to take a full account of the violence in the past. In a steamy rural patch of Alabama called Lee County, down along the Chattahoochee River, a young black man named Courtney Lockhart sits in a jail cell charged with armed robbery, assault, kidnapping, attempted rape, and murder, knowing that if he is convicted, he could face the death penalty.

Lockhart is twenty-five years old with large, expressive eyes, a round face, close-shorn hair, and a pencil-thin mustache outlining his upper lip. He was part of the Lethal Warriors brigade, but data suggest he was not part of the EPICON study. His acts were as bloody and senseless as Louis Bressler's or Jomar Vives's, but it appears no one from the army knew enough about Lockhart and his crimes to include him in the study. His case exposes one of the troubling aspects of crime in soldiers returning from war: no one knows how big the problem is.

Lockhart's story is almost too familiar. He grew up in a poor family, raised alone by his mother, who worked a swing shift in a paper factory. In high school he played football and basketball and ran track. He never excelled in school but he graduated on time in 2003 and was persuaded by recruiters visiting his school to join the army. In 2004 he was sent to Korea and assigned to the 2nd Battalion, 17th Field Artillery, the big-guns unit attached to the Band of Brothers brigade. That summer his battalion deployed to Ramadi. Lockhart was stationed right on the edge of the seething city at a massive forward operating base called Camp Ramadi. The day they arrived, thirteen rockets hit the FOB.

Almost every day mortars screamed into the camp, hitting random targets. The insurgent mortar teams usually disappeared into the city like ghosts. With no solid enemy to target, the massive, tanklike Paladin howitzers that Lockhart's battalion brought to Iraq sat idle except to occasionally lob preemptive 155 rounds out into the desert and scrubby farmland, trying to discourage any unseen enemies.[3] With a lack of artillery missions, the soldiers in the battalion were used as infantry troops. Just like the Band of Brothers, they cruised the IED-laden roads in Humvees. Twenty-one soldiers of the battalion were killed during their year in Iraq—almost double the casualties of the Band of Brothers. One morning, halfway through the tour, Lockhart was opening the door of his Humvee to climb out when a mortar landed no more than twenty feet away, almost killing him.

"I prayed for like an hour after that . . . I could not stop crying," Lockhart said as he sat at a cold, metal table in the Lee County jail, recalling the moment. It was the first time he had really talked about anything that had happened in Iraq.

One evening, he said, two mortar rounds came through the roof of the radio room where he was sitting. After that, he would lie awake at night, staring at the ceiling, waiting for a round to come through the roof. On another day, in April 2005, a lucky mortar from the insurgents dropped through the hatch of one of his unit's Paladins, setting off a series of explosions as, one by one, the 155 rounds stowed inside exploded. Three men in the vehicle were burned alive as Lockhart watched. "I used to play basketball with them, and we all just had to stand there and watch them die," he said. "We couldn't do anything. The fire was too hot. We just had to wait. Those guys, there was nothing left of them but their dog tags. I would try not to think about it, but I would have to drive past that burned-out Paladin every day."

The one soldier from that Paladin crew who had not been inside and survived, Stephen Sherwood, never recovered from the loss. He killed his wife then himself four months later.

Lockhart held himself together until the day his platoon sergeant, Neil Prince, left Ramadi to go on two weeks' leave in June 2005. Prince had always looked out for Lockhart in Ramadi and always made him feel safe. They constantly joked around. "He was my best friend, more like a father than anything else," Lockhart recalled. Then Prince's Humvee was hit by an IED near Khalidiya while driving to his leave. The sergeant and a twenty-two-year-old National Guard soldier were killed. Lockhart wept uncontrollably and refused to leave his bed. The only thing he wanted to do was load his rifle, walk out the gate into the wilds of Ramadi, and kill as many people as possible before he was killed himself. "After that," he said, "anyone who was not an American, I wanted them dead."

Like many others, Lockhart brought his hate and fear home when the brigade returned to Fort Carson in August 2004. He lied his way through the health assessments. He saw other soldiers punished, ostracized, or overmedicated if they said they had PTSD. He loved the army and didn't want that to happen to him, so he decided to deal with his problems on his own.

In the months after he returned, Lockhart started drinking too much and always carried a gun. He had problems keeping his anger leashed. Worst of all, he felt he had no place to go where he could relax and ease his nerves. His barracks at Fort Carson were not far from the artillery range. When the cannons practiced, it sounded like Ramadi. He would find himself trembling under his bed with no idea how he got there.

Lockhart started smoking pot to ease his nerves. It seemed to work. But during a company-wide drug test in February 2006 he was busted. His commander docked his pay, knocked him down to the lowest rank, and made him stay on post every weekend waxing floors. No one sent Lockhart to drug rehab classes, as is required, or asked him if he needed help.

On May 31, 2006, Lockhart got into an argument at a Fort Carson cafeteria. It started as a tiff over a fortune cookie with a guy he had never met. Lockhart's addled brain interpreted the minor slight as a serious threat. Neither soldier backed down until they were shouting in each other's faces. Lockhart was court-martialed for chest-bumping the other soldier and threatening to shoot him. For good measure, his commanders threw in his old marijuana charge. Lockhart never got a psychological screening after the incident. He was never offered counseling. Instead, he was convicted and thrown in a military prison for seven months, then sent home to Alabama.

His mother, Catherine Williams, said it was almost as if the army had sent back the wrong soldier. "My baby was a whole different person when he came back. There wasn't nothing the same about him," she said, sitting in the office of his attorney in 2010.

Lockhart spent most of his days shut in his bedroom. Loud noises sent him into a panic. He couldn't handle crowds. He kept having glimpses of sounds or sights from Iraq that he knew weren't there. One morning his mother tried to wake him up for breakfast and he started thrashing on the bed, kicking and punching. She yelled his name over and over as tears welled up in her eyes. "It was like he was fighting for his life," she said. "Finally he woke up and said, 'Mom, you can't do that no more.'" Another time she came home from work and spotted his hands peeking from under the bed. When she asked him what he was doing hiding under there, he simply said, "Nothing."

A month after Lockhart moved back in with his mom, she mentioned all his strange behavior to a friend at the paper mill who was in the Army Reserve. He told her the problems sounded serious and she needed to get her son help. He gave her an army phone number to call. She gave it to her son, but he never called.

"You know if you go in," he said when asked why he did not call, "they going to put you on a medication and another medication and say you are crazy, but you know you are not crazy."

Gradually, it started to seem that Lockhart had come through the worst of it. After a few months at home, he started coming out of his room more. He got a job as a laborer for a heavy equipment company and slowly started to earn small raises. After he had been at home a year he was spending more and more time with his family and his friends, playing basketball or just having cookouts in the yard. His family thought he was on the mend. Then, on March 4, 2008, almost three years after returning from the Sunni Triangle, he snapped.

Sitting at a table in the Lee County jail in 2010, his attorneys told him not to talk about what happened. But in a letter he wrote to his mother from jail shortly after his arrest, he said, "I woke up that day and realized I didn't have a life."[4]

The night of March 4, according to police, he drove twenty miles north of his mother's house in Smiths Station to Auburn University, where he spotted an eighteen-year-old freshman from the wealthy suburbs of Atlanta named Lauren Burk getting into her car. Burk had long brown hair that fell past her shoulders, an infectious smile, and a model's good looks. She had never met Lockhart and Lockhart had never met her. Lockhart forced her into her car at gunpoint and took the wheel. He drove north, up a rural highway that rolled through the pine forests and red Alabama hills. At a dark abandoned intersection between a low brick Baptist church and an old, neglected cemetery, he told her to take off her clothes. There was a struggle. Police say Lockhart shot her in the chest.

He pushed her out of the car and left her to die on the side of the highway. Then he drove back to an isolated parking lot behind the football stadium on the Auburn campus, doused the car with gasoline, and set it on fire.

Two days later Lockhart pulled a gun on a woman and her three-year-old son in a Sam's Club parking lot just across the state line in Columbus, Georgia, and demanded cash. The next day he attacked a seventy-two-year-old woman getting into her car in a Wal-Mart parking lot sixty miles north on the interstate to Atlanta. He tried to rob her, but other shoppers chased him away. Their description to police led to his arrest. After a short high-speed chase, he surrendered. That day police say he gave a detailed written confession. He later pled not guilty.

If Lockhart is convicted at trial, he could be executed by lethal injection.

Courtney Lockhart's story is in ways more disturbing than the others in his brigade who landed behind bars. It is not so much the crimes themselves, though they are coldly brutal and perplexingly random, but what they suggest about the brigade, Fort Carson, and the 1.5 million troops who have served in Iraq and Afghanistan. Lockhart had essentially been out of the army for two years before he snapped and went on a murderous crime spree.[5] That whole time, little suggested that he was at risk of such violence. Then one day all his simmering issues came to a boil. His story suggests that psychological wounds can fester for a long time. Even though combat in Iraq has died down, the personal battles of its veterans are still being fought every day. The wars in Iraq and Afghanistan may have unintentionally hidden vets like Lockhart all over the country, where they sit like 155 shells, waiting to go off.

The mistakes of the past were not erased when the EPICON delved into the underlying causes or General Mark Graham cleaned house at Fort Carson. By that time, many of the neglected troops had already been exported all over the country. Almost 1,200 soldiers were discharged from Lockhart's brigade alone between 2004 and 2008 for mental, medical, or disciplinary problems.[6] Countless others were medically retired, like Louis Bressler and John Needham. And that is only one group of soldiers from one army base. There are likely thousands and thousands more just like them. No one follows what happens to them after they are discharged. They just disappear into the civilian population.

There may be no other soldiers like Courtney Lockhart out there, or there may be five or five hundred. No one with access to the data that might be able to answer that question is even asking it. It does not fall under the mission of the active-duty military or the Veterans Administration. So far, no politician has pushed for an inquiry that could produce real answers. In 2009, the EPICON report recommended the army perform a service-wide follow-up study—a mega EPICON—to gauge the "possible link between deployment, combat intensity and aggressive behavior."[7] The Army's epidemiologists cannot undertake such a study without orders. It is likely such a study would only produce negative news, discouraging any leaders from issuing the order. As of this writing, no study has been done or even started.[8]

It is critical to accurately track and understand the issue of violence in veterans, and to continue to try to address it because, as a nation, we are not out of the woods yet. We're not even close. Violence in Iraq has dropped dramatically since 2007, but at the same time violence in Afghanistan has climbed to the highest levels ever. As of the fall of 2010, there are now 100,000 troops in Afghanistan. The IEDs, ambushes, and lack of defined enemies that proved so toxic in Iraq are just as vexing in Afghanistan and will likely produce the same kinds of casualties.

Not everything to come out of this dark chapter in history is tragic. Just as physical trauma in war helps advance medical science, the psychological casualties of Iraq have spurred research and programs to address PTSD. Since the start of the war, the Department of Defense has tried to correct its early missteps. Soldiers are now given more training to recognize combat stress and minimize it. Commanders are increasingly educated in how to productively manage troops instead of punish them. The army is preparing to place a "master resiliency trainer" in each combat platoon who will endeavor to strengthen troops' coping and stress thresholds in the same way other sergeants train them to be dead shots.

The steady stream of bad press about neglected PTSD cases coming out of Fort Carson and other installations also had an upside. It encouraged the Department of Defense to spend an estimated $500 million dollars on PTSD and traumatic brain injury research. This money is the biggest windfall for the field ever, and will likely propel understanding of the psychological fallout of war at a pace unimaginable in peacetime.

Research is already showing promising treatments to calm the unbalanced pathways of communication between the cerebral cortex and amygdala that cause some of the worst symptoms of PTSD. Some researchers are even trying to develop a "morning after pill" for traumatic stress that would prevent PTSD from ever taking hold.[9]

Naturally, there are drawbacks to this kind of advancement. The drug would potentially allow troops to endure more combat without debilitating fear reactions. Whether such a drug would then expose troops to more moral injuries, perhaps creating more and more Lethal Warriors, is an open question. It is disturbing to imagine a day when troops will be kept in combat using pills. There are no plans to do so, but given the enthusiastic use of sleeping pills and antidepressants in Iraq and Afghanistan, it is not unimaginable.

Where do the army-wide changes leave the Lethal Warriors? That too, is still unknown. It is conceivable that just as many will slip through the cracks of the new and improved system. In the end, the fate of these soldiers will likely rest not on the shoulders of big programs but of individuals—sergeants, lieutenants, captains, roommates, friends, and family—all who must make sacrifices to be sure their soldiers don't fall into despondent self-destruction. The army and Veterans Administration must arm these people who are closest to the troops with the tools they need to recognize a problem and get help.

The army can also achieve as much by focusing on other risk factors in addition to stress, namely guns and alcohol. Most of the Lethal Warriors who later got in trouble carried a loaded gun with them. Carrying a personal weapon off post is not necessarily illegal, and in the army culture it is hardly rare, but it is a huge risk factor. If Anthony Marquez or Louis Bressler, or any of the other soldiers who shot someone in reaction to what was happening at the moment had not been armed, they would almost certainly not be charged with murder and their victims would still be alive. The army gives only token warnings to soldiers about carrying weapons. Education should be increased and taken seriously, especially in light of the extensive reflexive fire training soldiers get. Alcohol can be just as dangerous. Almost all of the murders were committed when the killers were drunk. Again, it is likely that if they had been sober the killings would never have happened. If the army really wants to reduce crime, targeting the soldier culture of binge drinking is at least as important as targeting combat stress.

Young veterans are overwhelmingly resilient. In the course of writing the story of the Lethal Warriors, I have spoken to a number who went through hell after they returned from Iraq but are now doing fairly well. They healed on their own. In most cases, the body has a natural ability to rebuild. They have jobs. They have moved out of their parents' basements. Some are going back to school. Many of them said time was the best medicine. That is why minimizing exposure to guns and drugs and other high risk behaviors is particularly critical. Given time, most veterans can regain equilibrium. The risk is that some will upend their lives before that happens.

Ultimately, though, anything the Department of Defense or the nation as a whole does to try to ease troops back into civilian life is treating the symptoms, not the cause. The problem with violence in returning veterans is not a problem caused by poor screening or stigma or lack of treatment, it is a problem caused by war. And it is a problem that will not end until the wars do. If nothing else, the Lethal Warriors are a cautionary tale of the true costs of war on the home front.

These days Kenneth Eastridge is reading the classics.

Like the others convicted of murder, he is in prison. He spends much of his time in a small cell in Delta Correctional Center in the dry, western mesas of Colorado. He is set to get out of prison in 2018, but with good behavior he is eligible for parole in 2013. So far, his behavior has been very good.

To occupy his time Eastridge has read Dante's *Divine Comedy, Don Quixote, The Count of Monte Cristo,* and Niccolò Machiavelli's *The Prince.* He has read books on the ancient samurai of Japan and other warrior cultures that have helped him understand more about his journey around the globe, from Korea to Iraq to Colorado Springs and eventually to prison. He occasionally corresponds with Sister Kateri Koverman about what happened.

Like many of the soldiers now in prison, he is of two minds about the whole ordeal. On the one hand, he sees how much combat has damaged him. He still has occasional nightmares. He has a hard time watching the news. He is aware of how much conditioning he got as a new recruit—the shooting, the constant chanting about killing. "The army just pounds it into your head: kill everybody, kill everybody, kill everybody," he said in an interview late in the winter of 2010. "They don't want you to freeze up. They want you to train as you fight. They train [killing] into you enough times and it's instinct. You do it instantly, you don't have to think about it."

On the other hand, like many of the soldiers arrested for murder, he is still fiercely loyal to the army and the Lethal Warriors, and would give almost anything to be back in their ranks, fighting alongside his fellow soldiers. There is nothing he would rather do. Bressler felt the same way. So did Needham. Eastridge's greatest regret is that he screwed up his army career. He still sees himself as a soldier. When he gets out, he plans to try to join the French Foreign Legion.

"I hear they are still taking felons," he said with a knowing smile.

Obviously, despite all the advances in technology and weaponry, the need for men like Eastridge to conduct war on the ground is not going away anytime soon, so it is imperative that the military learns to care for troops. Call it Machiavellian, but the country will serve its long-term strategic and economic interests better by making sure troops are healthy and resilient. Maybe, Eastridge said, what the army really needs is a place where the hardest-hit troops could reenter civilian life gradually after deployments—something like a summer camp away from the stress of the real world where they could decompress for a few weeks or a month as a unit. Teach the soldiers how to resolve conflict there, he said. Teach them to let go of some of their fear. Go over and over peacetime scenarios in the same way soldiers trained for wartime scenarios. Otherwise, he sees a lost generation.

"There are guys like me all over the country now," Eastridge said. "We all went to war. You get used to it and you enjoy it to a certain extent. Then nothing else matters. You're afraid of normal life. There is no point to anything. Somehow you have to help these guys—change the mindset. If you don't, this kind of stuff is just going to keep happening."

POSTSCRIPT

WHERE ARE THEY NOW?

JOSE BARCO: After joining the army at seventeen, serving two combat tours, and being arrested for shooting a pregnant woman at a party in 2008, Barco was found guilty of two counts of attempted murder in 2009 and sentenced to fifty-two years in prison in Colorado.

BRUCE BASTIEN: After joining the army at nineteen and serving half a combat tour, Bastien was arrested for aiding in the murder of soldiers Robert James and Kevin Shields and the stabbing of Erica Ham in December of 2007. In 2008 he was sentenced to sixty years in prison in Colorado.

LOUIS BRESSLER: After joining the army at eighteen and serving two combat tours, Bressler was medically evacuated for PTSD after assaulting a superior. Bressler was arrested for the murders of soldiers Robert James and Kevin Shields and convicted of conspiracy to commit murder. In 2008 he was sentenced to sixty years in prison in Colorado.

KENNETH EASTRIDGE: After joining the army at nineteen and serving two combat tours in which he was hit by multiple IED blasts and diagnosed with PTSD, TBI, and depression, Eastridge was court-martialed in August 2007 and other-than-honorably discharged. Eastridge was arrested for aiding in the murder of soldier Kevin Shields in December of 2007. He was convicted of accessory to murder and sentenced to ten years in prison in Colorado.

ROBERT FORSYTHE: The medic served a tour in Kosovo and two in Iraq and was honorably discharged. After leaving the army he was arrested for drunk driving and reckless endangerment. He now is getting treatment for PTSD through the Veterans Administration and works as a medical consultant for the Lebanese military.

MARK GRAHAM: The two-star general was stationed to Fort McPherson outside Atlanta, Georgia after leaving Fort Carson in July 2009. He works for the U.S. Army Forces Command as a deputy chief of staff, coordinating the deployment and training of all army units.

RYAN KREBBS: The medic served two combat tours. He was medically retired with PTSD in 2009, is married with a child, and is attending college.

ANTHONY MARQUEZ: After joining the army at eighteen and serving one combat tour, he was injured by friendly fire in Iraq and became addicted to painkillers. He was arrested in October 2006 for the killing of Johnathan Smith. He pled guilty to murder and was sentenced to thirty years in prison in Colorado.

JOHN NEEDHAM: The California surfer joined the army at twenty-two and served one combat tour. He was medically evacuated from Iraq after a possible suicide attempt in September 2007 and medically retired from the army with PTSD and spinal injuries in July 2008. He was arrested for the fatal beating of Jaqwelyn Villagomez in September 2008. While awaiting trial for first-degree murder he died from an apparent opiate overdose in February 2010.

MICHAEL NEEDHAM: The father of John Needham quit his job working for a defense contractor after his son was arrested for murder, feeling that he could no longer justify supporting the United States war effort. He now sits on the board of a nonprofit that advocates for combat veterans.

GEORG-ANDREAS "ANDREW" POGANY: The veterans' advocate lives in Denver, where he is now director of military outreach and education for Give an Hour, an organization that coordinates volunteers who provide counseling to veterans.

RUDOLFO TORRES: The army specialist from California served one combat tour in Iraq and was preparing for a second in Afghanistan when he was arrested in the shootings of three people in Colorado Springs. He pled guilty to accessory to murder and testified against his friend Jomar Vives. He was sentenced to twelve years in prison in Colorado.

JOMAR VIVES: The army specialist from Hawaii served one combat tour in Iraq and was preparing for a second in Afghanistan when he was arrested in the shootings of three people in Colorado Springs. He was found guilty at trial for the deaths of Myra Cervantes and Cesar Ramirez and the shooting of Zachary Szody. He was sentenced in November 2009 to two life terms, plus 140 years. He is appealing his conviction.

NOTES

Unless otherwise noted, quotations are from interviews with the author.

INTRODUCTION

1. 911 recording of call reporting Kevin Shields's death, Dec. 1, 2007.
2. John Hazelhurst, "Colorado Springs Economy Remains at Mercy of the Military," *Colorado Springs Business Journal,* Aug. 24, 2007.
3. "Coalition Military Fatalities by Year," http://icasualties.org/Iraq/index.aspx.
4. Ibid.
5. Tom Roeder, "Brigade Likely to Be Home by Christmas," *Colorado Springs Gazette,* Dec. 1, 2007.
6. Ivan Shields, interview with the author, Jan. 18, 2009.
7. "The Band of Brothers" originally only referred to the soldiers in Company E of the 506th Infantry Regiment, but over time the moniker had been adopted by all companies in the battalion.
8. Dennis Huspeni, *Colorado Springs Gazette,* Jan. 9, 2008.
9. Extrapolated from the widely used metric of murders per 100,000 population used to determine murder rates, based on a battalion population of 500.
10. "Iraq War Vet Charged in Shooting Death of Fellow Soldier," *Lawrence Journal-World,* July 31, 2007.
11. Patrick Orr, "Armed Iraq Veteran Charged in Apartment Shooting," *Idaho Statesman,* July 30, 2009.
12. "War Blamed in Iraq Vet Shootings," Associated Press, Aug. 21, 2005.
13. Lolly Bowean and Megan Twohey, "Vet Accused of Killing Wife Weeps as Prosecutors Outline Case," *Chicago Tribune,* Mar. 1, 2010.
14. Tom Roeder, "Carson Soldier Kills Wife, Himself," *Colorado Springs Gazette,* Aug. 5, 2004.
15. "Combat Follows Soldiers Home," *Los Angeles Times,* Dec. 21, 2008.
16. Atul Gawande, "Casualties of War—Military Care for the Wounded From Iraq and Afghanistan," *New England Journal of Medicine,* December 2004, gives the number 1 in 10. A later study, "Evolving Mechanisms and Patterns of Blast Injury and the Challenges for Military First Responders," *Journal of Military and Veterans' Health,* January 2010, puts the rate between 1 in 10 and 1 in 20.
17. *Army Health Promotion, Risk Reduction, Suicide Prevention Report 2010,* U.S. Army, July 31, 2010, http://usarmy.vo.llnwd.net/e1/HPRRSP/HP-RR-SPReport2010_v00.pdf.
18. Department of Defense Personnel and Military Casualty Statistics "Casualty Summary by Reason, October 7, 2001 through August 18, 2007," Defense Manpower Data Center.
19. Army Medical Command, "Mental Health Advisory team (MHAT) V" report, Feb. 2008, www.armymedicine.army.mil.

CHAPTER 1

1. In interviews, several soldiers relayed hearing this phrase.
2. Stephen Ambrose, *Band of Brothers* (New York: Simon & Schuster, 1992).
3. Written instructions for the ceremony appear at 506infantry.org.
4. *Army Health Promotion, Risk Reduction, Suicide Prevention Report 2010,* U.S. Army, July 31, 2010, http://usarmy.vo.llnwd.net/e1/HPRRSP/HP-RR-SPReport2010_v00.pdf.
5. All information about Louis Bressler's childhood and decision to join the army comes from an interview with his mother, Theresa Bressler, Jan. 21, 2010.
6. Theresa Bressler, interview with the author, Jan. 21, 2010.

7. All information about Kevin Shields's childhood and his decision to join the army from an interview with his grandfather, Ivan Shields, and mother, Deborah Pearson, Jan. 18, 2010.

8. Ryan Krebbs, interview with the author, Feb. 25, 2010.

9. Soldiers interviewed universally used this term.

10. Charles R. Figley and William P. Nash, eds., *Combat Stress Injury: Theory, Research, and Management* (New York: Routledge, 2006).

11. David Nash, interview with the author, Mar. 20, 2009.

12. S. L. A. Marshall, *Men Against Fire* (Washington: Military Service Publishing Company, 1947).

13. Dave Grossman, *On Killing* (New York: Little, Brown and Co., 2009), p. 3.

14. Ibid., p. 252.

15. Both sides halted their propaganda broadcasts in June 2004.

16. "'Juicy Bars' Said to Be Havens for Prostitution Aimed at U.S. Military," *Stars and Stripes,* Sept. 9, 2009. Drinky-girl prostitution was said to be significantly curtailed in 2009 after an investigation by *Stars and Stripes* led to reform of the visa system.

17. Ryan Krebbs, interview with the author, Feb. 25, 2010.

18. Kenny Eastridge, interview with the author, Mar. 8, 2010.

19. Globalsecurity.org.

20. "Letter May Detail Iraqi Insurgency's Concerns," CNN, Feb. 10, 2004.

21. John Duval, interview with the author, Jan. 22, 2010.

22. Dick Cheney in an interview on *Meet the Press,* Mar. 16, 2003.

23. Associated Press, Mar. 18, 2004.

24. William "Wild Bill" Guarnere, Edward "Babe" Heffron, and Robyn Post, *Brothers in Battle, Best of Friends* (New York: Berkley Caliber, 2007).

CHAPTER 2

1. "Bush Calls End to 'Major Combat,'" CNN, May 2, 2003.

2. Casualty numbers from Society of the 1st Armored Division webpage, http://64.78.33.72/history/index.cfm.

3. "General: Iraqi Insurgents Directed from Syria," *Washington Post,* Dec. 17, 2004.

4. "Iraq Roadside Bomb Kills Three," BBC News, Feb. 19, 2004.

5. Untitled speech by General Mark Graham at the Suicide Prevention Command Chaplain Conference, Mar. 4, 2009.

6. Mark Graham, interview by the author, Feb. 10, 2010.

7. "The Soldier's Creed," http://www.armystudyguide.com/content/Prep_For_Basic_Training/Prep_for_basic_general_information/the-soldiers-creed.shtml.

8. "US FDA to Update Black Box Warnings for Young Adults Taking Antidepressants," *Pharma Letter,* June 2007.

9. Carol Graham, interview with the author, Feb. 23, 2010.

10. Ibid.

11. "A General's Personal Battle," *Wall Street Journal,* Mar. 28, 2009.

12. Carol Graham, interview with the author, Feb. 23, 2010.

13. John Nagl, the 1–34's operations officer, was a leader in innovative counterinsurgency tactics and later coauthored the army's counterinsurgency field manual and wrote the popular counterinsurgency book *Learning to Eat Soup with a Knife.* The strategies unveiled in Al Anbar province were later successfully used in Baghdad during the surge of 2007.

14. "Slain Soldier Remembered in Virginia as 'Awesome Guy,'" *Free Lance-Star,* February 2004.

15. Kentucky House of Representatives resolution no. 180, 2004.

16. Carol Graham, interview with the author, Feb. 23, 2010.

17. Ibid.

18. L. B. Cowman, *Streams in the Desert* (Cowman Publications Inc.,1925).

CHAPTER 3

1. *Mad Max* was a 1979 film about a dystopian future in which roving gangs of thugs cruise the highway in search of fuel. All missions in the battalion were named after movies according to Lieutenant Colonel Stephen Michael, interview with the author, Apr. 27, 2010.

2. Sergeant John Duval, interview with the author, Jan. 22, 2010.

3. Ibid.

4. Sameer N. Yacoub, "US Vows to Pacify Violent City, Residents," Associated Press, Apr. 2, 2004.

5. Bartle Bull, "With the Band of Brothers in Ramadi," *Radar,* May 2004.

6. Report by Captain Joshua Hähnlen, Battalion Intelligence Officer, 506infantry.org.
7. Although, soldiers said, it was readily available, particularly in Baghdad.
8. Battle summary by Captain William Jones, 506infantry.org.
9. Ann Scott Tyson, "Increased Security in Fallujah Slows Efforts to Rebuild," *Washington Post,* Apr. 19, 2004.
10. Battle summary by Captain William Jones, 506infantry.org.
11. Ibid.
12. Ibid.
13. David Nash, interview with the author, Mar. 20, 2009.
14. Kenneth Eastridge, interview with the author, Mar. 8, 2010.
15. John Duval, interview with the author, Jan. 22, 2010.
16. Ryan Krebbs, taped interview with the author, Mar. 4, 2010.
17. Tony Perry, "Polls Stand Empty Amid Sunni Stronghold," *Los Angeles Times,* Jan. 31, 2005.
18. Joseph Giordono, "A Year on the Edge: 2nd BCT Bound for Colorado after Grueling Tour in Ramadi," *Stars and Stripes,* Pacific edition, July 31, 2005.
19. "Bush Administration: Iraq Weapons Search Is Over," Associated Press, Jan. 13, 2005.
20. State Department spokesman Richard Boucher in a statement to the press, Jan. 11, 2005.
21. George W. Bush, speech, "President Discusses the Future of Iraq" Feb. 23, 2003, http://www.the moderntribune.com/george_bush_speech_february_26,_2003_plans_for_iraq_and_iraq_war.htm.
22. John Duval, interview with the author, Jan. 22, 2010.
23. "With the Band of Brothers in Ramadi," *Radar,* May 2004.
24. Video of the promotion ceremony shot by John Duval, April 4, 2005.
25. S. L. A. Marshall, *Men Against Fire* (Washington: Military Service Publishing Company, 1947).
26. Kenneth Eastridge, interview with the author, Mar. 9, 2009.
27. Kenneth Eastridge, interview with the author, Mar. 8, 2010.
28. Kenneth Eastridge, interview with the author, Mar. 8, 2010.
29. Interviews with Josh Butler, David Nash, Marcus Mifflin, and other soldiers all confirm the widespread use of stun guns.
30. El Paso County Sheriff interviews with soldiers from Anthony Marquez's platoon, October 2006.
31. Interview of Sergeant Cody Guerin by the El Paso County Sheriff's office as part of Anthony Marquez's murder investigation. Report filed Feb. 2, 2007.
32. Interview of Staff Sergeant Scott Martin Guerin by the El Paso County Sheriff's office as part of Anthony Marquez's murder investigation, El Paso County Sheriff's office report filed Feb. 2, 2007.
33. Anonymous sergeant from the 1st Battalion, 9th Infantry Regiment, interview with the author, Mar. 30, 2010.
34. Kenneth Eastridge, interview with the author, Mar. 8, 2010.
35. Lisa Chedekel and Matthew Kauffman, "Army Sees Record Number of Suicides," *Hartford Courant,* May 14, 2006.
36. Epidemiological Consultation 14-HK-OB1U –09, *Investigation of Homicides at Fort Carson, Colorado,* U.S. Army Center for Health Promotion and Preventative Medicine, July 2009.
37. According to soldiers in the platoon, an informal investigation into the incident, known as a 15–6, was conducted and, because the bullets used by some coalition and enemy weapons are similar, it could not be determined if the men were killed by friendly fire. However, Anthony Marquez said he was told what happened later by the soldier who fired on him. Another soldier gave a similar account to the author. The families of the dead soldiers were not given this information by the army.
38. Erin Emery, "Home Couldn't Harbor GI," *Denver Post,* Oct. 28, 2007.
39. Joseph Giordono, "A Year on the Edge: 2nd BCT Bound for Colorado After Grueling Tour in Ramadi," *Stars and Stripes,* Pacific edition, July 31, 2005.

CHAPTER 4

1. William "Wild Bill" Guarnere, Edward "Babe" Heffron, and Robyn Post, *Brothers in Battle, Best of Friends* (New York: Berkley Caliber, 2007).
2. Eric T. Dean, Jr., *Shook Over Hell* (Cambridge, MA: Harvard University Press, 1997).
3. Ibid.
4. "Tide of New PTSD Cases Raises Fears of Fraud," Associated Press, May 2, 2010.
5. David K. Kentsmith, "Principles of Battlefield Psychiatry," *Military Medicine,* Feb. 1986.
6. Willard Waller, *The Returning Veteran* (New York: Dryden Press, 1944).
7. Herbert C. Archibald, MD; Read D. Tuddenham, PhD, "Persistent Stress Reaction after Combat: A 20-Year Follow-up," *Archives of General Psychiatry,* May 1965.
8. William "Wild Bill" Guarnere, Edward "Babe" Heffron and Robyn Post, *Brothers in Battle, Best of Friends* (New York: Berkley Caliber, 2007).

9.   Charles R. Figley and William P Nash, *Combat Stress Injury Theory, Research and Management*, (New York: Routledge, 2006).

10. Benedetto De Martino, Colin F. Camerer, and Ralph Adolphs, "Amygdala Damage Eliminates Monetary Loss Aversion," *Proceedings of the National Academy of Sciences*, Feb. 2010.

11. S. Maren, G. Aharonov, M. S. Fanselow, "Neurotoxic Lesions of the Dorsal Hippocampus and Pavlovian Fear Conditioning in Rats," *Behavioral Brain Research*, Nov. 1997.

12. D. M. Amodio "Meeting of Minds: The Medial Frontal Cortex and Social Cognition," *Nature*, Apr. 2006.

13. Sterling C. Johnson, "Neural Correlates of Self-Reflection," *Brain* 125, no. 8, Aug. 2002.

14. B. S. McEwen, "Protection and Damage From Acute and Chronic Stress: Allostasis and Allostatic Overload and Relevance to the Pathophysiology of Psychiatric Disorders," *Annals of the New York Academy of Sciences*, 1032:1–7.

15. F. L. Woon, D. W. Hedges "Amygdala Volume in Adults With Posttraumatic Stress Disorder: A Meta-Analysis," *Journal of Neuropsychiatry*, Winter 2009.

16. The National Vietnam Readjustment Study (1983) estimated the lifetime number of cases at 30.1 percent and the current number to be 15 percent.

17. Judith Lewis Herman, "Complex PTSD: A Syndrome of Survivors or Prolonged Trauma," *Journal of Traumatic Stress*, vol. 3, 1992.

18. Jonathan Shay, "Achilles and Odysseus Today: What Homer Can Tell Us About Military Leadership," Rouman Classical Lecture at the University of New Hampshire, Aug. 2006.

19. B. T. Litz, et al., "Moral Injury and Moral Repair in War Veterans: A Preliminary Model and Intervention Strategy," *Clinical Psychology Review*, 2009.

20. Charles R. Figley and William P. Nash, eds., *Combat Stress Injury: Theory, Research, and Management* (New York: Routledge, 2006).

21. Ibid.

22. Hal Bernton, "Troops Suffer Long-term Brain Impacts From Shock Waves, Seattle Study Finds," *Seattle Times*, June 13, 2010.

23. Charles Hoge, et al., "Combat Duty in Iraq and Afghanistan, Mental Health Problems, and Barriers to Care," *New England Journal of Medicine*, July 2004.

24. Ibid.

CHAPTER 5

1.   Perry Swanson, "Protesters Tell Council Police Overreacted at Rally," *Colorado Springs Gazette*, Feb. 26, 2003.

2.   "Cities Jammed in Worldwide Protest of War in Iraq," CNN, Feb. 13, 2003.

3.   Tom Roeder, "Carson Soldiers Readjusting Well," *Colorado Springs Gazette*, July 1, 2004.

4.   Tom Roeder, "Toll of War Heaviest Here," *Colorado Springs Gazette*, May 8, 2006.

5.   David Olinger, "Deadly Duty for Fort Carson," *Denver Post*, Nov. 16, 2008.

6.   Tom Roeder, "Carson Soldier Kills Wife, Himself," *Colorado Springs Gazette*, Aug. 5, 2005.

7.   Pam Zubeck, "Putting a Cork in Crowd Troubles," *Colorado Springs Gazette*, Feb. 18, 2008.

8.   Tom Roeder, "Fort Carson DUI Rate High," *Colorado Springs Gazette*, May 26, 2006.

9.   U.S. Army Center for Health Promotion and Preventive Medicine Epidemiologic consultation no. 14-HK-OB1U–09.

10. Kenneth Eastridge, interview with the author, Mar. 9, 2009.

11. Ibid.

12. *Frontline*, "The Wounded Platoon," PBS, May 18, 2010.

13. Ibid.

14. Eric T. Dean, Jr., *Shook Over Hell* (Cambridge, MA: Harvard University Press, 1997).

15. Ibid.

16. Booing and disappointment were reported by numerous soldiers, including Eastridge, Krebbs, Nash, and Duval.

17. Joseph Schwankhaus, interview by Chris Buchannan and Daniel Edge, *Frontline*, "The Wounded Platoon." This segment of the interview was not included in the broadcast.

18. Tom Roeder, "2nd BCT Could Fight Again Soon," *Colorado Springs Gazette*, Dec. 10, 2005.

19. Daniel Zwerdling, "Soldiers Face Obstacles to Mental Health Services," *Morning Edition*, National Public Radio, Dec. 4, 2006.

20. Anonymous licensed social worker at Evans Army Hospital, interview with the author, Jan. 28, 2010.

21. Ibid.

22. Evans psychologist Douglas McNinch was recorded telling a sergeant, "I will tell you something confidentially that I would have to deny if it were ever public. Not only myself, but all the clinicians up here

are being pressured to not diagnose PTSD and diagnose anxiety disorder NOS [instead]." Michael De Yoanna and Mark Benjamin, "I Am Under Pressure Not to Diagnose PTSD," *Salon.com,* Apr. 8, 2009.
23. Stephen Knorr, Fort Carson Memo, June 7, 2007, made public by National Public Radio.

CHAPTER 6

1. *Denver Post,* Oct. 3, 2005.
2. "The Good Soldier," *Westword,* Mar. 20, 2008.
3. "Reduced Charges for Soldier Accused of Cowardice in Iraq," *New York Times,* Nov. 7, 2003.
4. Colorado Springs City Council, transcript of proceedings, Oct. 11, 2005.
5. Lionel Rivera lost the Republican primary for Colorado's 5th Congressional District seat in 2006. He remained as mayor. Term limits require him to leave office in 2011.
6. Georg-Andreas Pogany, interview with the author, Mar.16, 2010.
7. U.S. Army Center for Health Promotion and Preventive Medicine Epidemiologic consultation no. 14-HK-OB1U–09.
8. "President Visits War Wounded at Walter Reed," Armed Services Press Service, July 3, 2005.
9. Theresa Hernandez, interview with the author, Mar. 28, 2009.
10. Ibid.
11. Ibid.
12. Based on witness statements, El Paso County Sheriff's Office report, Feb. 2, 2007.
13. Ibid.
14. Ibid.
15. Ibid.
16. Interview of David Larimer, El Paso County Sheriff's Office report, Feb. 2, 2007.

CHAPTER 7

1. Conversation with Jose Barco and Kenny Eastridge based on an interview with Kenny Eastridge, Mar. 8, 2010.
2. James W. Willett, diary entry June 12, 1864, Bentley Historical Library, quoted by Eric T. Dean, Jr., *Shook Over Hell* (Cambridge, MA: Harvard University Press, 1997).
3. William Guarnere, Edward Heffron, and Robyn Post, *Brothers in Battle, Best of Friends* (New York: Berkley Caliber, 2007).
4. Charles R. Figley and William P. Nash, *Combat Stress Injury Theory, Research and Management* (New York: Routledge, 2006).
5. Conversation based on an interview of Kenny Eastridge by the author, Mar. 8, 2010.
6. "Dick Winters: Reflections on the Band of Brothers, D-Day and Leadership," interview by Christopher J. Anderson, *American History Magazine,* August 2004.
7. Joseph Schwankhaus, interview by Chris Buchannan and Daniel Edge, *Frontline,* "The Wounded Platoon," PBS, May 18, 2010.

CHAPTER 8

1. Kenneth Eastridge, interview with the author, Mar. 8, 2010.
2. Ibid.
3. "Counterinsurgency Operations in Baghdad," *Military Review,* May 2009.
4. "Bomb at Baghdad Market Kills 22 in Worst Such Attack in a Month," Associated Press, Feb. 21, 2006.
5. Kenneth Eastridge, interview with the author, Mar. 9, 2009.
6. M. E. F. Seligman and S. F. Maier, "Failure to Escape Traumatic Shock," *Journal of Experimental Psychology* 74 (1967), 1–9.
7. Paris Taylor, interview with the author, May 19, 2010.
8. The author was able to watch some of these videos with John Duval.
9. Robert Forsythe, interview with the author, Apr. 19, 2010.
10. Jose Barco, interview by *Frontline,* "The Wounded Platoon," PBS, May 18, 2010.
11. Kenneth Eastridge, interview with the author, Mar. 9, 2009.
12. Michael Cardenas, interview with the author, Apr. 5, 2009.
13. Paris Taylor, interview with the author, Apr. 18, 2010.
14. Robert Forsythe, interview with the author, May 21, 2010.
15. John Duval, interview with the author, Jan. 22, 2010.
16. Robert Forsythe, interview with the author Apr. 19, 2010.
17. L. Christopher Smith, "The Fort Carson Murder Spree," *Rolling Stone,* November 2009.

18. John Duval, interview with the author, Jan. 22, 2010.
19. Kenneth Eastridge, interview with the author, Mar. 9, 2009.
20. David Patraeus and James F. Amos, *Counterinsurgency,* Army Field Manual 3–24 (Department of the Army, December 2006).
21. Jim Keirsey, "Reflections of a Counterinsurgency Company Commander," *Army,* July 2008.
22. Ibid.
23. John Duval, interview with the author, Jan. 22, 2010.
24. Jose Barco, interview with the author, Nov. 30, 2009.
25. Robert Forsythe, interview with the author, Apr. 19, 2010.
26. Ryan Krebbs, interview by Daniel Edge, *Frontline,* "The Wounded Platoon," May 2010.
27. Robert Forsythe, interview with the author, Apr. 19, 2010.
28. icasualties.org.

CHAPTER 9

1. "Army to Award Bronze Star to APWU Members' Son," American Postal Worker's Union newsletter, May 29, 2009.
2. L. Christopher Smith, "The Fort Carson Murder Spree," *Rolling Stone,* November, 2009.
3. Ibid.
4. Ibid.
5. Ryan Krebbs, interview with the author, Mar. 4, 2010.
6. Kenneth Eastridge, interview with the author, Mar. 5, 2009.
7. Lt. Col. Stephen Michael, interview with the author, April 27, 2010.
8. Ibid.
9. Bruce Bastien and Robert Forsythe both confirmed Eastridge did these things.
10. This figure, first offered in an interview with Kenneth Eastridge, was confirmed by his squad leader, Michael Cardenas.
11. John Duval, interview with the author, Jan. 22, 2010.
12. This account is difficult to confirm. Bruce Bastien, Robert Forsythe, and John Duval confirm the shooting, but were uncertain of the casualties. The battalion commanders, Stephen Michael, denied it ever happened, saying if it did, he would have known about it.
13. Robert Forsythe, interview with the author, Apr. 19, 2010.
14. Leann Eastridge, interview with the author, Apr. 25, 2009.
15. Jeffrey "Sam" Althouse, interview with the author, May 10, 2010.
16. Ryan Krebbs, interview with the author, Mar. 4, 2010.
17. Jeffrey "Sam" Althouse, interview with the author, May 10, 2010.
18. Michael Becker, the California public defender assigned to John Needham's murder case, interview with the author, Apr. 29, 2010.
19. "An Ominous Feeling on Patrol—Then a Blast," Associated Press, June 18, 2007.
20. Jeffrey "Sam" Althouse, interview with the author, May 10, 2010.
21. Ibid.
22. All details of John Needham's injuries and treatment are from a summary he wrote of his deployment in December 2007. It was provided to the author by his father, Mike Needham.
23. Jeffery "Sam" Althouse, interview with the author, May 10, 2010.
24. Army CID, response to author's inquiries, May 2009.
25. John Needham's MySpace.com profile.
26. Mike Needham, interview with the author, February 2, 2010.
27. Marta Vives, interview with the author, Mar. 28, 2009.

CHAPTER 10

1. Conversation based on interview with Kenneth Eastridge, Mar. 8, 2010.
2. L. Christopher Smith, "Fort Carson Murder Spree," *Rolling Stone,* November 2009.
3. Ibid.
4. Ibid.
5. Theresa Bressler, interview with the author, Jan. 21, 2010.
6. Tira Bressler, police interview, Dec. 6, 2007.
7. Colorado Springs Police Report by detective Derek Graham, December 10, 2007.
8. Ibid.
9. All quotes and descriptions of the murder of Robert James are from a taped police interview of Bruce Bastien, Dec. 10, 2007.

10. Ibid.
11. El Paso County Coroner's Report for Robert James, Aug. 9, 2007.
12. Bruce Bastien, police interview, Dec.10, 2007.
13. Colorado Springs Police report of domestic violence arrest of Bruce Bastien, Aug. 3, 2007.
14. L. Christopher Smith, "Fort Carson Murder Spree."
15. Tira Bressler, police interview of Aug. 8, 2007.
16. "Army Health Promotion, Risk Reduction, Suicide Prevention Report, 2010," July 31, 2010, http://us-army.vo.llnwd.net/e1/HPRRSP/HP-RR-SPReport2010_v00.pdf.
17. L. Christopher Smith, "Fort Carson Murder Spree."
18. Kenneth Eastridge, interview with the author, Mar. 9, 2009.
19. Ibid.
20. Erica Ham, interview with the author, Mar. 10, 2010.
21. Erica Ham, interview with the author, Mar. 10, 2010.
22. Bruce Bastien interview with Colorado Springs Police Department, Dec. 5, 2007.
23. Ibid.
24. Ibid.
25. Kenneth Eastridge, interview with the author, Mar. 9, 2009.
26. Bruce Bastien, Colorado Springs Police Department interview of Dec. 5, 2007.
27. Ibid.
28. Tira Bressler, Colorado Springs Police Department interview of Apr. 25, 2008.
29. Bruce Bastien, Colorado Springs Police Department interview of Dec. 5, 2007.
30. Ibid.
31. Ibid.
32. Louis Bressler and Tira Bressler, jail phone conversation recorded by the El Paso County Sheriff's office, Dec. 5, 2007.
33. Ibid.
34. Details and quotes of Bastien's confession from police interview of Bruce Bastien, Dec. 10, 2007.

CHAPTER 11

1. The entire exchange between CID Agent Kelly Jameson and Bruce Bastien is based on a taped Colorado Springs police interview of Bruce Bastien, Dec. 12, 2007.
2. Kenneth Eastridge, interview with the author, Mar. 9, 2009.
3. John Duval, interview with the author, Jan. 28, 2008.
4. Jose Barco, testimony in Colorado's 4th Judicial Court, Oct. 2009.
5. "The Wounded Platoon," *Frontline*, PBS, May 18, 2010.

CHAPTER 12

1. Colorado Springs Police Department detective Derek Graham, interview with the author, Feb. 10, 2010.
2. Captain Zachary Szody, court testimony in Jomar Falu-Vives murder trial before the 4th Judicial District Court, Colorado Springs, Nov. 2, 2009.
3. Colorado Springs Police Department detective Bradley Pratt, interview with the author, Mar. 18, 2010.
4. Nate Gabriel, interview with the author, Apr. 19, 2010.
5. Though Jomar Vives's name is officially Jomar Falu-Vives, and that is what he was referred to in the press, everyone in the Army knew him as Jomar Vives. Conversation based on author's interview with Brad Pratt, Feb. 8, 2010.
6. Johlea Vives, interview with the author, Mar. 2009.
7. Ibid.
8. Colorado 4th Judicial District minute order for the proceedings of Jomar Falu-Vives's divorce and child custody hearings.
9. Colorado Springs Police report summarizing an interview with Rudy Torres and other suspects in the Jomar Vives homicide investigation, Aug. 21, 2008.
10. Ibid.
11. Hailey Mac Arthur, "Judge: Falu-Vives' MySpace Profile Not Relevant to Trial," *Colorado Springs Gazette,* June 23, 2009.
12. Jomar Vives, Colorado Springs Police interview by Detective Bradley Pratt, July 29, 2008.
13. Rudolfo Torrez, Colorado Springs Police interview by Detective Derek Graham, July 29, 2008.
14. Ibid.
15. Ibid.
16. Ruodolfo Torres, Colorado Springs Police interview by Bradley Pratt, Jan. 9, 2009.

17. Rudolfo Torrez, Colorado Springs Police interview by Derek Graham, July 29, 2008.
18. Ruodolfo Torres, Colorado Springs Police interview by Bradley Pratt, Jan. 9, 2009.
19. Ibid.
20. Ibid.
21. Ibid.
22. Ibid.
23. Alonso Hernandez, Colorado Springs Police interview by Bradley Pratt, Aug. 27, 2008.
24. Ibid.
25. Ibid.
26. Alonso Hernandez, Colorado Springs Police interview, Aug. 2008.
27. Leo Robledo, Colorado Springs Police interview, Aug. 2008
28. Rudolfo Torres, Colorado Springs Police interview by Bradley Pratt, Jan, 9, 2009.
29. Alonso Hernandez, Colorado Springs Police interview by Bradley Pratt, Aug. 27, 2008.
30. Rudolfo Torres, Colorado Springs Police interview by Bradley Pratt, Jan. 9, 2009.
31. Ibid.
32. Alonso Hernandez, Colorado Springs Police interview, Aug. 2008.
33. John C. Ensslin, "Unrepentant Falu-Vives Receives Two Life Terms," *Colorado Springs Gazette,* Nov. 20, 2009.
34. Jackie Bastien, recorded phone call to Bruce Bastien at the El Paso County Jail, Dec. 11, 2007.
35. Dave Grossman, *On Killing* (New York: Little, Brown and Co., 2009), xxiii.
36. Paris Taylor, interview with the author, May 17, 2010.

CHAPTER 13

1. Mike Needham, interview with the author, Feb. 2, 2010.
2. Conversations recreated from author's interview with Mike Needham, Feb. 2–3, 2010.
3. John Needham, letter to Assistant Inspector General Randy Waddle, Dec. 18, 2007. While the allegations were investigated, they were found to be unsubstantiated and no charges were ever brought.
4. The inspector general's office said it investigated John Needham's accusations and found them to be unsubstantiated.
5. Mark Benjamin and Michael De Yoanna, "You're a Pussy and a Scared Little Kid," *Salon.com,* Feb. 12, 2009.
6. Dialogue based on an interview with Mike Needham, Feb. 3, 2010.
7. Steven Mirin, American Psychiatric Association Medical Director, testimony before the House VA Appropriations Subcommittee, April 2002.
8. "Concerns Mount Over Waiting Lists at Veterans Affairs Mental Health Centers," Fox News, Feb. 13, 2007.
9. "In Tide of PTSD Cases, Fear of Fraud Growing," Associated Press, May 3, 2010.
10. Ibid.
11. Mike Needham, interview with the author, Feb. 2, 2010.
12. John Needham's MySpace page, provided by Mike Needham.
13. Mike Needham, interview with the author, Feb. 2–3, 2010.
14. Ibid.
15. Ibid.
16. Ibid.
17. Ibid.
18. Sarah Sevino, interview with the author, Feb. 3, 2010.
19. "'Mentally Unstable' Iraq Veteran Arrested in Death of Girlfriend, 19," *Los Angeles Times,* Sept. 3, 2008.
20. Vik Jolly and Salvador Hernandez, "A Short, Turbulent Affair Ends in Death," *The Orange County Register,* Sept. 3, 2008, http://www.ocregister.com/news/needham-162983-inside-deputies.html.
21. Scott Martell, "Iraq War Vet in Murder Case Found Dead; Faced Other Charge" *Orange County Register,* Feb. 26, 2010.

CHAPTER 14

1. U.S. Senate, Committee on Homeland Security and Government Affairs, *Hurricane Katrina: A Nation Still Unprepared,* December 2006.
2. Ibid.
3. Evans Army Hospital data, April 2009.
4. *Colorado Springs Gazette,* November 2007.

5. Evans Army Hospital data, April 2009.
6. Evans Army Hospital data, April 2009 and November 2009.
7. "Salazar Seeks Review of Carson GIs' Alleged Spate of Violence," *Denver Post,* Oct, 18, 2008.
8. Ibid.
9. Nick Palorino, interview with the author, Mar. 19, 2010.
10. Epidemiological Consultation 14-HK-OB1U –09, *Investigation of Homicides at Fort Carson, Colorado,* U.S. Army Center for Health Promotion and Preventative Medicine, July 2009.
11. Ibid.
12. Ibid.
13. Ibid.
14. Ibid.
15. "Fort Carson Says Its Suicide Rate Is Falling," Associated Press, September 1, 2010.
16. Georg-Andres Pogany, interview with the author, Mar. 16, 2010.
17. Carol Graham, interview with the author, Feb. 26, 2010.

CHAPTER 15

1. Heidi Vogt, "Military Keeps Soldiers at Combat Site," Associated Press, July 31, 2010.
2. Ibid.
3. Courtney Lockhart, interview with the author, January 11, 2010.
4. Cathy Williams, interview with the author, Jan. 12, 2010.
5. Courtney Lockhart is appealing his court-martial and will not be formally discharged from the army until the appeal is settled. As of this writing, it is still pending.
6. Epidemiological Consultation 14-HK-OB1U –09, *Investigation of Homicides at Fort Carson, Colorado,* U.S. Army Center for Health Promotion and Preventative Medicine, July 2009.
7. Ibid.
8. Dr. Amy Millikan, U.S. Army Center for Health Promotion and Preventive Medicine, interview with the author, June 4, 2010.
9. Matthew J. Friedman, "Prevention of Psychiatric Problems Among Military Personnel and Their Spouses," *New England Journal of Medicine,* January 2010.

INDEX